PENGUIN BOOKS

I WISH MY PARENTS UNDERSTOOD

Lesley Jane Nonkin is a staff writer at *Vogue* magazine, a contributing editor at *Young Miss*, and has formerly been on the staff at *Harper's Bazaar*, *The New York Daily News*, *Women's Wear Daily*, and *W*. She has spent three years studying the concerns of American teenage girls.

I Wish My Parents Understood

A Report on the Teenage Female

Lesley Jane Nonkin

PENGUIN BOOKS

PENGUIN BOOKS
Viking Penguin Inc., 40 West 23rd Street,
New York, New York 10010, U.S.A.
Penguin Books Ltd, Harmondsworth, Middlesex, England
Penguin Books Australia Ltd, Ringwood, Victoria, Australia
Penguin Books Canada Limited, 2801 John Street,
Markham, Ontario, Canada L3R 1B4
Penguin Books (N.Z.) Ltd, 182–190 Wairau Road,
Auckland 10, New Zealand

First published in the United States of America by Freundlich Books 1985
Published in Penguin Books 1986

LIBRARY OF CONGRESS CATALOGING IN PUBLICATION DATA
Nonkin, Lesley Jane, 1957–
I wish my parents understood.
Originally published: New York: Freundlich Books, 1985
1. Adolescent girls—United States—Attitudes.
2. Dating (Social customs) 3. Adolescent psychology.
I. Title
HQ798.N66 1986 305.2'35 85-21749
ISBN 0 14 00.8668 4

Printed in the United States of America by
R. R. Donnelley & Sons Company, Harrisonburg, Virginia
Set in Palatino

To Jeffrey—
with all my love

Acknowledgments

My greatest appreciation goes to Jamie Adams, who so kindly lent his time and expertise in statistics, all in the name of friendship, to help develop and analyze the *TeenAge* Relationships Survey—it would have not been possible without him; to Bill Weber and Andrew Calkins at *TeenAge* for believing in the project; to Vidar and Frank Jorgensen for seeing it through; to Ron Porter for the excellent tabulation and extra computer runs. Thanks also to Phyllis Schneider and Deborah Purcell for assigning me the *Young Miss* article that was the seed for this book and for putting me in touch with *TeenAge* Magazine.

Of the many people and organizations that helped me track down teens, I cannot forget: Sharon Dunseath and the Universal Cheerleaders Association; Polli Howard and the Future Homemakers of America, Inc.; Tom Burkley and The Congressional Seminar of The Washington Workshops Foundation; Brian Foss and Cynthia Hearn Dorfman and A Presidential Classroom for Young Americans. Though I did not quote from them directly, I would like to thank Dr. Leonard Reich, clinical child psychologist for the Health Insurance Plan of New York; Dr. Anne C. Petersen, professor of human development and head of the Department of Individual and Family Studies, The Pennsylvania State University; Dr. Leah Blumberg Lapidus, diplomate in clinical psychology, American Board of Professional Psychology, Columbia University, Teachers College, for the time they spent with me, helping me grasp the overall teenage picture.

And of course, my gratitude to Kathy Beckett for introducing me to my agent, Wendy Lipkind; to Amy Claire Bartlett for her wonderful editing and encouragement; to the 1,300 girls who took the time to respond in person or on paper; to the innumerable friends and associates who helped put me in touch with them. And lastly, to Larry Freundlich for taking the time to listen to my idea.

Table of Contents

Author's note

Before reading this book, girls may want to fill out the blank questionnaire provided in Appendix I to see how their answers compare with those taken by TeenAge *readers. Parents may find it interesting to respond to the survey* as if *they were teenage girls; the difference in answers, I'm sure, will be quite revealing.*

I Wish My Parents Understood

Introduction

This book, by its very nature, is about love and hate, fear and excitement, moving away from childhood, coming together with the adult world. It's about triumph and defeat, about learning to give as well as to take, about coping with fulfillment as well as with loneliness. It's about "getting it together" at a time when everything seems to be coming apart.

For no one can talk about what girls like and hate about boys without addressing the full range of tantalizing, sometimes disturbing, emotions and issues "they" bring with them—issues that can consume our teenage years. Because even if we aren't worried about boys—about what they're doing, thinking, saying—then our best friend is. Or all our friends are. And if we aren't confused about which invitation to accept to the senior dance, then we're wondering if we should go at all. Or our mother's wondering. Which makes us wonder.

So like 'em. Hate 'em. We've got to deal with 'em. I say "we" because we are all, from fourteen to forty, somewhere in our hearts, still "girls." Because boys are still "boys," and all the crazy things they do—or don't do—are still a part of the society we live in. Getting a handle on "them" starts right here, with a sharing of experience, and with confessions from girls all over the country about what they really, often secretly, like and hate about boys.

How it all got started

Shortly after I was asked to write a story called "What You Like and What Bugs You Most About Boys" for *Young Miss* Magazine, the raw material for the article—five ten-pound manila envelopes of readers' letters—arrived on my desk at work. I immediately became fascinated with them, carrying them with me on subways and buses, everywhere I went. At home I spread hundreds of letters across my bed, feeling like a modern-day "Miss Lonely-hearts." I just couldn't believe so many girls were still in the dark about boys! Surely something must have changed in the ten years since I had gone to high school!

But no. The stories were the same. Boys all over America still didn't call back after a date, still treated girls like "dumb bunnies," still didn't know how to be friends after a breakup. All the wacky, irrational antics that had plagued me as a teen were still going on. Even more worrisome were the girls (like me) who ended up, as a result, feeling jealous or angry, who (like my friends) tried new clothes, new drugs, cigarettes, even sex, to succeed with boys. Some of the stories were candid and funny; others heart-wrenchingly sad.

And I began to wonder. What if those girls knew what I know now? Would the letters have been any different? Could a little insight take the heartbreak, the misery, the sting out of those teenage years? Would a little understanding collapse the endless hours of anguish, of waiting by the phone, praying, "Oh, please, please let it be him!" into a more reasonable, less paralyzing time warp? (I remember Patty Duke asking the operator to call her back just to hear the phone ring.) If a girl knows that other girls feel it's okay to ask a boy out, will she simply take the initiative herself—and give *him* a call? Will boys who treat girls badly get the boot sooner if a girl has the power of group opinion behind her kick? Will girls who treat boys badly—often as a perverse means of getting or keeping them—be able to recognize their own self-defeating behavior in another girl's actions?

I couldn't help thinking it might all be different.

I also wanted a chance to explore my own adolescent frustration with boys, to understand why they always seemed like such alien beings to me. Why even though my friends and I spent half our waking hours like voracious buzzards pecking over their emotional anatomy, dissecting their personalities, sinew by sinew, bone by bone, we'd always come away as confused as ever, unsatiated, dying for more. Why boys like Peter D., a gorgeous college freshman I met at the New York Aquarium laboratories one summer (those were my "scientist" days) would torment me with beautiful crayoned envelopes—but no letter inside! Why he failed to "show" for my senior high dance, leaving me on the bedroom floor in tears and a new skirt I'd bought just for the occasion. Or why in eleventh grade, poor Mark T., who my friends said couldn't walk down the street and chew bubble gum at the same time, wrote me love poems and put up with my fickle ways because I was too afraid of group opinion to admit I liked him. They are answers I want, every girl wants, because they are part of the universal experience of growing up female.

This book is also an attempt to understand what makes those very popular high-school girls tick, what keeps those gutsy, self-confident amazons unflustered around boys. Why they can hold court in their rooms while ladies-in-waiting brush out their long tresses, emulate their dress, elect them to school office; why they can hold court on the dance floor while *all* the best-looking guys trip over themselves to fetch them brownies and lemonade, to steal just one moment in their aura. Why, I've always wondered, are some girls like them, while others pinch their waistless, breastless figures, and wonder what Ms. Popularity has that they don't. Is it not what these girls have, but, as gossipers may say, what they're willing to "give out" that makes them popular? Or is there something more complex in their charm that draws boys, like a bug-zapper draws mosquitoes?

Twenty-seven, I think, is the perfect age for me to examine such adolescent mysteries, because it's a time of reflection, when I've just leapt over the fence of growing up but my senses are still as accessible as an adolescent's. I haven't forgotten the piquant thrill of pining away for my first crush or the heartbreak of catching Terry C., my eighth-grade love, making out with another girl! Yet I also understand now, that we're not the adults we think we are as teens; that I wasn't as invincible or all-knowing as I thought then.

This book also addresses one of the strongest messages behind the *Young Miss* letters—that girls want to talk about boys! That they want to air their opinions and hear what their friends are thinking. That they want to know how other girls deal with peer pressure, drugs, drinking, and the ever-changing kaleidoscope of sexual mores. They want what boys have always found in all-night "bull" sessions, but with more depth, anonymity, a broader scope of experience to draw from. They want perspective, and girl-to-girl communication.

Why? Because today's social setup is no longer the simple "dating" system our parents grew up with. Instead of relationships that begin with proms and end with wedding cakes, we have an endless array of competing, often conflicting, arrangements in between. One group pressures us to sleep with our boyfriends; another pressures us not to. One clique says we should date around, another says we should "go steady." One wrong turn and we can easily end up in a crowd or with a boyfriend we don't really like. Even worse, we can end up doing something we may regret later.

The "maturity crunch"

Clearly, relationships in a souped-up computer-communication age move faster than ever. Embarrassments I felt in tenth grade about "my first slow dance" occur in eighth grade today. Really big issues that hit my freshman year in college—like sex, careers, drugs—now confront high-school girls. It's as if we're experiencing a kind of "maturity crunch"—where teens are expected to handle more and more complex issues at an increasingly younger age.

With the high divorce rate, the breakdown of organized religion and family, and a blurring of sex roles that gives rise to stars like Boy George, where can we turn for answers about sex and boys? Even those of us with parents equipped to handle the subject may feel silly or uncomfortable actually talking about it over breakfast. Teachers don't have time to get involved; magazine articles gloss over it in a sentence.

As a result, we turn to friends—the kind of friends I hope this book presents. Friends who have been down the same rocky road we're traveling, who have experienced the same emotions. And if our friends can't give us answers—and some problems don't have any—then it simply helps to know we're not alone. If this book serves no other purpose than to show one girl or her parents that she's not the only one confused about relationships, then it will have been a success.

Boys will find here an inside track on girls' "locker room" talk. Parents and educators will find it a helpful glimpse inside a puzzling social world. For all of us it is a glance into the world of the future, and a look back at the past; a chance to see that courtship hasn't really changed since the time of Romeo and Juliet. It's still a game. Only the rules are different.

Tracking down teens

Since the *Young Miss* letters contained less than adequate information for a book, I tracked down every teen I could find in one place at one time: girls in Orlando, Florida, for a national cheerleading competition; in Washington, D.C., for a meeting of the Future Homemakers of America, Inc.; for the Congressional Seminar of the Washington Workshops Foundation; at Marymount College of Virginia. I nabbed New York City punks and "Main Line" Philadelphia preps, California beach bunnies and Kentucky beauty queens, tall girls, fat girls, some with bad skin, others who were gorgeous. Girls who were popular homecoming queens, those who could only dream of what a date is like; those who talked my ear off for hours, others who merely shrugged. Hundreds of interviews, countless bags of pretzels, and who knows how many cases of diet soda later, I confirmed the message behind the *Young Miss* letters: girls all over America have exactly the same gripes and good words about boys! And they have a lot of them! One thousand and six additional surveys from *TeenAge* Magazine readers confirmed the facts again.*

* See Appendix I, *TeenAge* Relationships Survey.

The demise of the "sexual revolution" and the rise of a new sexual etiquette

I found that the sexual revolution of the Sixties has left an extraordinary amount of confusion in its wake. While many teens complain about the pressure to lose their virginity by senior year ("If you're still a virgin," one girl explains, "they think you're a lezzie or that there's something wrong with you"), truly *casual* sex remains taboo. Even among the "sexually liberated," one must be "in love" before having "acceptable" sex; sleeping with a boy on the first date, or even within the first two weeks, is justified *only* if a relationship develops later. One girl who cherishes the sexual freedom she found in Denmark during her junior year abroad laments that she'll have to change her ways now that she's "back in America."

Even boys are expected to show *some* degree of sexual restraint. While many girls have given up the fantasy of marrying a "virgin" (word has it that the last one in America was seen leaving via pterodactyl), they don't want a guy who's too experienced either. Somehow a guy who's slept with more than three or four girls before he's out of high school seems slightly undiscriminating, even "sleazy." The level of acceptable sexual experience for both sexes has merely been rolled back to a new standard, where at three or four experiences you're still socially acceptable. After that you're a "sleaze."

Of course, there is the other, more familiar, side of the sexual coin—the traditional girls who, like their mothers (and like me at the time), reject this "pressure" and the peers who have "compromised their morals" by giving in to it. They can't understand what the hype is all about, or fathom their friends' fascination with sex. Some are morally, others religiously, opposed to it. Often they view themselves as islands in a world seething with sexual revolution.

Ironically enough, and contrary to most popular belief, there seems to be very little "revolution." The tide of sexual liberation seems merely to have retreated to a different shore, leaving teens with a new kind of sexual etiquette that's not terribly unlike the more clear-cut one of the Fifties. Promiscuity is still taboo; sex and love still go hand-in-hand, if not directly to the altar, then to another kind of socially sanctified setup.

SOUTHERN GIRLS AND THE ENTRENCHED OLD DOUBLE STANDARD

Southern girls, who historically gravitate toward a more traditional kind of life-style, find the new etiquette especially hard to deal with. South of the Mason-Dixon line, where virgins are more strident and outspoken, many non-virgins feel a need to "cover up." If they sleep with their boyfriends (and more do than you think), they play it close to the vest, telling no one, not even their best friends. The idea, one girl told me, is to do whatever you want, but keep your reputation clean. She should know. She had mastered the "sweet and innocent" act so well that when an enemy finked to the class about her sexual escapades, no one believed him! Double standards are certainly not new, but it's hard to believe that in this day and age they carry such weight! (This is the same double standard that baffled me when I went to Duke University in North Carolina, where I was shocked to discover all the sweet, virginal sorority girls were indeed "getting it"—but all under wraps.)

SEXUAL IRRESPONSIBILITY: SEX WITHOUT CONTRACEPTION

What is truly disturbing, however, and what needs close attention from teens as well as adults and educators, is the alarming number of girls who are having sex without birth control. They are not the well-publicized urban kids for whom getting pregnant may seem a statement of identity. Instead, they are well-informed middle- to upper-class girls who say they don't want to get pregnant but believe it can't happen to them, or who feel that sex with birth control is "contrived" or "unromantic." Many are afraid or unsure of where to get contraceptives; many fear their parents' reprisals for doing so. The difficult task of meshing romance with reality is one that leads many to exclude contraception altogether. (One Pennsylvania girl told me that it wasn't until she took her best friend to have an abortion that she finally got contraceptives herself—even though she'd been sleeping with her boyfriend for over a year. A third friend however, would not get birth control, still believing that it "couldn't happen to her.") The result: an unfortunately high pregnancy rate.(Curiously enough, though many girls don't fear *getting* pregnant, almost all fear *being* pregnant; the number who go through unnecessary "scares" and last-minute pregnancy tests is amazing!)

THE SELLING OF SEXUALITY

Are teens to blame? Not entirely. Day after day, the media chips away at their moral fiber with taunts and teases about terrific sex, about the boys they'll catch if they wear designer jeans, name brand sweaters, sexy sandals; rock songs screech in their ears about juicy sexual relationships awaiting those adventurous enough to try it; a barrage of best-selling romance novels wrap sexual reality in fantasies sweet enough to swallow like candy. And no one, but no one, says anything at all about birth control! What dime-store heroine or soap-opera beauty, in the middle of a rapturous love scene, has stopped and said, "Oh, pardon me while I get my diaphragm"; and of course, we are *all* those heroines.

Even worse is the lingering sexist notion that a girl is not "supposed" to plan ahead for sex; that sex, for her, is supposed to be a spontaneous, overwhelming expression of love and passion that takes control of her senses and absolves her of guilt—while a boy can guiltlessly carry condoms and plan ahead for sexual conquests from the day he turns thirteen. A society that teaches girls to be deferential to boys, and not to be assertive when it comes to sex, especially spur-of-the-moment unprotected sex, is also to blame. Clearly, we need not only sex ed but "girls' ed."

AN ASTOUNDING IGNORANCE

I was also astonished to hear that "sex ed" courses, when and if they are offered at all, come too late, often in the junior or senior year of high school, long after most girls are sexually active.* Many are co-ed, which makes it difficult for shy girls to speak up. Still more are mere excuses for sex ed courses, taught by gym teachers or equally inappropriate instructors. I even heard one hair-raising

* According to Planned Parenthood of New York City, most schools do not offer a "defined curriculum" in sex education, even though many Americans mistakenly believe that the schools are doing "the job," so they don't have to. In fact, only three states—Kentucky, Maryland, and New Jersey—along with the District of Columbia, require sex education at all; only seven others encourage it.

story about a science teacher gone "creationist" who refused to discuss the basic facts of life. "The only thing she managed to get across to the five already pregnant girls in the class," says the New York teen, "is that the baby is not in the stomach . . . where it can be digested by stomach juices, but in the uterus!"

Even in classes that manage to get the facts across, teens feel that the emotional side of sex has been ignored altogether, so that this part of their education is left to the scriptwriters of *All My Children* and *General Hospital*. And at this difficult juncture, even the best mother-daughter relationships break down: "My mom and I are best friends; we can talk about anything," says girl after girl, "except sex." According to Planned Parenthood in New York City, though most parents would like to involve themselves with their children's sex education, a recent study showed that 90 percent have difficulty doing so! No wonder teens are sexually irresponsible—they are classroom pilots with textbook knowledge, but little "feel" for flying! (My research also rips a hole in the oldest anti-sex ed argument around—the idea that sex ed encourages kids to experiment. The *TeenAge* Relationships Survey shows that the number of non-virgins in the study group does not change whether they've had sex education or not.)

The new economics of independence

In contrast, there is an amazing new kind of responsibility, a praiseworthy awareness of the economics of independence. Many girls reject their parents' dependent, throw-all-your-eggs-in-one-basket life-style—one that involves getting married, settled in, even pregnant, before the high-school or college diploma can be hung on the wall. They want to work first. Even those who plan to marry early mention part- or full-time jobs as alternative types of emotional and financial support. Girls from wealthy families, or with capable fiancés, want to work for the sense of reward and identity it brings. The status of "just a housewife" has declined to such a low level that some teens are embarrassed to admit, especially to their friends, that they have no career aspirations at all.

Unfortunately, the phrase that often follows "I want a career" is "so that I can support myself in case of divorce." Sad but true.

Teens of the Eighties, even those from happy households, are painfully aware of the emotional price many parents, especially women, pay for their economic dependence. It is for that reason that although they all still want to get married, they want to do it later—in their late twenties, early thirties, after they've had a chance to establish themselves and a career. They also want fewer kids—perhaps one to four. Social fad or economic fact, they know it is difficult to raise a family, especially a large one, on a single income.

Separate and still unequal

The most startling moment in my research came when I heard girl after girl qualify statements about wanting equal pay for equal work with: "But don't get me wrong, I'm not a women's libber," "But I'm certainly not for ERA; I don't want to be sharing bathrooms with men or going off to war," or "But women and men just aren't equal and they never will or should be," as if equal opportunity was completely unfeminine and threatened to destroy our society by transforming women into men. The idea that women could gain the *same* rights as men, without becoming the same sort of creatures, is lost on a whole generation of girls.

For that reason, boys still have the upper hand in dating, are still expected to ask for and pay for the date—even if the girl is wealthier—and are still expected to make the first moves (any girl who does is "sleazy"). Dropping hints, manipulating, conniving remain the only "respectable" ways girls can catch a male eye. Most approve of the traditional stronger-male/weaker-female stereotype, too, claiming they want a taller, older, more mature man, one they "can look up to." Even those with plans to work full time want the male to retain the title "breadwinner." Girls in the Eighties consider being successful a balancing act—being a superwoman both at home and in the office.

There are some rumblings of change, however: a Kentucky beauty queen who wants to go to medical school; a preppy New Bedford girl who watched her mother support her father and enjoy it, and who wouldn't mind doing the same herself; a college freshman who asks guys out on "real" dates—they even cook the meals—and knows how to handle it when they turn her down; the overwhelming rejection of machismo and boys who treat girls as inferiors; the dislike of peers who act "dumb" around prom time just to get a date. There's even a glimmer of hope in the ubiquitous desire to be more assertive—to ask boys out. "Then we're free to make a choice too," explains one girl, "so we don't have to sit around waiting, trying to beautify ourselves while we wonder if he'll ask us out. If we want a guy, we should be able to go for it!"

Teen speak

Dating lingo has also undergone a metamorphosis. Except in the South, where traditional terminology lingers, "dating" has been almost completely eclipsed by less binding phrases like "going out" or "seeing" someone. And in the South, a girl hasn't arrived on the dating scene until she can "car-date," because the idea of her mom driving her to a school dance is babyish; and she won't car-date someone until she's "talked with" him for quite a while—not on the phone, mind you, but in person as a casual date or friend. All over the country, "nerds" (social rejects with horn-rimmed glasses and ankle-high "flood" pants, whose only dates are calculators) have become "dorks," "dweebes," and "geeks"; and "acting cool" is "staying chill." Great-looking or "tough" guys—"the bees' knees" in the Fifties—are "bad" in the Eighties, and in Manhattan, where "breaking and rapping" reigns, any guy is "in" as long as he doesn't talk or dress "bebop." To have sex is "to make," "to put," or in some cases, "to celebrate your love." Of course, just "fooling around" can mean anything from a tickle fight to intercourse.

Problems with parents—a new kind of generation gap

Much to my surprise, teens from all over America say they have one wish when it comes to parents: that adult attitudes toward teen sex, drugs, and drinking would become more realistic. "I want them to know that it's not just me who has these problems," many girls say. Or they think their parents "would die" if they ever found out what really "goes on." One girl went so far as to warn me not to whitewash the present youth culture: "I hate articles in teen magazines that treat us like innocent babies," she said. "Don't do that in your book. We know what's going on and we can handle talking about it."

Indeed! In all my naiveté, I assumed that today's teens would find less of a generation gap with their parents than those of previous decades. I figured that parents who were ten or twenty years older than I would have a certain tolerance for different behaviors. Even if they didn't participate in it, they were at least acquainted with such social phenomena as divorce, the drug culture, "the Pill." They might not approve of it, but at least "pot" was not some alien drug that had just drifted onto the scene. But I guess I was wrong.

This is not to say, of course, that every teen concerns herself solely with drugs and sex and boys. The majority, in fact, say "you can still have fun without drugs, sex, or drinking." But it is important to point out that these kinds of options are around—in varying degrees—within every community. Every girl from Memphis to Manhattan, no matter how sheltered, must at some point confront them. Parents who communicate well with their teens know this is true; parents who find it hard to communicate should learn more about it.

A DANGEROUS LACK OF COMMUNICATION

Another problem, one that stems from a sad lack of communication, comes from parents who lay down the law, sometimes harshly, and just blindly assume that their daughter abides by it. Granted rebellion is part of adolescence—everyone smokes cigarettes just because they're not supposed to—but some parents are strict to the extent of alienating their teens. Dozens of girls talk about not being allowed to date before age sixteen, and tell me they dated anyway by climbing out of windows, meeting boys at the malls. Harmless enough. But some continue seeing boys their parents don't like and then are afraid to ask for help when they need it—when they think they're pregnant or when the boy is becoming unmanageable. Perhaps they're driving and drinking with a boy whose name their family doesn't even know. While some girls can handle that kind of responsibility adequately, it's risky. If it was my kid, I'd want to talk to her about it, know who she's seeing, what she's doing, rather than pretend to myself she wasn't doing anything at all.

I was also surprised at the number of parents unwilling to loosen their grasp and give girls the trust they need and deserve at such an age. Girls whom I found to be smart, level-headed, responsible, but whose parents thought they were incapable of caring for themselves, largely because they were female and needed to be "protected." Many cited brothers who'd been allowed, if not pushed into, freedom much earlier. Yet they are left frustrated, angry, and resentful.

On the lighter side of parent-teen conflicts is the remarkable, ultimately amusing, array of conflicting complaints I've heard about parents' attitudes toward boy-girl relationships. Some girls want parents to show more interest; others say "don't pry." Many girls say they hate being teased about boys; others claim their parents take the whole dating situation far too seriously. Any way you slice it, it seems, parents—like boys, as you'll see in later chapters—lose.

The irony of change

There is irony in the things teens say they would like changed about the dating system. "People shouldn't judge somebody by their reputation or label someone a slut because she sleeps around," says one Texan who spent an hour describing how after she had sex with her boyfriend, she convinced everyone she was still a virgin. "Boys shouldn't date just bodies," says a New Jersey girl who picks boys by looks only. "Girls should ask guys out," say almost all girls, but later admit that they are too chicken to try it. These are ironies, not to laugh at but to learn from. They are the kinds of conflicts that arise whenever we say we want change, the kinds that have been with us and our social system from time immemorial.

An irony emerges, too, in the way male/female relationships don't change. If I were to alter the ages and drop the few references to high school and football stars, this could easily be a book about women and men. Said one unmarried thirty-five-year-old friend after hearing some of my interviews, "The sad thing is, as you get older, guys still act the same."

There is a certain charm, I think, about the fickleness of these teenage years, about the contradictions that arise as we try to wriggle out of our old baby skins and emerge as mature-thinking adults. Perhaps the ultimate joy, at least in looking back, is the innocence of self-discovery, when we all at once realize, much to our own chagrin, that we've been caught—half in, half out of our new cocoons. We don't know who we really are—adult or child—or what we really want—jocks or poets. But we are forgiven—because we are only teens, and in a time of such raging confusion, how are we supposed to know what we like and hate about anything—especially about boys!

—Lesley Jane Nonkin
August 1984

Section One

What Girls Like About Boys

1

"So," our mother asks, "who is this Mr. Right?"

We all think we know him. In fact, we can all picture him as he rides into our life on his white steed. He's definitely dashing, charming, wonderful. But then what? Is he preppy and self-assured, or painfully shy, yet thrilling? Does he have a brawny worked-out physique, or a lanky one? Is he a rock, movie, or TV star we know by name, or someone as mysterious and unidentifiable as a fashion model?

Not surprisingly, he is all of the above. And for every girl there is a completely different Mr. Right, sometimes a whole range of them. For some girls he is tall and dark, for others blond and stocky. Some want him cool and aloof to inspire the chase, others want him sensitive and up-front. Just as many girls "die" for romantic boys who bring them flowers as "die" of embarrassment when they receive them. Mr. Right comes in as many different shapes and sizes as sweatshirts from a department store—and each girl has a different fit in mind!

My interviews also point out that the guy we end up with may actually look and act nothing like the guy we dream about. Our fantasies may dictate that he must be gorgeous, but gorgeous guys, like gorgeous girls, lose their magnetic pull when a bad personality surfaces. We may want him to be fun, daring, humorous—fine for a few dates, but when it comes to relationships, we may go for someone more practical. Things such as money, race, religion, social savvy, or dress may have little room on our imaginary menu—but may be very important when deciding whom to go out with or whom to marry. As one married teen puts it: "We all dream about tall, dark, and handsome, but usually end up like I did with short, stout, and red-headed."

Though we don't like to admit that our friends influence us at all, group opinion can throw us toward blonds and intellectuals, away from brunettes and radicals. It can lead us to pick a boy solely for his looks, make us break up with someone we really like. Many aspects of a boy's physical and mental anatomy are subject to whimsy; what we like or hate today may not be what we like or hate tomorrow.

Are we who we date?

The boy we choose also depends upon who we are. And the *TeenAge* Relationships Survey confirms what I found in my interviews—that girls of the Eighties seem to fall into five categories: Twentieth-Century Fast Trackers, Sweet Southern Belles, Modern Traditionalists, Supersonic Daters, and Strong Individualists. Each group has a specific set of personality traits and values that sets it apart from the others and helps explain why girls like so many different types of guys.

THE TWENTIETH-CENTURY FAST TRACKER

Genuinely independent and self-sufficient, the Twentieth-Century Fast Tracker grasps liberation by the horns and rides it wherever it takes her. She wants to marry in her late twenties—after she's had time to play the field, work on her career, and make the most of her education. She rarely wants to be "just a housewife," and is the only one to vote overwhelmingly to support a househusband—i.e., if his ego can handle it! Because her identity comes from within and never from the boy at her side, the Twentieth-Century Fast Tracker is most noted for her openness to many different types of boys and her willingness (more than any other girl) to overlook boring clothes, bad looks, lack of money (she'll make her own), differences in religion and race. The only thing she really cares about is a great personality.

She's also less impressed than others by candy, flowers, and having car doors opened for her, more open to boys who let her split the cost of a date (because it makes her "feel independent") and who let her make a few of the "first moves." When it comes to asking boys out, though she may not have already done it, it's definitely on her mind. For unlike any other girl, the Twentieth-Century Fast Tracker feels wholeheartedly that things are "liberated enough today" to try it, and gives the thumbs-up indication that she'll do it in the near future.

Though she smokes and drinks as often as many other girls, she is exceptionally drawn to level-headed Mr. Straight (a guy who doesn't drink, smoke, or do drugs) and is more often than others repelled by "cool, aloof guys who offer a challenge." While she's no less likely than most other girls to be a virgin, she is the least likely to want to talk to her parents about her social or sexual life.

THE SWEET SOUTHERN BELLE

At the opposite end of the spectrum is the Sweet Southern Belle, a girl who doesn't necessarily come from the South but who has a conservative enough attitude to say she does. A modern-day Scarlett O'Hara in every sense of the word, the Sweet Southern Belle has very little interest in liberation or equality because, as tradition has it, she gets the best of both worlds: enough modern reality to let her have a career if she wants one, enough old-fashioned respect to have a "gentleman" cater to her needs. What she cares about most is that he fits in with the old world she comes from—particularly, overwhelmingly, that he comes from the right racial and religious background.

Since she evaluates much of her self-worth by the quality of the boy she snags, the Sweet Southern Belle snaps up the most successful, older boy in the crowd—perhaps the captain of the football team or a boy with money—and cares more than any other girl about looks and the impression his good manners make on parents. A die-hard conservative, she is also more easily won than others by fancy courtship rituals and is more likely than others to applaud a macho image. Though she's twice as likely as the Modern Traditionalist to believe that "no girl is a virgin when she marries anymore," she's *not* more likely to approve of premarital sex or to have already lost her virginity.

THE MODERN TRADITIONALIST

Less right-wing than the Sweet Southern Belle, yet still steeped in family tradition, is the Modern Traditionalist, who clings with one hand to a Fifties kind of Doris Day image, while embracing the reality of modern marriage and economics with the other. The backbone of the nuclear family, she is the only one who consistently places a home and family before a career and is open to the idea of being a housewife. While she completely rejects role reversals—especially the househusband idea espoused by many Twentieth-Century Fast Trackers—she does expect to work when she's married and often says, as is the current vogue, that it's primarily "to support herself in case of divorce."

The hallmark of the Modern Traditionalist is her conservative (yet somewhat contradictory) view of sex. She believes it's important to be a virgin at marriage, often wants to marry one, and heartily disapproves of premarital sex. Yet she is no more likely than most other girls to be a virgin! In keeping with her traditionalist point of view, however, she *is* the least likely to have asked a boy for a date and the least likely to ever want to. She also drinks and dates more than the Strong Individualists. Like the Sweet Southern Belle, she wants a boy to take control—to make the call, pick her up, pamper her with presents—but does not care as much about his race and religion. Her point of view has been moderated by today's eased-up mores and reality.

THE SUPERSONIC DATER

Out in a fast lane all her own is the Supersonic Dater, who adores love and romance on the wild side. Almost always dating, she's nearly twice as likely as other girls to be seeing just one boy, and for that reason rejects group dates more than others. Because of her rebellious or adventurous streak, she's a drinker and much more often a smoker. While the majority of Supersonic

Daters don't do drugs, they are considerably more receptive to the idea than any other girls, and are more inclined to say that pot and coke are "cool" in their group. Unlike anyone else, the Supersonic Dater is a little more willing to give a wild boy with a similarly fast-lane personality a break, yet surprisingly still applauds Mr. Straight.

She stands out because of her significantly low virginity rate—only 29 percent—and the chance that she will say, more often than others, that sex is "fun" and "acceptable." She is also the most likely to say that she wishes her parents understood that sex is more common today than when they were growing up. Though Supersonic Daters are more likely to have already asked boys out, they're not role-reversers by any means; like many other groups, half of them still want the boy to pay for the date—even when it's one they initiated! When it comes to a boy's religion, they're very liberal, falling neatly between the really forward-looking Twentieth-Century Fast Trackers and the slightly more old-fashioned Strong Individualists.

THE STRONG INDIVIDUALIST

The rest of the girls fall into a category that defies classification because the girls in it like to reap the best of all possible worlds. They like to mix the level-headedness of the Twentieth-Century Fast Tracker with the family orientation of the Modern Traditionalist; like the Sweet Southern Belle, they like the boy to pay for a date and yet many reject her overriding interest in money, etc. A complex mix of movers-and-shakers and laid-back realists, the Strong Individualists pick and pull from every category, whenever need be.

2

Good Looks: Beauty or the Beast?

What do girls from all groups notice first? Good looks. In our be-fit, be-beautiful society, an attractive body or face is like the gleam on a new sports car—it catches our eye. It's the reason we dress in the latest fashions, cover our blemishes, and coordinate the colors on our pen-and-pencil sets. Surrounding ourselves with pretty objects, or attractive boys for that matter, is just another part of the American dream.

Unfortunately, we are also taught that we mustn't "judge a book by its cover," that we should really accept a date with Richard Gere, Robert Redford, or Rick Springfield because of his "great personality," that we should be able to see through greasy hair and ripped jeans to view the "real" boy inside. Nice try, "but let's face it," says one girl who speaks for most, "if I see a kid walking down the street, I am attracted to his looks, not his personality!"

The only problem with looks comes when we place too much emphasis on them. Then like Kate,* a fourteen-year-old Supersonic

* All the names have been changed, because girls felt freer to bare their true feelings if anonymity was guaranteed.

Dater from New York City, we can end up judging boys superficially: "I turned a guy down and I think it had to do with his looks," she says. "I'm still friends with him and now my best friend is going out with him. If she doesn't mind, then I think it's fine. But I know some people sort of make a face when I tell them that they're going out." Though it's great to watch all our friends drool when we walk into study hall with the class knockout, we can sometimes carry the importance of their response too far. Then the desire just to be seen with him becomes more important than the relationship itself, and we hang in there for the wrong reason. His great looks can be such a hook, in fact, that even a terrible personality won't shake us loose.

Falling for the beast

Blonde-haired, blue-eyed Christy, a Modern Traditionalist from Paoli, Pennsylvania, fell into just such a trap. At seventeen, she has the kind of enviable take-charge attitude that makes her a leader in her group, which she asserts "is known for always dating the best-looking, most athletic guys in the class." For that reason Christy, who attends a "Main Line" public high school, values surface appearances highly, and has never dated a guy who wasn't good-looking. While she is certainly no knockout herself—her jaw's a bit too square, her hair, which she pulls back in a turquoise plastic clip, a bit too frizzy—she is none the less attractive, and boys, it seems, have never been hard to come by.

A few years ago she began dating Paul, the five-foot-eleven, dark-haired, green-eyed captain of the football and baseball teams. "He was really, really handsome, incredibly good-looking, really well-dressed, well-groomed," she says, crossing her legs on her bedroom floor, getting comfortable against her bed. "He was the best-looking guy in the class. Obviously it was his looks that first attracted me to him, it was just the first thing I noticed." She also noticed that he was a grade younger. But that didn't matter. After a rocky relationship with an older guy, it was good to feel in control.

Though they cared about each other a lot, there was also a barrier between them. "Paul needed someone who was willing to be there for him always, to be totally into him, and I'm just not

What Girls Look For in Boys

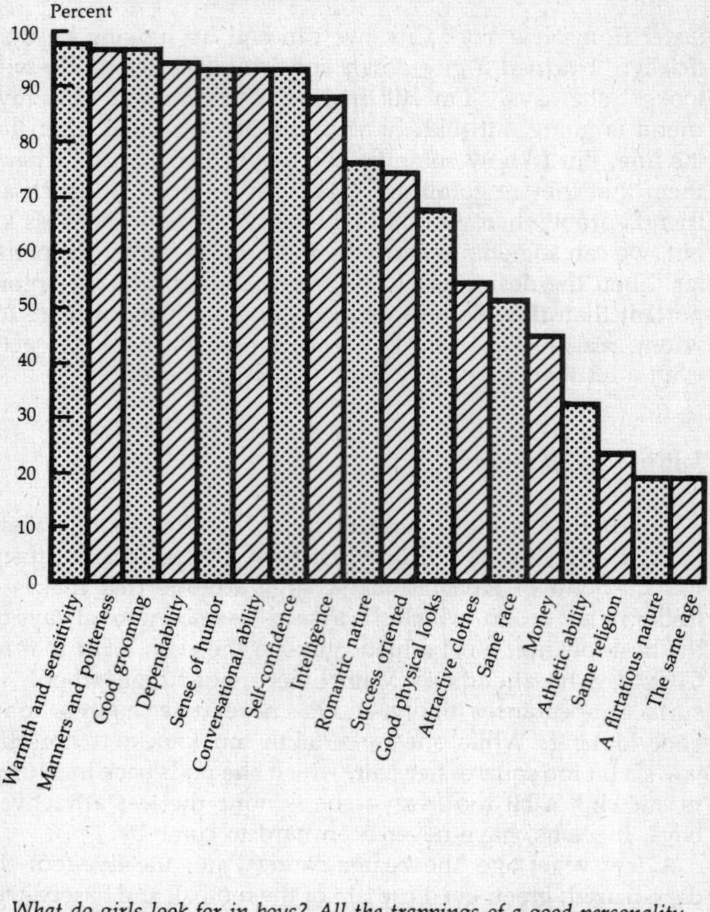

What do girls look for in boys? All the trappings of a good personality mixed with traits that are sure to make him successful in later life. What gets top ratings? Warmth and sensitivity at 98%, manners and politeness at 97%, good grooming and dependability at 94%. Not far behind come a good sense of humor, conversational ability, and self-confidence at 93%, intelligence at 88%, a romantic nature at 77%, and an orientation toward success at 75%. The surprises: good physical looks only received 68%, attractive clothes only 55%, the same race only 52%, money only 46%. Even more startling, athletic ability was rated important by a mere 33% of the girls—while the same religion came in at 24%. The two personality duds? A flirtatious nature and the same age which only 20% of all girls found important at all.

like that," she says in a somewhat raspy smoker's voice. "We'd go to parties together and I'd go downstairs with people and he'd sit upstairs by himself. He didn't like me to be around other people and friends—only with him. He was very possessive, chauvinistic, egotistical—but I knew that from the start. I tried to talk to him about it, but honestly don't know if he understood what I meant; he was just used to being such a big deal all his life."

She frowns, playing with the cord on her pink sweatshirt, worn inside-out over a turquoise polo shirt with a stand-up collar. "It actually got to the point where I really didn't even like him that much, but because I enjoyed his good looks, I put up with the relationship. I didn't want to go out with him anymore but I couldn't break it up either. I just kept putting it off, hoping it would get better. Sometimes I was so annoyed by his behavior, I was even mean to him."

That summer, however, Christy decided that time away from the situation would give her better perspective, so she went to visit her mother in Michigan. After much realistic brooding, her thoughts on Paul changed. "I realized that it wasn't worth it anymore. It was just empty. The looks had worn off and I was bored. We talked about it before I went off again to the shore for another two weeks, and agreed that there was no point in continuing it. When I came home again, he was already dating another girl, Jackie, and he was really happy."

She sighs, pushing the fluffy bangs from her eyes. "My friends still say, 'But Christy, how could you have broken up with him? He was so-o-o-o good-looking!' But it had really gotten to the point where I didn't even think he was attractive anymore; it was such a total turnoff."

I ask her how she feels now when she sees Jackie and Paul together at school: "It makes me really jealous! I'm jealous that she can put up with him and I can't! I see how good-looking he is and it bothers me, but I know that if I had him back it would be the same as before and I don't want that." (Well, clearly she does and she doesn't. Christy would like him back—but only on her terms.)

What to do differently next time? "I won't date a guy just for his looks anymore." She smiles sheepishly, as if she's just discovered a profound truth. "Personality is very important."

Unfortunately, Christy's experience is not unique. Though almost all girls in the *TeenAge* Relationships Survey say that they'd never hang in there for looks, when pressed in an interview they almost always concede that they give good-looking guys with creepy personalities a second, third, even fourth chance to come around. Why? Because even if they don't, another girl will. A few "Pauls" date themselves out or end up with bad reputations and a smaller pool of fish to draw from. But more often than not, girl after girl has to rescue herself from his gravitational pull by realizing her self-worth is not measured by the guy she "catches," and by forcing herself to see him and his good looks realistically. Says one East Texan who squirmed away from her "Paul": "Eventually, I figured out that in our school there are a lot of really cute guys and I could find one with a good personality instead of one who was just a zero."

Though it's impossible to say what makes some girls place so much emphasis on good looks, the *TeenAge* Relationships Survey does indicate that girls who rate a boy's looks as "important"—68 percent of those surveyed (85 percent of Sweet Southern Belles, only 56 percent of Twentieth Century Fast Trackers)—have a very different value system from those who don't. Perhaps because looks-conscious girls are appearance-conscious in every sense of the word, they are more than twice as likely as girls not interested in looks to judge a boy by his clothes and money, and more likely to gravitate toward jocks—because of their attractive bodies. They are also more embarrassed than others by poor grooming and less likely to give an unattractive boy with a great personality a break. So is it any surprise that more than a quarter of all looks-conscious girls are just like Christy and feel an attraction to cool, aloof guys who offer a challenge?

The case of "The Frog Prince"

Personality can also have the opposite effect and transform a frog into a prince. Then a boy's warmth and sensitivity, intelligence and thoughtfulness outweigh any less-than-perfect physical traits. "When you get older, looks are going to decline," points out Devon, a Twentieth-Century Fast Tracker (seventeen, Melbourne, Florida). "Personality, and the love that has arisen from that personality, is going to keep the relationship going. Many

Looks-Conscious Girls vs. Non-Looks-Conscious Girls: How They Value Other Superficial Qualities

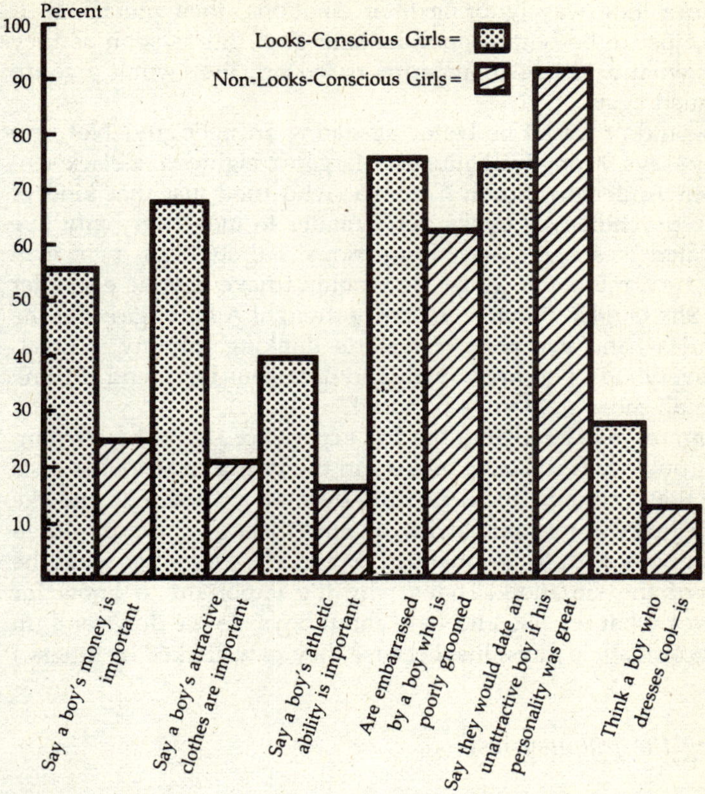

According to the TeenAge *Relationships Survey, looks-conscious girls, 68% of those surveyed, place more emphasis on all other superficial qualities than those who aren't. For instance, 56% of looks-conscious girls say a boy's money is important, while only 25% of others agree, and a startling 68% of looks-conscious girls say a boy's attractive clothes are important while only 21% of others agree! Twenty-eight percent think a boy who dresses cool—is, while only 13% of others agree. Because they like an attractive worked-out body, 40% of all looks-conscious girls say a boy's athletic ability is important, while only 17% of others agree. And, though the majority of all girls say they are embarrassed by a boy who is poorly groomed—looks-conscious girls are more critical. Seventy-six percent agree while only 63% of others do. And though most girls go along with a current cliché—that they'd date an unattractive boy if he had a great personality—looks-conscious girls aren't quite as charitable.*

girls go a long way ignoring their emotions, their morals, their values, just to be with a good-looking guy. But as soon as they realize what a real relationship is based on, they won't give up that much again."

So wouldn't we all be better off dating an ugly guy? Not necessarily, says Strong Individualist Margaret, eighteen, a black senior from Anderson, South Carolina, who tried just that kind of reverse psychology. "Looks don't matter to me—every guy I've ever dated was ugly, ugly. I'm serious. I thought an ugly man would treat me better 'cause he wouldn't have anyone else after him." She laughs. "That's just crazy though! A lot of girls get the same idea—and everyone else starts thinking the guy is great. Then everybody you know wants to date your boyfriend. I think I made all those ugly guys popular!"

(Margaret may be joking, but her experience shows how whimsical popularity is. If social brokers in the ruling crowd all at once decide that a certain "look" is cool—even an anti-esthetic one like torn-up holey jeans, mohawks, or pins through the nose—then stock in boys with those qualities skyrockets, no matter what the reality of the situation. That's why it's important to know for ourselves what we like and hate about boys, so we don't end up with incompatible guys, just because they're well-liked by others.)

Passing the jealousy test

Looks can also be a problem because they give the outside world—parents, friends, or enemies—something to hang an opinion on. While many of our girlfriends are caring and considerate enough to accept any boy we like, some may make remarks that make us feel uncomfortable. Some "friends" may be jealous if we date a really good-looking guy, others may be jealous if we date at all. Then peer pressure can become as irritating as sand in the eye. "They wouldn't dare say anything if I was going out with a wicked good-looking guy," says Pamela (sixteen, Norwell, Massachusetts), a Strong Individualist who has a sweet little doll's face, and a sneer in her voice that betrays it. "But if he was not great-looking, I wouldn't tell them because they'd say, 'Yuck! How can you like him?' Most of the time I have to like someone who's nice-looking, who the group approves of. Most of the time, those guys are idiots too, so I don't go out with anyone I really like. I wish there was less pressure and that they would keep their opinions to themselves."

Nice wish. But many girls, like boys, like to talk. And when they run out of things to say about themselves, their boyfriends, their teachers, their parents, they dig into other people's lives. Gossip, though not necessarily malicious, is for some a way of life. When it becomes negative, as in Pamela's case, it's best to take the advice of one very level-headed Twentieth-Century Fast Tracker from New York: "I liked this guy on TV, Jason Bateman," says Norma, fourteen, who hasn't really begun to date. "He seems obnoxious on the show but like a good guy to me because he's really humorous. My friends don't consider him good-looking and make fun of me for liking him. I won't let anyone stop me from liking him though. Otherwise I'll never find anyone I really like—especially when it comes to marriage. Girls our age like anyone their friends like. They really haven't established their own ideas yet—they just pick out guys who are good-looking."

Pressure to please doesn't have to come from the outside. It can simply be our own wish to "fit in" with the group and find a boy who will do likewise. Says Bobbi (sixteen, Ashland, Kentucky), one of the Strong Individualists, "If you like somebody, you want everybody else to think he's cute too, you know? It makes you feel better. Then of course, you don't want everybody thinking he's beautiful 'cause you don't want everybody going after him. But I don't want people thinking that I'm dating a dud or saying, 'Oh, God, what a jerk she is!' I know that it's not right, 'cause I shouldn't worry about what other people think, but that's the way I feel sometimes." (And it's the way most girls feel most of the time.)

It doesn't even have to be negative—as one New Yorker reveals: "My friends encourage me to go for guys just because they're beautiful. They've told me I'm foolish if I don't. My own feelings are more important though. I don't ignore their advice, because it can get me interested in a guy. But the right personality has to be there. If it is, then their enthusiasm just speeds matters up."

3

Other Elements of Beguile

So what is it exactly about a boy's physical appearance that turns us on? What do we really look at first? Is it a great pair of legs or a great pair of eyes? Is it muscles or mustaches? Terrific hair or terrific feet? Surprise of surprises: preferences fall above or below the neckline—with half the girls I interviewed saying they are bowled over by the curve of his lips, the other half by the curve of his hips!

That model's face

Without doubt, however, eyes—in a whole range of colors from "really weird blue" to "light, light, pale brown"—can reel us in from across the room or across the street. Because they pout, laugh, or cry with the boy we like, they reveal his personality, and betray all his secret, intriguing emotions. "There's a guy my friend likes and she thinks she can tell he's sweet and gentle because of his eyes," says Jennifer, fourteen, a thin, hyper, black Strong Individualist from Manhattan, who has depth-defying black eyes herself. "I agree. I'm always attracted to eyes first because they're the windows to the soul. In fact, I probably won't go out with a boy whose eyes I don't like." (As trivial as it seems, boys, this is the truth!)

Hair also reveals personality. We know that a conservative crew cut isn't likely to join us at our favorite underground dance club; pink tips and orange roots won't make it at the country club. Clean, neatly styled hair reflects a strong self-image, while a greasy mess sends just the opposite message. Says one girl for all of us: "If he doesn't care about his hair, how can he possibly care about me?"

That "Olympic" body

And what about his body? In this fitness-crazed era any guy who isn't running marathons or working out every day of his life is labeled a "wimp," a "dweebe," or just plain "dorky." Undeveloped bodies, it seems, are as much of a turnoff as undeveloped minds, and few girls can find excuses for them. "If they're skinny and scrawny," says Barbara, nineteen, a Modern Traditionalist from Norwell, Massachusetts, "it shows! They should be out lifting weights! Friends put pressure on me to judge a boy by his body. They say, 'Why are you going out with him?' I say, 'He has a great personality.' They don't understand. I guess they think he's not masculine or mature."

Indeed! At a time in our lives when everyone's body and mind is changing faster than a Baskin-Robbins flavor of the month, dating someone physically "under par" is like playing hopscotch at the Olympics—it leaves us with the sneaking suspicion that we, unlike everybody else, have somehow not quite arrived. It's no surprise then that physically mature boys, who seem in control of their bodies, have a sticky kind of confidence that attracts girls like flies. "After all," says one girl, "who wants to date a klutz?" Explains another: "If he never did a sport in his life but had a great body, then that's fine with me. I hate flab, but more than that I can't stand some guy who's trippin' over his feet and embarrassin' me—especially when we're dancin'."

On the other hand, to the ever-fluctuating teenage mind, too much muscle can be a threat. "In gym class I often look at the boy's bodies first and I like them firm, muscular, but not like Arnold Schwarzenegger," says one girl. "Those guys are disgusting; they can't even lie down on a bed comfortably! If God wanted them to have all those muscles, he would have made sure they were born with them."

THE ALLURE OF HUNKS AND HEROES

Physical and therefore social confidence may well be the reason why a third of girls in the *TeenAge* Relationships Survey rate athletic ability "important." While "hunks" and "jocks" obviously have attractive, healthy, sexy bodies, most also have attractive social lives. And though the majority of sports-minded girls say they gravitate to jocks through "common interests" (believe about half of them!), others are simply drawn to the dazzle like moths to a bright light. "Athletic ability is fun—so is going out with the captain of the football team," says Patty, fourteen, Piermont, New York, a Supersonic Dater and connoisseur of jocks. "Most girls like to be able to brag, 'My boyfriend plays football.' Many think it makes them look good. For others, it's just a good excuse to socialize." One savvy Northeasterner even told me that hitching up with the most popular jock on a new high-school campus was the key to her success with the "in" crowd—even after they broke up.

There also seems to be a kind of prestige attached to many athletes, especially in small towns where high-school and college sporting events attract more attention than all the honors students lumped together. Then quarterbacks assume the importance of "war heroes," as opposing sides of the community whip up the troops with tailgating parties, all-day parades, all-night beer blasts. Dating the captain of the football team, says one Blackford, Indiana, girl, is tantamount to being First Lady in the White House. (A terribly anachronistic and sexist Americanism, I realize, but one that still seduces many girls. Hopefully, in the future, boys will bask in the glow of the increasing numbers of female athletes.)

But athletes are not universally adored! "They turn me right off!" exclaims Marsha, a seventeen-year-old Modern Traditionalist from Norwell, Massachusetts, whose fiancé roller-skates—the closest she'll ever let him get to competitive sports. "I dated a couple of jocks and I wouldn't do it again. All that mattered to them was sports and friends—not me! They were conceited and thought they were superior to everyone else in the class. If they were seniors, they expected the freshmen girls to look up to them. They were basically on ego trips." Other complaints: jocks "think they rule the halls," "run the school," "can sleep with any girl they want," "carry team spirit too far." Says Pamela: "They all cluster together—like a team—even when they date. If you go out with one, they all give you their advice. And they talk too much. I know one guy who went out with this girl and had his friends in the back yard watching them make it. When they were done, all the guys clapped." This sweet, shy, pale blushing flower of a girl is now steaming. "To say the least, the girl was not pleased."

The *TeenAge* Relationships Survey points out that the main difference between the Pattys who get turned on by athletes and the Pamelas who get turned off is their own athletic interests and abilities. "Jockettes"—girls who rate athletic ability as an important male attribute—almost always explain it's because they're into sports themselves. Jockettes are also much more likely than other girls to value a boy's money, success, and prestige (over twice as many want to date the captain of the football team!), to look for attractive clothes, and pleasant physical looks. They have a traditional bent: jockettes are 36 percent more likely than others to expect a boy to pay for a date, and 24 percent more likely to want him to make the first sexual moves. So it's not surprising that Sweet Southern Belles have the highest proportion, 47 percent, of jockettes.

(But just dating a boy for his body can be dissatisfying. "I usually notice the physique first," says one girl, "because I'm nearsighted. I've known girls who just go for the body though. They're usually quick affairs, one-timers. They're over soon.")

SOME LIKE 'EM TALL

As expected, the old standard—that girls prefer tall boys who make them feel secure, at ease, the way Mother always said it should be—still holds, sometimes even to the point of pure irrationality. "I'm five-three so I couldn't date anybody shorter," claims Margaret. "A short guy might be the best thing for me or the nicest guy in the world, but I'll pick a tall guy first." It seems tall boys, like tall buildings, give us a sense of protection and security.

Jockettes vs. Non-Jockettes: How They Pick a Boy

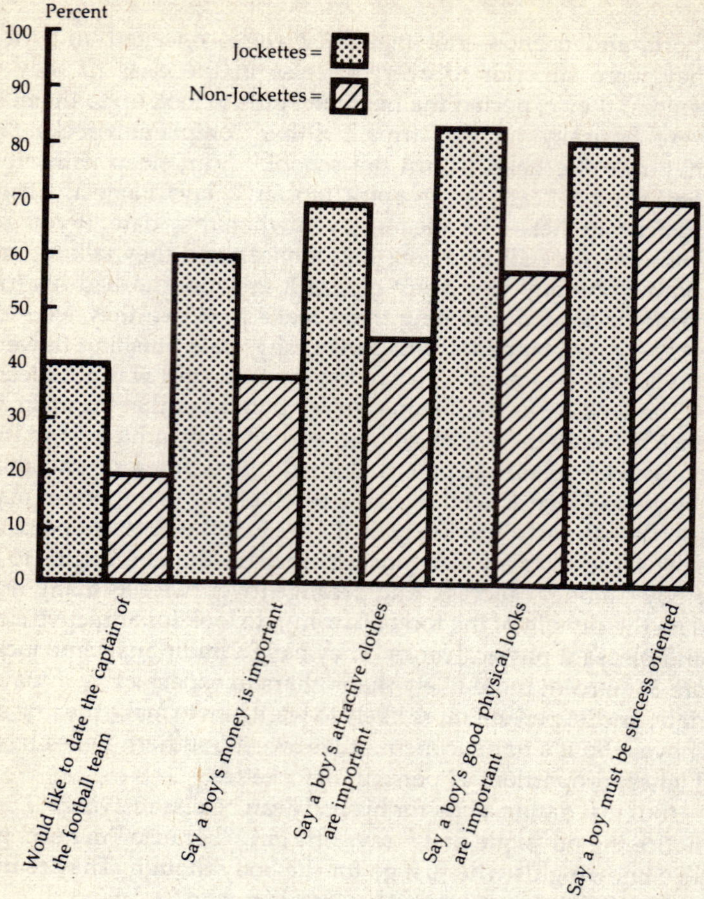

Jockettes, girls who rate a boy's "athletic ability" as important on the TeenAge *Relationships Survey, place more emphasis on a boy's status and success qualities than girls who don't consider athletic ability important. To begin with, 82% of jockettes say a boy must be success oriented, while only 71% of others say the same; 41% of jockettes would like to date the captain of the football team (the image of status and success) while only 20% of non-jockettes say the same. And, 60% say they consider how much money a boy has, as opposed to only 38% of others who do the same. Not surprisingly, jockettes are much more concerned with his physical looks, too: 84% saying that a boy's physical features are important, compared with only 58% of others who say the same.*

Dating a shrimp, we often worry, may look silly, like we've settled for second best. (This is especially true if you happen to be a shrimp yourself because short girls are often pursued by peewees afraid to ask a taller girls. I'm ashamed to admit I even held one five-foot-two guy at bay throughout my senior year—even though my friends said he looked like Robert Redford—because he didn't fit my preconceived notion of maleness. In the middle of that tumultuous college sea, I wanted a giant rock to cling to; he was a short, inflatable raft.)

Luckily for all of us, male idols like Dustin Hoffman and Dudley Moore dispel such truly tasteless notions, so that some girls even admit they like 'em short. "The guy I'm datin' now is about the same height, maybe shorter, so I just don't wear heels," says Joan, sixteen, a five-foot-eight strawberry-blonde "punkette" and a Strong Individualist from Ocean Springs, Mississippi. "One of my best friends is seein' a guy who's eight inches shorter than she is—that's a lot! They look really funny!" (She laughs a Bugs Bunny laugh.) "But they've been datin' so long that she doesn't even think about it anymore. People pointed it out to her in the beginning: 'How can you date him—he's so short!' But he's nice; she liked him and that's what counted. If you know a guy well enough, you can overlook many things like that."

Neatness counts!

One thing we can't overlook, however, is bad grooming. Often mistaken for poor "fashion sense" or unattractive "physical traits," or used as a euphemism to eliminate true losers from our address book, grooming is the quality that separates the winners from the losers, the "men" from the ragamuffins. It was the most important item on the *Young Miss* list; in third place at 94 percent on the *Teenage* Relationships Survey, and is mentioned in nearly every personal interview. Sweet breath, beautiful teeth, clean clothes are not only esthetically pleasing, but have social implications as well. "It's nice to be seen with someone who looks and smells nice," says one girl. "It makes me feel more secure. It means you can show him off in front of your friends. Who wants a dirty guy? It's embarrassing. If I take the time to look good, I expect him to also!" Says another: "The majority of boys I know are pretty poorly groomed—even the older guys. I don't understand it. If they just cleaned themselves up they would be acceptable. Even if they weren't good-looking they would get another look from me."

Saturday night fashion fever

With the question of good grooming comes the question of "style." While many charming guys can be forgiven simple fashion naiveté (one girl's date showed up at a black-tie banquet wearing white athletic socks), over half the girls in the *TeenAge* Relationships Survey say dress is important, perhaps because, like feathers on a bird, it helps them identify their social species. "Yes! I admit it," says Carmen, sixteen, Coral Gables, Florida, a Modern Traditionalist jet-setter who abhors alligator shirts and kelly-green pants. "A well-cut outfit, clothes that fit properly, are turnons. A guy who has designer name tags on each piece of clothing is a turnoff, as is someone who wears his clothes too tight." Rachel, fourteen, a no-nonsense jeans-and-sweatshirt kind of Strong Individualist from New York, agrees: "If I don't like the way he dresses, it means we probably have very little in common. Guys who are slobs or who wear black shirts with yellow flowers and green ties are gross! A normal guy would wear jeans and a shirt."

Dress can even be a personality indicator: "If he dresses like a nerd, then I can't help labeling him one," says one girl. "If he dresses really cool, then I assume he is. Designer jeans usually turn me off; I like New Wave!" Yet the total irony is that just as many girls love cords as jeans, and just as many go for "preps" as hate them. And while most girls complain that boys don't dress up enough, others say terrific dressers intimidate them. It all depends on what we've been brought up to admire. Clearly, dress is as whimsical as popularity.

Clothes, of course, can also revamp drippy "fives" into startling "tens": "Sometimes a guy, like the one I'm dating now, isn't that good-looking at all," says one South Carolinian, herself an admitted clothes horse. "But the way he dresses is so neat, so nice. It makes him look great. There's no reason why a guy can't dress well—it just shows he takes pride in himself."

4

"What do you see in him anyway?" our mother persists

"Personality!" we reply.

Ah, yes, personality—the great equalizer. Like the skillful hand of a magician, it sometimes lets a wonderful, yet less than perfect, guy slip through our lines of defense. Then suddenly, when we least expect it, reveals him as our Jack of Hearts, our Mr. Wonderful, our Mr. Right. Personality is first on the lips of almost every girl I interviewed, heads every *TeenAge* Relationships Survey, and often outweighs looks, athletic ability, even grooming. We *notice* looks first, but personalities are what relationships are made of!

Mr. Sensitivity

Ironically, the aspects of personality we like best—warmth and sensitivity (topping the *TeenAge* Relationships Survey at 98 percent)—are those most at odds with the cool, aloof exterior boys are encouraged by society to cultivate. "A guy should be warm and sensitive," says Helen, sixteen, black, a Strong Individualist from Upper Montclair, New Jersey. "Unfortunately, in some cases society has him thinking he's got to be leather-tough. But he can be masculine and feeling at the same time. He can even cry—he's human, too. I had a guy cry to me; it was interesting. I was kinda sad, kinda glad that he felt he could do it. I like it when a guy feels sensitive and doesn't stick to guns and football. They can be interested in babies and flowers. It's nice to pick a flower and say, 'This smells good.' Society says boys have to block that emotion out—but they miss a lot."

Girls who tout male sensitivity have even gone so far as to alter their definition of "masculinity." "There's nothing wrong with warmth, sensitivity, emotions," says one Los Angeles sixteen-year-old. "I don't know why boys think they're incapable of showing them. It's an asset to their whole being and makes them much more manly. If I met a guy like that, I would respect him, because he had no fear of his feelings."

Communication, warmth, and pure affection are exactly what first drew Fatima—a bright, sensitive Hispanic junior and Modern Traditionalist from a Manhattan Catholic girls' school—to Roberto. "My boyfriend freshman year was really—ah, poor Roberto—ugly!" she sighs, riveting her huge, round black eyes on mine, her only earthly anchor as she drifts away on memories of past infatuation. Her lips are dark, full; her long black hair is layered, luxuriant. I'm prepared for anything; her lovelife is like hurricane season on *The Love Boat*. "He had acne, bad teeth. I actually fell in love with him though—we became so close. He just popped into my life when it was really important; when I was having problems with my mother."

Her black corduroy minidress, lace-up boots, and tights are no match for the clammy fire-escape stairs of my office building—the only private place we have for a rushed interview, so she tightens her coat around her neck: "It all began when my best friend said she wanted me to meet her boyfriend's little brother, Roberto, at the park. Only the night before, I'd had the worst fight ever with my mother about going to a party alone because my girlfriend had backed out. I made a big fuss. I guess I really didn't want to go either but I slammed the door in her face, which really got her fuming. So she hit me with the sole of a slipper. It was the first time she'd hit me!—so I cried all night. When I went to the park the next day, I wasn't in any state of mind to remember that

Roberto would be there. I'd heard lots about him from my friend, but it didn't cross my mind."

A clear plastic ice-cube earring tumbles from her ear and she quickly replaces it. "We played volleyball and I taught him Five Hundred Rum. Eventually, we put down the blanket and had a picnic. We were both a little shy in the beginning but he began to open up. I found out later that when he saw me get out of the car he told his brother he thought I was good-looking."

At one point, she says, everyone was making fun of the slipper bruise on her leg. "You could see it 'cause I was wearing shorts. They were all asking me if I was a sadomasochist. I ended up telling Roberto what had happened with my mother. When we were going home in the car together, he suddenly, unexpectedly, put his arm around me. We went out for one year and two months from there."

The kind of caring that Roberto exhibited is very different from a sexual overture—and worlds more important. It's the kind of warmth girls long for in boys, the kind that keeps them coming back for more, well after any infatuation with beautiful exteriors has faded. It's the kind of warmth that made Ginger, an eighteen-year-old quintessential Supersonic Dater from Atlanta, Texas, fall in love with Robbie's hug. "I loved the way he used to hold me. It made me feel so good. No one has made me feel that good before or after," she says, batting her giant blue eyes at me. "I felt really happy when I was with him. We could talk about my arguments with friends, even about my father, a former policeman who set unusually strict curfews and who was making it the unhappiest time of my life." She twists a lock of blonde hair around her little finger—clearly, a habit she reserves for boys—and fluffs the pleats on her floral printed dress. "Robbie was wonderful!

"You know those times when you're upset and you can't figure out what's wrong?" she asks. "Well, one time I was over at his house and I didn't even know what was bothering me. He got really frustrated and said, 'I don't know what you want me to do.' I wanted him to just hold me. I didn't want to have to say it; I wanted him to just do it on his own—and he did. He said 'Oh, I'm sorry. I don't know what it is but I want you to feel better.' I was just crying and crying and Robbie just held me. But as hard as I was crying, I was happy."

Clearly, Robbie and Roberto had the right stuff. But believe it or not, there are some girls who'd rather their guy didn't: "I like a guy who shows his feelings for a girl, but I don't like someone too mushy," says flaky, modelesque Virginia, seventeen, a Strong Individualist from Penn Valley, Pennsylvania. "This one guy was just too nice to me and I had to break up with him because I didn't like it. He'd go to church and stuff; he was too queer, straight, and yicky. I don't like guys who treat me nicely all the time; I get bored with them. I like a challenge." (Virginia's "relationships," I find out later, are more like a tug-of-war between the "beautiful people.")

"P.D.A."

And a note on P.D.A. (Public Displays of Affection): while many girls find open signs of caring and friendship very gratifying, too much of a good thing can be a turnoff. "I hate guys who are all over you in public," says one proper Southerner. "It's strange because I'm real affectionate. I love to hug and touch people. When I'm with a guy, I'm affectionate too, but when we're in public I don't like to put my arm around him. Maybe hold hands. But none of this kissy mushy stuff. I don't like people walking down the mall hanging all over each other. It drives me crazy. I like to do it in private." Another girl says it's so embarrassing that she "pretends like it's not happening."

A little romance

Closely allied with sensitivity, though not a top priority, is "a romantic nature." Baskets of roses delivered to our doorstep, books of poems written about us, long, pensive walks along the beach at sunset, seem to fulfill our expectations about what romance should be—and any boy who can pull it off seems to have something "extra," at least for the 77 percent in the *TeenAge* Relationships Survey who love it. "I'm so romantic, my friends get sick of it," says Jennifer, who is accustomed to being spoiled by her father. "I wouldn't even worry about what a guy looked like if he brought me flowers; being pampered conquers all. Once I saw a guy on *General Hospital* sprinkle a girl's bed with rosebuds and I went crazy!"

Romance allows boys to express caring as well as creativity, to show that we really are—at least for the moment—the center of their universe: "Don, the guy I'm going out with, is so romantic," says Julie, a seventeen-year-old Supersonic Dater from Berwyn, Pennsylvania. "We'll go out to dinner and he'll excuse himself to buy cigarettes, come back with roses instead. If I need something—a cigarette, a match—even in the middle of a meal, he'll run out and get it. Little things like that mean a lot; they show he's really thoughtful." Julie's list of "little things" also includes a gold bracelet that Don bought during a stroll through the mall one day. "I said, 'Look at that!' because mine had broken a week before. Then he said, 'I'll be back in a minute,' and went to buy it for me. I couldn't believe it."

Julie may be overly impressed with Don's spending power, but most girls agree it's the thought—a card, a gesture, a compliment at the right moment—that counts. Presents that take the place of necessary communication can have a negative effect. "This shy guy started getting on my nerves," says one girl. "He didn't really know or understand me and definitely couldn't talk to me. He did things that annoyed me but I couldn't get mad at him because if I did, he sent me roses. He sent me roses all the time. I love them to death, but it's like he went overboard with it. If I get a rose I want it to be special, not just 'Cheer up, you're in a bad mood.' He thinks a rose takes care of everything. That made it especially hard when I was trying to tell him I wanted to date other people."

Too much romance, too soon, can be a turnoff as well—especially for younger girls who are easily threatened by overt signs of male interest. "I hate it when a boy opens doors, brings me flowers," exclaims Laura, thirteen, a Modern Traditionalist from Englewood, New Jersey. "It makes me laugh because I think he's trying too hard. Besides, no one our age does it." One Kentucky girl found that a guy who brought her roses on the first date raised her expectations so high (she really thought he was Prince Charming) that she was crushed when he turned out to be a mere mortal.

Mr. Manners

Good manners, like a romantic nature, tend to indicate that a boy is aware of other people and the world around him, give us clues about his upbringing and an idea about how he'll fit into our socioeconomic group. For that reason, "manners and politeness" get a 97 percent approval rating in the *TeenAge* Relationships Survey, making them the second most important attribute a boy can have. Also 86 percent say their primary function is to make a good impression on parents. Obviously, if mom and dad are sticklers for "good manners," but he tears into a lunchroom hamburger like a starving wild boar from Africa, we'd better not invite him home to dinner!

The key is, as one girl puts it, "No embarrassment, *please!* A boy must be polite—especially in front of grown-ups. He must show good judgment by the way he talks in front of them, too. It has nothing to do with etiquette. It's just that I hate a guy who starts talking and whispering about girls in a room full of grown-ups. It just shows how immature he is."

Many Southern girls equate manners with "respect." And one transplanted New Yorker has become so spoiled by Dixie "manners" that she finds it impossible to cope with anything less. "I'm not really into the lady bit," says Claire, sixteen, a sharp-shooting, jeans-and-silk-blouse, Twentieth-Century Fast Tracker, from Lexington, Kentucky. "In fact, I've had some guys complain that I'm the only girl in the school who can open her own doors! But the guy I went out with last weekend didn't open the car door for me and it kinda bugged me, 'cause now I'm used to it. It's bad, but I kind of thought that since it was the first date he'd try to impress me a bit more."

She tucks her pale bare feet under her legs, slips a gold good-luck charm nervously up and down her necklace. "When I first got to school, a friend got mad at my Northern 'liberation,' saying 'I always try and open the door for you but you never give me the chance!' But we'd be talking and so I'd just naturally go on ahead. Well, I'd just never thought about it! A lot of Kentucky girls have grown up with it, but I haven't. Now it's funny. On a first date especially, I look for it. It shows a little respect, that he's out to impress me."

(I never will forget my friend Diane, an anachronism from Atlanta who still believed in white gloves, tea parties, hair spray, and true "gray" Southern gentlemen. One of the hottest tickets on Duke's campus, she was shocked by her first date with a "Yankee boy" who forgot to open her car door. "I just sat there and waited for that rude boy to come back and open it," she harrumphed. "Don't your mothers teach you any manners?" Many Yankee boys were shell-shocked by such gentility—especially when they waited till Friday afternoon to call girls for a date, only to find that the perfect Southern gentleman had booked them weeks in advance. Transplanted Southerners, as Claire says, can be the worst manners critics of all.)

5

The Press for Success

As much as we all love romance and great manners, we don't want a lackadaisical Romeo hanging around our locker all day, spouting sonnets and yanking petals from daisies. We are a very practical generation; he must also be successful!

Excuses for the "Me" Generation

We've heard them all before, time after time, the put-downs of the "Me" generation, the kids of the Seventies and Eighties who are interested only in getting ahead, making a living. About humanities courses that have been replaced by more "in-demand" technical or practical training, how no one gives a damn anymore about what they learn, only about the grades they get. But it's no surprise! Given the economic outlook for the country and the world—inflation, gross unemployment, spiraling deficits—teens have a right to be nervous! If Ph.D.s can't find work, then we know that getting a job, especially one we like, is difficult; acquiring a home, a car, the kind of life-style we were raised with, will be harder than that. "Making it" has become a fact of life; "success" has become a hallmark of the Eighties, a theme of this book.

It's a comprehensive success as well. Not just something academic, but physical success—trim, healthy bodies that are dexterous, athletic; and romantic success—good, sensual, sexual lives, guys who "know what they're doing." We want a "successful marriage," because we're willing to wait so long to enter it, to be sure we're mature, established adults who can handle that kind of responsibility. Achievement has become such an end in itself that some girls use it as a screening device: "I'm not dating anyone now, even though I'd like to," says one New Yorker, "because I'm too busy finishing school and filling out college applications. Besides, the guys that call seem so young, so unconcerned about their futures. I'm not even interested."

We apply success to our "Superwoman" outlook on life, to our hope for careers that will make us feel independent, worthwhile, secure. To our hope for home lives that will be fulfilling and meaningful. For such reasons, the vast majority of girls in my interviews and in the *TeenAge* Relationships Survey are attracted to "Superboys"—well-groomed, intelligent males with all the markings of social and economic thoroughbreds. Today we may be less interested in a boy's "background" than in the "ground" he plans to gain.

"It's important to get into a good college 'cause it's so hard to get jobs now, with all the cutbacks," explains a politically minded South Weymouth, Massachusetts, Twentieth-Century Fast Tracker, Sarah, fourteen. "So everybody's really trying to get ahead. I think that's important. It determines the kind of boy a girl wants to date too, because before you go into a relationship, you want to make sure it's going to work. That means having similar ideas and backgrounds so that a success-conscious girl will end up dating a boy like herself."

Like many girls, Sarah notes, "There's no longer any pressure to hide the fact that you're ambitious. I think most boys are turned on by girls who are independent, who *don't* need them; it's attractive. Besides, I plan to be successful, so I don't want a guy who'll resent me if he's not." Sarah also craves money, reasoning that "if he isn't concerned with money, then he probably isn't concerned with success."

For girls from less affluent backgrounds, success can be number one. "I want my guy to be a strong achiever like myself. That's why I like athletes—because they portray a picture of being successful," says Margaret, whose father is a supervisor in a nylon plant, her mother a lab technician at a hospital. "Athletes try to play the best they can so they can go pro. They're the kind of people I like to associate with. I certainly don't want to be poor; I'm as poor now as I want to be!"

Money is the easiest yardstick by which to measure accomplishment, but certainly not the only one. "Sure, money and making it are important," says Audrey, eighteen, a brown-haired, brown-eyed all-American girl from Friendswood, Texas, in a pink-and-white floral dress. "We're always psyched for success but are we ever really satisfied? For some people success is having lots of money. For others it's having kids, a nice house. In any case, it's important to have goals in life, to reach for them, not just be a bum lying around. New ideas, new challenges keep you alive and young.

"It's hard to describe success for myself," continues this hard-core Modern Traditionalist, "because I'm never satisfied. As soon as I complete one goal, I'm looking for something else to strive for. It keeps me going and I hope my husband will be like that, too."

Examined closely, this press for success may not even be completely our own idea: "Right now it isn't important to me whether my boyfriend wants a career or not 'cause we're just going to college," says Lara, seventeen, a Strong Individualist from Seabrook, Texas, who's also a picture-perfect brunette in a miniature striped bikini (we're poolside in Orlando, Florida, during a cheerleading competition). "But if he wasn't motivated and just wanted to work in a car wash or something, I'd think twice. It was my mom who first asked, 'Lara, what's he going to do?' I never really thought about it before, but I guess she's right."

Mr. Popularity

Another measure of success, especially on the teenage level, is popularity. Though a popular guy doesn't necessarily have more going for him, we may be led by the circus around him to "think" he does. If nothing else, it boosts your ego to hang on to someone everybody else likes. "Hopefully, there is something appealing about him to you as well as to others," says Kendal, seventeen, a sweet Southern Belle and a curvy, cat-eyed beauty contest winner from Clearfield, Kentucky. "Though it's not really important to have other people interested in a guy I date, it's nice to know they want him, too."

Many girls think that dating a popular guy will make them more popular, help them break into the elite clique, win them prestige. Many think that popularity is like wet paint—something you can brush up against and be anointed by. "Prestige matters to about 75 percent of the kids in my class," snaps Audrey. "But we other 25 percent end up happier. Why else do you think the divorce rate is so high?"

Minds over muscles

In order to be successful, the boy we like must also be intelligent—not "brainy-bookworm" smart, say 82 percent of all girls in the *TeenAge* Relationships Survey, but street-wise, with "a good head on his shoulders" and a gift of common sense. "My boyfriend's not going to college," says one girl, "but he's got a lot of know-how, is making a lot of money, and will definitely move up the ladder." Intelligent types make better decisions—like knowing not to drink and drive, or not to bring a girl home late when she has a strict curfew. Suzanne, fourteen, a Supersonic Dater from Paoli, Pennsylvania, broke up with her old boyfriend, George, because "He was slack on grades and cared only about partying. That's why he flunked out; he wasn't responsible—and I like responsible guys. Irresponsible guys are always misjudging things. They don't really care about what others think or what they're going to do in the future. I'd rather have a man who can find a job, support himself and a family."

Girls like Ginger, who dreams of running for public office some day, demand even more awareness "I like to talk about what condition the nation's in, about politics and war. But I have a hard time finding guys like me," she says. "My current beau doesn't want to talk about stuff like that. So I just avoid the issue and bring it up with girlfriends. He's not well-informed and that's his own fault. I want someone who cares about the world and what's going on. It's philosophical, but I can't stand somebody who's just floating through life, just living in their own little world."

The rapper

It also takes a certain amount of intellect to be "a good conversationalist," a top-of-the-list quality on the *TeenAge* Relationships Survey that makes any relationship easier, more relaxing, and comfortable. It's especially important when we're caught in the car alone with a new date listening to our own heart beat, the air-conditioning hum. "I like to carry on interesting conversations, not just sit around with a dud, trying to find things to talk about," explains Carmen. "One night, for example, Juan, my crush (I've never had a long-term boyfriend) and I stayed up all night talking about religion, the devil, and society. They were things worth talking about. I don't think most guys are inclined to think that way; it wouldn't be the first thing on their minds."

Ah, but we don't want an Einstein either! "If a guy gets all As, people say 'E-e-e-e-w, I can't believe you get all As!' They joke about it," says Strong Individualist Noel (fifteen, Bronx, New York), a tall, thin, vivacious black girl who attends one of Manhattan's super-social private schools with the likes of Mick Jagger's kid. "It's considered nerdy and antisocial, 'cause it means he'd rather go home on Friday and study than talk on the phone. Then when he comes in Monday, all he can talk about is the bio test—which is still two days away! It's not cool in our school to be too smart or too different." Nor is it "cool" anywhere for a guy to flaunt his intelligence, because it can be intimidating. "I don't like it when guys are overly intelligent and use huge words just to impress me," says Fatima. "For instance, I once met this guy at my cousin's wedding who was trying to get to me by talking to my cousin. When she asked him a simple question: 'What does it take to get into your college?' he turned it into a lecture. He should have answered simply and left his giant vocabulary for business. He tried to impress me and just ended up turning me off."

If he can't take a joke—forget him

Top of nearly every list, only second behind warmth and manners, with a 93 percent rating on the *TeenAge* Relationships Survey, is humor, which sets a relaxed atmosphere, relieves tension, and helps us get serious points across in a pleasant way. In fact, if many of us can't date a guy with a twisted mind, we'd rather not date at all. "I just like guys who are funny and like laughing," says Rachel. "It puts me in a different mood. One guy I know is like that and I eat lunch with him every day. I can go into lunch totally pissed at everybody and not wanting to talk. Then he puts food on his lip and lets it hang there, letting everyone look at it. It's silly but funny. Once I bet him he couldn't last one whole period without being funny around me and found out he couldn't! With other people, however, he can be more serious."

"Humor is a vital part of any relationship," sums up Devon. "You've got to be able to laugh at yourself or you're not going to make it. I mean, with all the stupid things I do, I'd be a nervous wreck if I took them all seriously. Humor is really an important consideration in a guy. If he can't laugh then there's no future in our relationship."

6

The Quest for an Older Man

Age, because it influences a boy's personality, can make the difference between the mature, steady lion we long to be with and the hyperactive sand flea who does nothing but annoy. Try as we may to debunk clichés like "younger boys are too immature," or "girls mature faster than guys"—it just can't be done; there's just too much evidence to the contrary.

"A lot of guys my age are really immature," says Holly (seventeen, Livingston, New Jersey), a Strong Individualist who only goes for older guys. "They play cat-and-mouse games—like following you around, or waiting to find out if you like them so they can act hard to get. Many simply can't decide whether to ask you out at all and spend most of their time debating should I or shouldn't I? I'm just not into that." Other problems: Younger boys are "confused," "strut down the hall like Mr. Bigshot when they land an older girl," "don't have any future goals," "are boring conversationalists," "act hyper and obnoxious—especially around girls they like," end up "throwing things at you instead of talking to you." And many are just plain unattractive: "You see some guy who has a really gorgeous face but a little scrawny body," says Noel, "and you think, 'I really can't wait till he's older and bigger. But for now—hands off.' "

There's such a stigma attached to dating younger boys that the idea of choosing one willfully is out of the question. "I once dated this younger guy. He was fifteen and I was sixteen and we met at the beach," says Jean, seventeen, a Strong Individualist from Pikeville, Kentucky. "But every time I was with him, I felt inferior because I felt people were saying, 'Oh, look at her with that little young guy. There must be something wrong with her.' He looked up to me instead of down to me. It felt weird, like I was his older sister instead of his girlfriend."

In praise of younger men

In rare cases, however, dating a younger guy works. "A girl in our class liked a younger guy and it was a real scandal," Noel notes. "But he was really cool; he didn't act younger. He was even taller than her, one of the few guys who matured early. After everyone found out who 'the younger guy' was, they didn't care. It's just the idea that frightens most girls away. It can happen, but the girl is usually embarrassed about it. As in this case, she tried to keep it hidden as long as she could, until it eventually came out."

A few girls even say there's an advantage to dating a younger boy—control. "Age doesn't matter, maturity does and that's not measured in years," says Didi, eighteen, Bedford, New York, a Supersonic Dater with a cigarette voice, double-pierced ears, and a healthy appetite for males with cars and money. "When I was seventeen, I went out with a guy who had just turned fourteen and it was fun. It made me feel like I had control, which I liked for a change." She tosses her long wavy blonde mane in the air, lights a cigarette. "With most younger guys you don't have to worry about them being sexually aggressive. If you say no, and put your foot down, they usually listen; it lets you decide the pace. Older men, on the other hand, can provide too much of an age gap. I dated a twenty-six-year-old when I was fifteen and there were too many differences, too many people asking if he was immature—or why else was he hanging out with a fifteen-year-old? I finally decided I didn't need to take care of someone who couldn't take care of himself."

The older, the better

For most of us, however, older "men" represent "security" because no one's likely to hassle us or say we're rocking the boat if they see us with someone two or three years our senior. They are also more likely to be emotionally "settled," self-confident, and secure, to have money, cars, and an ability to take us anywhere we want to go. In short, older boys have everything younger boys lack, plus none of the hassle.

"I love older guys!" exclaims Carmen. "I've never gotten along with guys my age. Maybe I'm just too mature for my years, but I just can't relax unless I'm with older people. They rub off on me and it's hard to go down to a younger boy's level after being up there." Agrees another, "An older boy is more interesting, more mature, more likely to do romantic, intriguing things."

But if it's control we seek with young whippersnappers, it's lack of control we fear with older guys—the notion that like out-of-control kites they may drift beyond our tether—or worse, take us flying away with them! "With someone much older, I would feel weird," says Nicole, a thirteen-year-old Strong Individualist from Fort Lee, New Jersey. "He might be more sexually experienced and I wouldn't want him to try things on me. Besides, it would never happen. Most high-school boys don't even know that we junior-high girls are here."

Indeed. In some school systems where age and structural barriers have become social barriers, junior-high girls are unofficially banned from conquests on the high-school level. Nonconformists, who are brazen enough to cross the line, are viewed as traitors, objects of envy or suspicion who have to be shot down by public opinion as soon as possible. "Last year when I was in seventh grade I went out with a ninth-grader and everyone called him a cradle robber," says Emily, thirteen, Cliffside Park, New Jersey, a Supersonic Dater who attends a private junior high. "They said he must be hard up because he couldn't find someone his own age. Older kids thought I was a slut and started talking about me. It finally embarrassed me so much that I had to stop dating him."

Says Patty, who encountered similar resistance at another school: "I like boys to be a few years older because at my age, they can't get any younger! But I went through so much grief last year for dating a junior. Everyone assumed I was sleeping with Jake after two weeks and that I was a slut. It was a horrible year for me. Many of my friends were terrified of going into high school, afraid that people would hate us. Now, in high school if people assume things, they don't say it. They just keep their mouths shut. They know if they keep it up someone older will tell them to shut up. They were used to dictating; now they're dictated to."

The result? Many girls like Gia, thirteen, a Strong Individualist from North Bergen, New Jersey, feel so constrained by public opinion that they keep their desire for older boys a secret. "I really prefer older guys," she confides, "and can't wait until I'm in high school so I can go out with them. But right now the only boys I can go out with are those my age; in our school, dating someone older is considered slutty. They think you're gross and that he's a cradle robber. For instance, I once fooled around with a guy who was three years older and I got a lot of grief. Maybe it's because they assume you go farther with an older boy; maybe it's the sexual thing, I don't know."

Dating a boy who's much older can give our parents reason to worry that we're getting in over our heads. "I dated a guy who was five years older than I," says Supersonic Dater Dale, seventeen, Norwell, Massachusetts, "and when his parents moved away, he and his brother got their own apartment and started college. His parents cut down on his money so he couldn't come see me as often and my parents wouldn't let me go to the apartment alone. As a result, the relationship just fizzled out. We still care for each other but there's just too much of an age gap." Logistics alone can make an affair all but impossible to continue. One girl dated a guy in his thirties when she was fifteen. "It lasted two weeks. He was in the city and it was a big secret. I had to commute and finally said forget it."

And when he's ready to "settle down" but we're just "pulling up roots," the age gap can suddenly become a "gape." "The only thing that causes problems is that right now I'm getting out of school and I have to decide if I want to go to college or work," says Vanessa, seventeen, a lean, leggy, plastic beauty-queen type (definitely a Sweet Southern Belle) from Kimper, Kentucky, who's been dating Tom, a divorced twenty-two-year-old, for over a year. "I know that if Tom thought I was wavering he'd start pushing me into staying home. I made it clear when we first started dating that I wanted to go to college but now I'm not so sure." Vanessa, one of those girls who manage to look genteel even in a yellow sweatsuit, runs her long, aristocratic fingers through her mass of brown curls.

"We've talked about marriage 'cause he's worked, has enough money, and is ready to settle down. He asks me when I'm going to be ready but I just ask, 'What do you mean?' Though I know he doesn't want to stop me from going away to school, the whole issue gets me confused."

What about a job, a career, financial security? I ask. "Oh, I don't need to worry about that," she drawls sweetly. "Mom and dad are in the coal business; I could always go live with them." Just then a single diamond ring on her left hand flashes in front of my eyes. "It's not what you think." She laughs, catching my surprise. "It's not an engagement ring from Tom, just a present from my d-a-a-a-a-a-d-d-y!" (I learned later that many Kentucky girls sport such tokens of affection from parents and beaus. So much for being a coal miner's daughter!)

Still, some strong-minded girls actually like the mental game of chess that older boys afford. "He's got to be at least a little domineering," says Bobbi, a heavy-set blonde with thick blue eye shadow, curls tucked up under a baseball cap, a skimpy black bikini. "I'm a domineering person and I don't like to be the one who takes over and says, 'We'll do this and we'll do that.' I like a challenge." She grins. "There was one guy who was a lot older than me—I was ten and he was seventeen. We got along real good because he wouldn't jump when I said jump—oh, gosh, no. We didn't have any conflicts though. I never let him domineer me, but I liked to let him try—just a little bit."

7

Money: Princes and Paupers

Talk of money—especially when it has to do with what we look for in boys—is in most circles so taboo that not one girl I interviewed made an off-the-cuff reference to it. It wasn't until I examined an old *Seventeen* Magazine survey that listed money as a dating factor in the Seventies, that I began to inquire about it and got a torrent of opinions that ranged from the ubiquitous "it's not important," mumbled by "nice girls" trained not to talk about nasty subjects, to gutsy monologues on the advantages of dating rich boys. Many teens, especially those under sixteen, even admit they're simply too young, or too coddled, to grasp (or admit) its importance!

In any case, money reveals itself as an important factor in social acceptability, one that can make us feel socially at ease or out of our league with a boy, comfortable at dinner with his family, uncomfortable with his friends on vacation. Like most girls I interviewed, the majority in the *TeenAge* Relationships Survey agree hands down that money isn't important for a date; when it comes to marriage most quickly change their tune. Then only a fraction of them have the guts to stick by their idealistic guns. "I'd never marry a guy just for money," says Devon. "There'd be no relationship. Money would help a lot; it would make life a lot easier, but when you get old you may lose it. And there's got to be something else there to keep the relationship alive. Of course, most girls will date a wealthy guy! But girls who stay with them only for that reason are using them and it really bugs me. That really, oh man, hurts."

Audrey, unlike most Sweet Southern Belles, agrees. "We did this rating game the other day, ranking a boy's qualities on a scale of one to ten and I listed wealth as nine—nearly the least important. My father, a drafting teacher, and mother, a dental hygienist, use their money well and don't waste it. We live nicely, have nice things, but not like many of my wealthy friends, who have cars and enough outfits to last four months without wearing the same thing twice. But I don't think they're any happier than me. Love, respect, religion, morality, are more important to me than the diamonds they get for Christmas. I just need enough money to live comfortably."

The majority of girls, however, believe money does matter—especially in later life when it comes to maintaining the status quo. "I'd like my husband to have enough money to take me places, get a big house, travel," says Christy, who isn't about to settle for anything less than daddy provided. "Around here there's nothing to do without it! It's important to be financially secure. I plan on working, too. I'm not going to be Miss Housewife running around like the Main Line women here, playing paddle tennis all morning, golf all afternoon. That's boring."

It is also "attitude." "I want to say money's not important—but it is, because the future is very important," says Rita, sixteen, a black Supersonic Dater from Bronxville, New York. "I don't want him necessarily to be rich, but he can't be crude. It's a snobbish statement but I don't want a guy wearing sneakers to a formal affair! He must dress well and not act like a low-life. It's breeding more than money."

However, less affluent girls say money is the passport to the kind of life they envy. Such is the case of a Strong Individualist named Mickey, a super-cynical wisecracker whose big white teeth, raspy outdoors voice, clear blue eyes, and freckles say she should have been born to the elite side of Virginia society, instead of to Galax, a stiflingly small blue-collar town with one restaurant, one disco, and absolutely nowhere else to go on Saturday night. Crisp, aloof, determined, Mickey at seventeen wants a career, no husband, no kids—but lots and lots of money—dates that have it, too.

"I like the idea of dating somebody who can show me a good time," she says, scrunching her tall, thin frame accordion-style onto the couch of the conference room where we meet. "It's my dream to have some guy pick me up at the front door, bring me roses and jewelry, open the car door for me, take me to a nice restaurant. If he doesn't have money, he can't do that easily." She shoots me a sideways glance, half for impact, half for approval. "I don't ever want to want for anything material."

Crossing her arms, bouncing one blue-jeaned leg on her knee, she continues. "Where I come from no one has money, so the guys I've dated don't either. When I get to college, I want to date a guy with a car. I'm not sayin' that if I met a nice guy who didn't have one that I wouldn't date him, but I'd rather he did. Then he can take me to parties, snow and water skiing. If he has no money he'll end up watching football games at my house, drinking beers."

Like more "monied" girls, Mickey equates million-dollar bank accounts with sophistication, something she says is an absolute must: "If we're in a restaurant looking at the menu and the waiter comes over and asks if he can help us, and my date says, 'Shucks, I don't know yet,' that would be a total turnoff," she explains. "If he says, 'Please come back in a few minutes and take our order,' that would be fine. He has to know what's going on, be sophisticated and intelligent about it." (Interestingly enough, "sophistication" was an important concern of girls, considered to be "materialistic," in the Twenties. By the Fifties, it was replaced by an overall desire for less materialistic qualities, like "a great personality.")

Since money plays an important part in any marriage, Mickey says dissimilar values cause friction. "How? Lord, like when Mrs. Jane Doe wants to buy a fur coat and Mr. Doe wants to buy a pickup truck, then who gets the money? That's why a woman should have her own career. If she wants to buy a fur coat, let her. She can use her own money. That sense of independence is important."

The *TeenAge* Relationships Survey shows that girls who choose a boy primarily for his money or earning power are unlike Mickey and tend to hold more traditional values across the board than girls who don't. For that reason they are more likely to be Sweet Southern Belles, least likely to be Twentieth-Century Fast Trackers. Perhaps because some come from traditional families themselves, they're much more inclined to feel a boy should pay for a date and that a man should support a household, are remarkably more concerned that he "fit in" with their own religious and racial backgrounds, that he present an attractive appearance to the outside world through the clothes he wears. Because money-oriented girls are also more concerned than others that their men be successful, they place a greater emphasis on intelligence, athletic ability, and early signs of leadership. In fact, money-oriented girls are 40 percent more likely than others to want to date Mr. Successful—the captain of the football team.

He is what he drives!

Even though the improved economic situation for women in the Eighties has made dating a boy just for his car less acceptable, there are still some who think "wheels" are number one. "Having a nice car is important," says Gigi, seventeen, a Sweet Southern Belle from Ashland, Kentucky, who thinks that like a diamond, cars should be flaunted. "My boyfriend has a Trans Am and it's nice. You know, just getting in and out of a nice car looks good; it's prestigious. My boyfriend's lucky he's got one. I'd still date him if he didn't, but it makes it nicer." "It's awful, I know," concedes another, "but a guy is always better looking in a Z-28, Ferrari, Corvette, or Mazda RX-7. Besides, no one wants to go out in a car that might not start."

Girls from the South don't really consider themselves as "dating" until they can officially "car-date"—i.e., be alone with a boy, cruising carelessly away from the strings and strains of meddling parents, so cars for them are symbols of independence. And for those who live great distances apart, cars are a necessity. "We go out of town to date," says Janice, a seventeen-year-old Strong Individualist from Ryan, Oklahoma, "to Duncan, Oklahoma, forty-five minutes away or Wichita Falls, Texas, which is about an hour. Those are about the closest places that have movies or anything

Money-Conscious Girls vs. Non-Money-Conscious Girls: Traditional Values

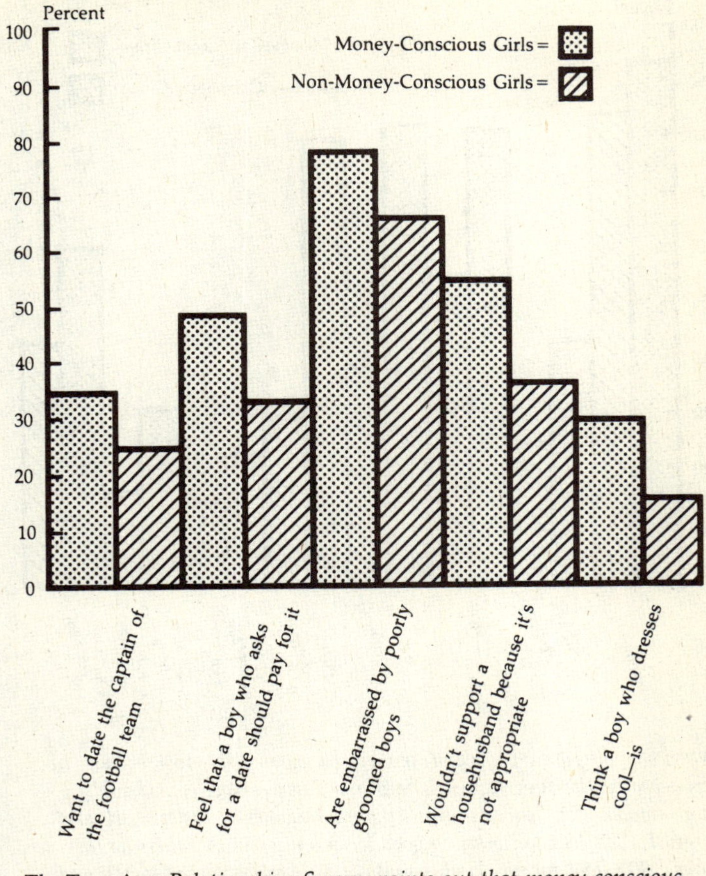

The TeenAge *Relationships Survey points out that money-conscious girls (those who said money is "important" or "very important" on the* TeenAge *Relationships Survey) possess more traditional values than non-money-conscious girls. Forty-nine percent feel that if a boy asks them out he should pay for the date while only 33% of others agree; 55% would refuse to support a househusband on the grounds that it's not appropriate, while only 37% of others agree, and 35% are attracted to the stereotypical high-school hero—the captain of the football team—while only 25% of others are. Though all girls emphasize a boy's good grooming, money-conscious girls are quicker to reject "Sloppy Joes" (78% to 67% for others). They are also more likely to use a conventional, superficial measurement like clothes to judge him: 30% of money-conscious girls say a boy who dresses cool is, only 16% of others agree.*

Money-Conscious Girls vs. Non-Money-Conscious Girls: Looking for Mr. Successful

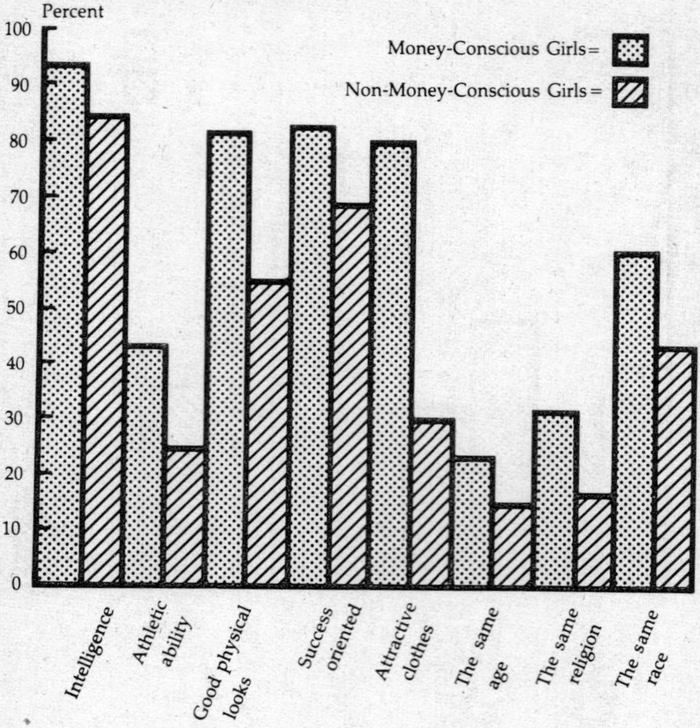

When shopping for a boyfriend, money-conscious girls, 46% of those interviewed on the TeenAge *Relationships Survey, place considerably more emphasis on "success" traits than non-money-conscious girls. As a result, 82% look for winning good looks (only 55% of others do the same), 80% look for nice clothes (only 30% of others do the same), and 23% look for the same age (only 15% of others do the same). Since money-conscious girls also want to make sure their guy has the "right" credentials to make it in this world, 61% want him to be of the same race and 32% say of the same religion, reflecting much greater concern with "fitting in" than non-money-conscious girls who come in at 43% and 17% respectively.*

Of course, there's nothing to stop any girl from coming right out and saying she wants a successful man—because all do. It's just a matter of degree: 83% of money-conscious girls rate "success oriented" as important while only 69% of others say the same.

good to do. If you don't have a car or can't borrow one, you can't really date."

Luckily, not all girls judge boys by their ignition keys. One told me she was totally turned off when her date, the richest (and weirdest) boy in town, said he loved his six sports cars more than anything in the world—more than money, parents, girls. "Just what I thought," says one seasoned philosopher, Grace (sixteen, a Strong Individualist from Catlettsburg, Kentucky), "boys with beautiful cars are usually spoiled brats!" Says another, "I'd never date a boy because of the car he drives; what has it to do with his looks, personality, views, and morals?"

8

Religion

On a train speeding toward Paris, a wiry Alsatian boy raced to a secret rendezvous with his rosy-cheeked lover from the Midi. When he arrived at the station, however, he found waiting for him, not his lover, but her angry father, who'd intercepted their letters the way he planned to intercept their love affair. For she was a Catholic and he was a Protestant—and her father was unable to abide by an interfaith marriage. As a result, he banished them both from his sight forever, a mistake he retracted only one year before his death in order to see his already grown-up grandchildren. Not fiction but fact, this was the true-life love story of a couple I lived with in France, a couple with the happiest, most loving, "together" family I've ever seen. It's a story with such a happy ending that it's sad to think religion could ever stand in the way of joy—an outlook that seems to be shared by many teens today and at least 65 percent of girls in the *TeenAge* Relationships Survey.

Except in the South, where Christian sentiments are strongest, most teens echo the trend across the country that suggests attitudes toward meeting, dating, and marrying interreligiously are easing. "A recent study revealed that interfaith marriages have doubled in the past decade," says William D'Antonio, Ph.D., executive officer of the American Sociological Association. "And a recent Roper opinion poll showed that 70 percent of Protestants, 85 percent of Catholics, approve of Protestant-Catholic marriages, while 62 percent of Protestants, 82 percent of Catholics approve of marriages between Jews and non-Jews. Public attitudes are very supportive of intermarriage, and behavior is following it." (An interesting observation, especially at a time when everyone is touting a "new conservatism.") Reasons for the relaxed atmosphere include: fewer people, especially teens, practicing "institutionalized" religion, and more and more young adults going away to college, moving out of restrictive family controls and exclusive neighborhoods. When one New Yorker says, "It's stupid to break up two people in love just because of their religion," she may really be speaking for many.*

As in many classic romances, the religious barriers come not from ourselves—we're surprisingly liberal—but from our parents, who pressure us to maintain family tradition and marry within our faith. If we happen to fall in love with someone who isn't exactly what they had in mind, we can be caught in a terrible, age-old battle. Like Colleen (seventeen, a Supersonic Dater from Lansdale, Pennsylvania), a Lutheran who was dating Allan, a Jew, we can find ourselves having to make the difficult choice between parents we respect and a boyfriend we love.

Ivory skin, full round cheeks and chin, pastel eyes, and soft blonde curls give Colleen a maternal look, an aura that seems physically as well as mentally warm, cushy, inviting. Even the clothes she wears—a white sweatshirt, sneakers, faded jeans—look easygoing. Just back from an eye-opening year in Denmark (where she experimented with sex, drugs, a more liberal youth culture), Colleen finds her new values and her old conservative background have begun to clash. "My parents said 'go out with whomever you want.' So I went out with a couple of black guys and had no problem," she begins. "They said, 'Fine, don't tell your grandparents and never marry them—it would cause too many problems for the kids.' But now there's a problem with my

* This doesn't mean teens' *personal* interest in religion has declined. A recent Gallup Youth Survey shows that many teens still read the Bible on a regular basis and consider themselves to be "religious."

current boyfriend Allan [a 210-pound weight lifter and football player] because he's Jewish and my parents say, 'Don't marry a Jew; don't marry a Catholic.' My cousin married a Catholic and had to bring up the kids that way. It hurt my mom's side of the family a lot. They said she shouldn't have compromised herself.

"It's frustrating because I asked him, 'What do you think about the kids?' " she continues, rapping a pencil angrily on the table. "He said, 'Well, I want my kids to have Christmas.' I said, 'Good, that works out really well.' He said he'd also like them to have a Bar Mitzvah. I know a lot about Jewish culture so that doesn't bother me at all. He also doesn't go to synagogue much, so that wouldn't be much of a problem, even though I go to church almost every Sunday. He even said he'd join me once in a while as long as I didn't expect him to participate. That's fine with me—if he's with me, then he acknowledges what I believe, and he's not against it. He says, 'Okay, you have one belief; I have another.' Fine. That's what happens on a lot of other issues.

"If he was Catholic, that would be another problem," she adds. "Not too many Catholics are lenient enough to say, 'All right, you can go to the Lutheran church and I'll go to the Catholic church'—they want you to get married Catholic and I don't think I'd like that."

Colleen saw a lot of interreligious and interracial relationships "work" when she attended a "very mixed" junior high school in another town: "We whites were in the minority. A lot of mixed relationships turned out well. Nothing shocks me anymore."

But parental disapproval eventually forced Colleen and Allan to break off. "It was really tough for a while. They were making little comments all the time. I'd get so frustrated, I'd take it out on him; so we broke up. But both of us were really miserable—even our friends were begging us, for their sakes, to get back together. It drove us so crazy that four months later, he said, 'I can't take it any longer; let's get back together and ignore what your parents are saying.' " The conflict wasn't resolved until Colleen talked to Allan's parents about it. "They like me. I call them mom and dad, they call me dear; it's really a good relationship. They told me not to worry—my parents will eventually come around. Then I realized my parents have really never liked anyone I've gone out with, no matter what religion they were. I think they're just overly protective because I'm their only girl."

Religious conflict can erupt even when one person practices and the other doesn't. "It's weird 'cause I don't consider myself a certain denomination," says Claire. "I was baptized Catholic but I don't practice and my views are certainly not Catholic at all. My religion is believing in myself. If I could find somebody who could understand that, it would be great. I tried explaining it to my old boyfriend Mel, who was a practicing Catholic, but he'd just keep asking, 'Don't you believe in a supreme being?' And I'd say, 'Well, I don't know.' We'd always end up in a fight because we couldn't agree."

Mel was also a religious hypocrite. Even though he had an easy time accepting premarital sex—which goes against all Catholic doctrine—"He had a hard time accepting contraception, so we never used any," Claire points out. "It must originate in his religious background. He thought the pill was too much of a commitment and he didn't like any other method. In the end, we just ended up abstaining—I couldn't handle going through each month worrying that I was pregnant. I was so nervous the last time we had sex that I had a pregnancy test. He freaked. That ended it. It wasn't worth it and he stopped calling."

Of course, those who don't "practice" at all find religion is rarely an issue. "I've never really gone to church," says Bobbi, "so I wouldn't date or marry a boy for his religion and I wouldn't make my kids any certain religion either; I'd let them choose their own—if they wanted one at all. I believe in God, and try to do right by my standards, and hope those are His, but I think that being a good person is really what counts."

Devout worshipers like Audrey (Catholic) are like the about 24 percent on the *TeenAge* Relationships Survey who would disagree heartily. "For others I think it depends on their religion and how serious they are about practicing it. But for most people, religion plays a very large part in dating, especially in marriage. It's probably the most important aspect for me. Sure people can date and 'get by' with the differences, but when it really comes down to living the rest of their life with someone, raising their kids a certain way, more people than you think will change their minds."

The *TeenAge* Relationships Survey indicates that it's not just religious interests but an overall conservative personality—like that of the Sweet Southern Belle or the Modern Traditionalist—that separates the Audreys from the Bobbis, because girls who

Religion-Conscious Girls vs. Girls Who Are Not Religion-Conscious: Traditional Values and Attitudes

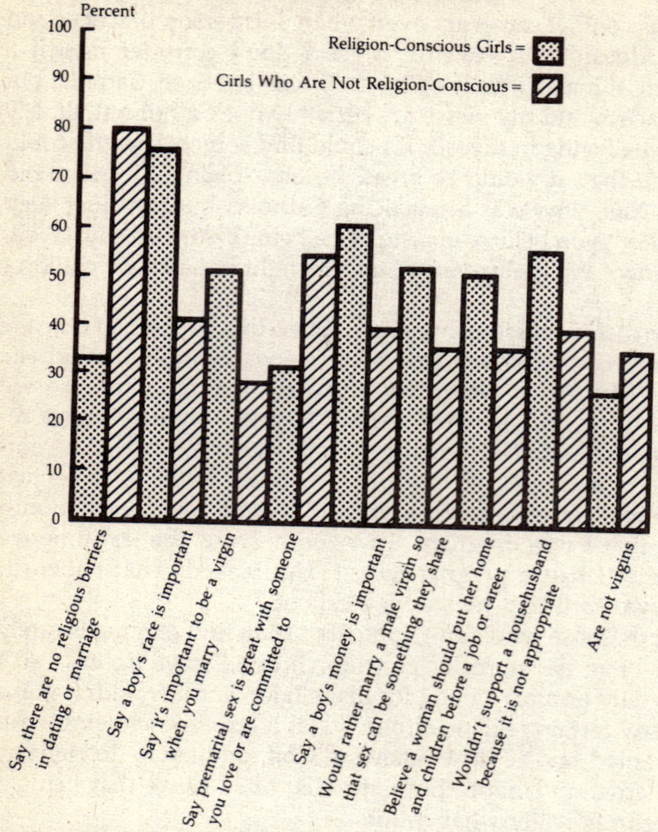

Religion-conscious girls, 24% of those surveyed, have more traditional values than girls who are not. For example, 80% of non-religion-conscious girls say there are no religious barriers in dating or marriage while only 33% of religion-conscious girls agree, and 76% of religion-conscious girls say a boy's race is important while only 42% of others agree. Religion-conscious girls are also more likely to judge a boy by his money: 61% say it's important compared to only 40% of others—and value the traditional family.

As far as sex goes, religion-conscious girls are much less liberal. Fifty-two percent say it's important to be a virgin at marriage, while only 28% of others agree, and 53% would rather marry a male virgin, while only 36% of others agree. Surprisingly, the number of religion-conscious girls and non-religion-conscious girls who have lost their virginity are not too far apart: 27% of religion-conscious girls are non-virgins as are 36% of others.

pick boys for their religion are also more likely to believe a woman should put her kids and home before a job, and feel that a woman should not support a househusband because it's not appropriate. They are also more likely to choose him for traditional reasons, i.e., athletic ability, clothes, looks, money, and success. But here's a surprise: though religion-conscious girls are 86 percent more likely than non-religion-conscious girls to say it's important to be a virgin at marriage (and 46 percent more likely to say they want to marry one), they're only 14 percent more likely to *be* virgins—most probably because eased sexual mores in the Eighties have even begun to cross religious boundaries!

9

Race

I don't know when "race" becomes a part of our social consciousness. I can only say that for me it wasn't until the late Sixties, when I entered the fifth grade at a rough, newly integrated public school, that the idea of racial differences, the question of interracial dating even occurred to me. All my girlfriends were "doing it," and when Jennifer informed me that Gary, a chubby, ebony-skinned boy in my math class, liked me, I was as coolly interested as any white fifth-grader could be. But before we even had a chance to exchange glances in the playground, my parents had me transferred to a neighboring school where the environment was less violent, the education better, the atmosphere, consequently, much "whiter."

The following years in private school, we limousine-liberal "preps" treated our token blacks with the reverence afforded Sunday school shoes, cherishing them for their difference and uniqueness, but never really incorporating them into our everyday lives. We elected them to office, cast them as leads in plays—once, ironically, as Mary Poppins—but never, ever invited them home to dinner.

By college, especially since it was in North Carolina, the wedge of racial consciousness had effectively severed all romantic ties. "They" sat at "their" tables in the lunch hall, had "their" own fraternities and sororities and even consolidated "their" wings of the dormitories, always on the ground floors. By senior year our only exchanges were forced, fleeting glances in lecture halls and labs, unintimate stares that seemed to acknowledge our mutually chosen isolation. And then we did what all "enlightened" students did in the "changing" South of the Seventies—we elected a black student-body president one year, a black to play the mascot the next.

Because there was so little contact, so little real possibility of any interracial dating, I'm sure we would have felt like most of the girls I interviewed (both black and white) and like 32 percent of respondents in the *TeenAge* Relationships Survey, safe enough to say that race was never a dating issue, and we would have mimicked the same old worn-out cliché—that "all men are created equal." Barring a few rednecks who are probably more honest about their prejudices, most girls are taught it's not polite to judge a boy by his color—or at least to admit it in public. Race, like money, is not a quality we mention freely.

"I don't see any racial barriers," says Claire, who is white and from Lexington, Kentucky. "But the social pressure against it, especially in the South, is just impossible. I've got a white friend who started a relationship with a black guy; it was so important to keep it a secret that when rumors eventually went around, it had to be ended. The pressure was too great. When I lived in Florida and Philadelphia I saw many mixed couples, but not in Kentucky—there's not one." In Florida, when Claire dated a Filipino boy with dark skin, "people always said, 'Oh, I'm surprised.' But there was no real problem. At this school something like that wouldn't work at all."

Helen, a black New Yorker, found the same pressure when she dated a white boyfriend from Switzerland. "It was fine for me because my mother was understanding but for Larry it was terrible. His dad thought it was okay but his mother was cool and aloof to me, and they were always fighting about it. It was making him really upset. Finally I said, 'Why don't we just be friends?' I knew he wouldn't break up because he'd be afraid it was for racial reasons. But we were becoming two very unhappy people." Helen hopes that in the future if "we're really in love, we can overcome any obstacles that society puts in the way."

Other girls claim society's rules and regulations are too hard to ever break down. "I'd hate to say I don't believe in interracial marriage or dating because that means I really don't believe that all men are created equal," says Dierdra, seventeen, a white Strong Individualist from Salt Lake City, Utah. "But you know, somehow I feel you shouldn't. The kids aren't really of one race or another so they'll have identity problems. If there aren't kids, I'd be tempted to say it's okay, but I've been brought up to believe you shouldn't date interracially. It would be especially looked down upon in my community."

Racial prejudice, like religious prejudice, seems to stem more from parental and community pressure, than from our own minds, explains eternal optimist Roxanne (eighteen, white, a Strong Individualist from Belcourt, North Dakota), who thinks girls will grow more lenient with age. "Where I'm from, there are few religious barriers but strong racial ones. When kids get older and out on their own, I believe they'll change their minds. A lot of what they think is due to their parent's backgrounds, attitudes, social upbringing. When they're exposed to other life-styles, their opinions will no doubt change."

Curiously enough, the number of black-white marriages across the country has actually increased—from 65,000 couples in 1970 to 164,000 in 1983—though it still represents less than half of one percent of all married couples. "Not really that much change," says Steven Rawlings, family demographer for the Census Bureau.

While on the *TeenAge* Relationships Survey the Sweet Southern Belles appear to be the most race-conscious and Twentieth-Century Fast Trackers the least, the survey also reveals that race-conscious girls—those who say a boy's race is important—come from all groups and focus on tradition, and a boy's success potential. That's the reason why race-conscious girls are 74 percent more likely than non-race-conscious girls to say the boy they marry must have a lot of money, why they're 65 percent more likely to want to date the captain of the football team, and why they're

Race-Conscious Girls vs. Non-Race-Conscious Girls: Traditional Behavior

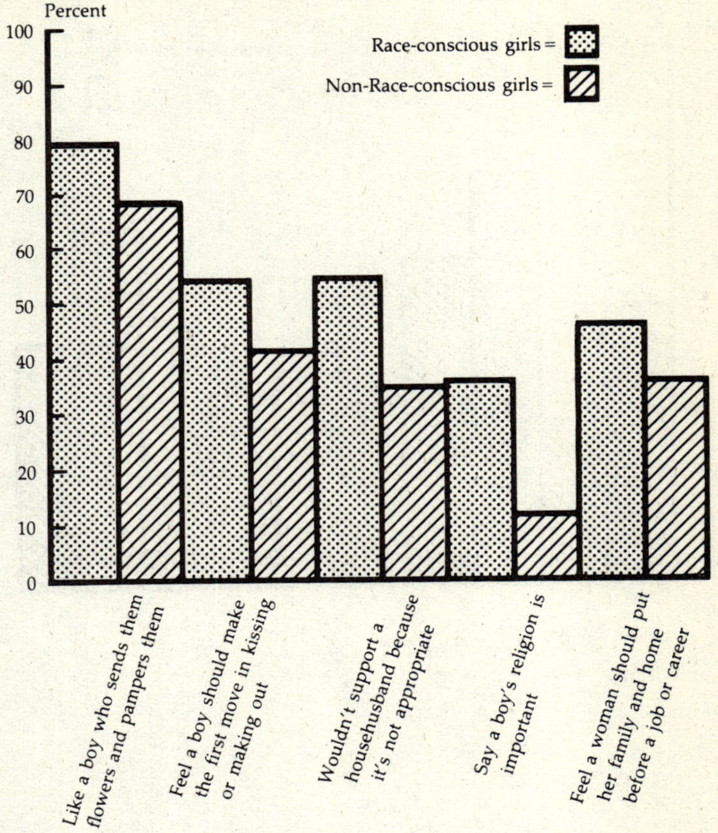

According to the TeenAge *Relationships Survey, race-conscious girls, 52% of those surveyed, are more traditional in their social outlook and dating habits than non-race-conscious girls. For instance, while most girls like a boy to pamper them, send them flowers and open the door, race-conscious girls place more emphasis on it: 79% say it's important while only 68% of others agree, and 54% of race-conscious girls also feel that a boy should make the first sexual moves while only 42% of others agree. Race-conscious girls place more value on a boy's religion: 36% say it's important compared with only 12% of others. And, when it comes to the future, race-conscious girls are more likely to opt for the conventional model of the nuclear family. Fifty-five percent say they wouldn't support a househusband because it's not appropriate (only 35% of others agree) and 46% say a woman should put her family and home before a job or career while 36% of others agree.*

Race-Conscious Girls vs. Non-Race-Conscious Girls: Interest in Successful Boys

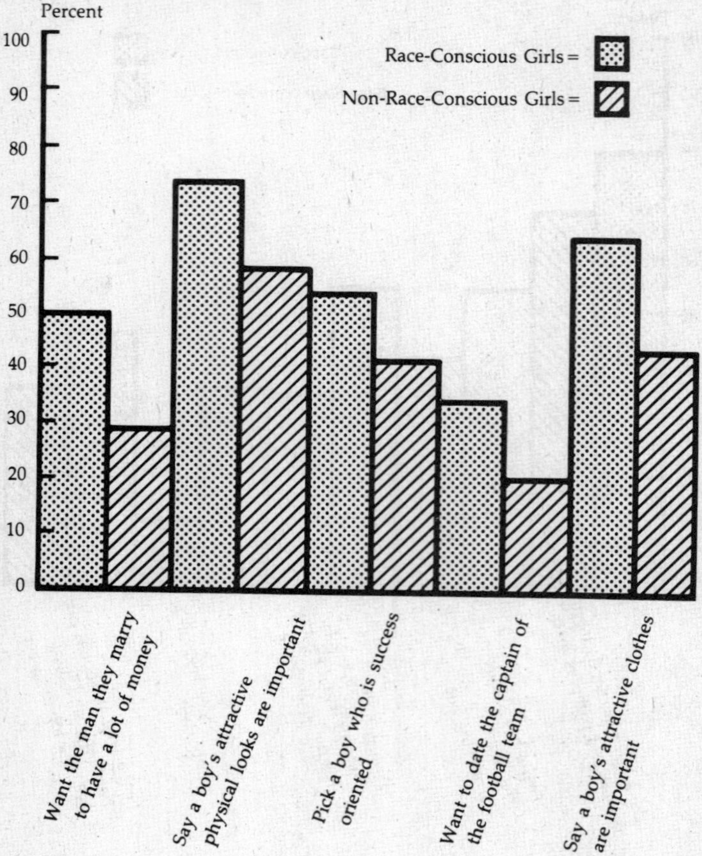

The TeenAge *Relationships survey shows that race-conscious girls are more likely to pick a boy who is successful, or who will be successful in later life, than girls who aren't. For instance, 50% of race-conscious girls say that they want the man they marry to have a lot of money while only 29% of others say the same, and 34% of race-conscious girls say they want to date the captain of the football team compared with only 20% of others. Naturally, race-conscious girls will feel that an attractive—and acceptable—physical presentation will help any boy become successful. Therefore 74% say that a boy's good looks are important while only 58% of others agree, and 64% say that his clothes must be attractive compared with only 43% of others. But race-conscious girls won't hesitate to say it's success they're after: 54% say they pick a boy for his success orientation while only 42% of others say the same.*

also more likely to choose a boy for his looks and clothes. Their traditionalism shows up in their greater tendency to want boys to pamper them and make the first sexual moves, and in a stronger, more conventional, feeling about the importance of a mother's role and "saving oneself" for the wedding night.

Section Two

Dating and Relationship Problems

10

Springing the Peer-Pressure Trap

Like Santa Claus, the Tooth Fairy, and the Easter Bunny, peer pressure doesn't exist. That, at least , is what many girls I interviewed said. Because like the "Can you guess what this is?" pictures in puzzle magazines that zoom in so close on flowers or spider webs that petals look like satin bed sheets and delicate filaments look like fishing-boat ropes, peer pressure is often disguised by lack of perspective. None the less, 74 percent in the *TeenAge* Relationships Survey admit that being like (or unlike) the crowd governs their attitudes toward sex, drugs, drinking, and boys and suggest that approval from friends (or lack of it) is the most common reason why they pick boys they don't really like.

The problem is that peer pressure invades every aspect of our lives: it influences the clothes we wear, the makeup we buy, the places we go to dance. It may be easy to shrug off when our friends make fun of the purple stretch pants our mother makes us wear, or it may be impossible to ignore when we walk into a party given by a group we don't fit in with. It's what drives some girls to get drunk at eighteen because "everyone else" does, to race to second base in order not to feel left behind. It's even the reason why girls found it easier to admit peer pressure exists on paper than in person.

"There's a lot of pressure to conform," says Grace. "A lot of people try to pass it by, but I noticed it a lot when I was younger and would do things like swearing because my friends would say, 'Come on.' It was really just a feeling of not wanting to be left out. Like I'd go out to lunch with some friends even when I didn't want to, because I was afraid they'd say I was boring, or I'd pick the cheerleading uniforms they liked and would spend more money on them than I wanted to, because I was afraid to say anything. I see a lot of really insecure younger kids go along with the crowd just to be liked. Luckily, as you get older it changes. Now I do what I want to do because I know I'll turn out better in the end. I realize I'm the only one who can decide how good I am; other people can't do that for me. My friends can't push me around anymore, because I feel like I'm starting to become myself."

Fear of being laughed at is what makes peer pressure so successful, says Jean: "You know you have your own opinion about life and the way you want to live it, but you hear somebody else's idea and you think, 'Well, maybe I should change mine because I don't want to stick out, don't want people to laugh at me.' I've seen people laughed at! It's funny, when I stick to my ideals it feels good, like I really stood up for myself, like I know what I'm doing and that I'm right. And when I give in I feel terrible and think, 'I didn't want that! Why did I do that?' But it's like I'm always afraid people will say, 'You're weird; you're crazy.' "

And of course they do. Not necessarily maliciously, but because for many teens it's hard to imagine anyone not wanting to think like the crowd. For instance, when I interviewed girls in groups, they would say, "It's not necessary to talk to us privately; we all think alike." But when I got them alone, they all had very different views on everything from sex to school. But they weren't about to let their friends know! Heidi, fourteen, a Supersonic Dater from Berwyn, Pennsylvania, explains it best: "Once Mariel and I and some friends were watching the commercial for *All the Right Moves* and we were like, 'Oh, wow, Tom Cruise is such a fox!' But Mariel was the only one who said he wasn't. She doesn't think he's ugly but she doesn't see anything special in him either. No one could believe it and everyone was on her case all night. I thought she was crazy too, because he's sexy and cute, but I also feel it's her own business. I don't know why she thinks that way but she does."

Just as friends influence who we like, they can also influence who we don't like. Says Lara, whose boyfriend had been treating her badly for some time: "I guess you could say that my friends contributed to breaking us up because his behavior made me feel real stupid in their eyes. It really helped to catch him with another girl but I would have broken up anyway. Group pressures always affect you. Not at first—if you really like somebody no one will say anything. But if a guy starts treating you badly your friends start saying, 'Hey, what are you doing?' Obviously, I listen to me first, but I definitely hear them."

The most negative elements of peer pressure come to bear with drinking and drugs. While many girls say neither are considered "cool" in their group, others claim they are, and feel pressured by group opinion to go along. "Peer pressure exists for sure and there's a lot," says one Strong Individualist. "There's a particular pressure to drink because there's nothing else exciting to do and 'cause if you don't drink, you get called a 'Goody Two Shoes.' If you won't go to parties because there'll be drinking then you're considered an outcast. But if you go to a party and just say, 'No thanks,' then it's fine 'cause it's your own decision. People don't really hassle you openly about it, but it's there." Some girls even find themselves in the unsavory position of "pressurer." "I go along with drugs and drinking at a party (pot is the only halfway acceptable drug, very rarely coke) because I like to," says Didi. "I don't do it just 'cause it's around. If I don't do it, kids will say, 'Aw, come on. Don't you want some? You sure?' But it doesn't influence me. It's not like you're uncool if you don't. Once though I found myself doing it to other girls. We were partying and I wanted them to have a good time. I guess I also do it if a person's in a bad mood and I want to snap them out of it."

Pressure is greatest for younger girls. "I don't smoke, drink, or do drugs heavily because it's not good for me and I only do the things I want to do," says Marsha. "But when I was a freshman and sophomore I went along with the crowd at parties, because I wanted to fit in with the older crowd. But when I got to be a senior I found out it wasn't something I really wanted to do. Now I'm really independent and not inclined to do something I don't believe in."

Strangely enough, girls who bear up under pressure and keep their individuality are often admired. "One of my friends doesn't drink or smoke pot or anything," says Suzanne. "I respect her for it. I think it's good that she can make that decision for herself. I've never really heard anyone make fun of her and I don't think it bothers her. I think most teens care what others think though, because they care what their appearance is. I can tell others are dying inside because they're doing something someone else wanted them to do, or because they think it's cool or that they're gay if they don't. It's weird because it's the same wherever you go, with girls, with decisions, with teenagers. Everyone's always wondering, especially sexually (my friends all did this), should I or shouldn't I? No one's ever really sure what they should do."

Coping with pressure to conform can at best be difficult. If we don't give in, we must accept ourselves as outsiders like Marion, sixteen, a Twentieth-Century Fast Tracker from Freeport, New York, who says, "There's definitely peer pressure. If you're not like everyone else, you're weird. Take it, I'm weird! If kids try pushing drugs on me I'll walk out of the party. My friends pretty much understand that I don't want to take it. I get tipsy on half a can of beer so I know my limits." Or like Rachel: "There's no peer pressure, because if I'm in a group doing drugs and I don't want any, I stay chill. I just say to them, 'No.' "

Or like Devon, we can choose to ignore it. "Peer pressure's my pet peeve. It's a problem all right but not as great as everyone is always saying. There's pressure not to be an outcast, but that's where you come into being your own person. It gets really lonely at times, but if you're different there are rewards you can reap, too. Like for being different I got elected to school office. People are now just realizing what I've done in my life. After the first years in high school you realize that if you're different, nobody's really going to care. People may pick on you but you get to a point where you don't care. Maturity gets you there. You say, if I know this guy is a jerk and he's picking on me, then who cares? You also learn to come back with something. It doesn't have to be nasty, just a statement of your point—like, 'Leave me alone! Don't pick on me because there's no reason to!' "

Or we can simply take the stand Norma does: "I don't go along with the rest of the kids in any situation, simply because I don't want to," she says. "I know how to say no because I've done it before. I think peer pressure is bullshit because no one ever pressures you into it. They say, 'Do you want some?' and I say no. Other people might think I'm square for what I do but I don't care."

11

Why Must I Be a Teenager in Love?

So what is being in love like? It's a question that consumes our conversations at the beach (when we're supposed to be doing French translations), makes us daydream about "him" at night and stay up till dawn talking with friends. Is it warm, comforting, spiritual, like the tenderness we feel for parents and friends? Or jolting and electric like the passion we see on TV? Is it the mix of joy and terror that claws at our throats every time our "crush" asks us a question? Or the way our head races when he breezes by in the hall? Night after night we try to define it. But to no avail. We are romantic junkies with an itch for love. And every time we scratch it, it only gets worse.

Love, television style

Confused, yes, but gullible, no; we can tell the difference between "true love" and cheap imitations the way a good connoisseur can tell the difference between good and cheap wines. Boob-tube portrayals are "too idealistic," "too fairy-tale-like," "too unrealistic" to be taken seriously. *The Love Boat*, while fun to watch, is certainly not the kind of "love-style" we expect to lead. "Love's not always the bed of roses it's made out to be in books, magazines, and movies," says one sixteen-year-old. "Not everything in real life turns out so right. They never show couples in unreconcilable arguments, so I know it's fake. Every couple argues and doesn't get along well at times. I see it with my parents, friends, and boyfriends. I think it's normal. I watch TV love and fantasize about how I wish it could be. I like love stories, but I know the difference."

Nor do we expect TV sex to cure real-life problems. "Right now, I know a boy I could love, and it seems that if it were a problem in the movies, he would automatically fall in love with me," says Ruth, sixteen, a Strong Individualist from Whitefield, Connecticut. "But in real life that's not the way it works. Love in the movies is sex, and sex is too precious to throw away like that."

Teen vs adult love—a matter of degree

Unlike teen love, adult love is expected to "endure friction better," "be less influenced by friends," be more realistic. "When you're younger, you're more naive and careless," explains Kari, a fresh-scrubbed, preppy Strong Individualist, sixteen, from Gainesville, Florida. "Experience in relationships is important. Adults have gone through much more than we have and just have more grown-up outlooks. Their love takes into consideration things like jobs and money, while we just go to the prom. Ours are not very real relationships." Hypothesizes Patty: "Once you get to be around thirty years old, you probably look more for stability than for fun and excitement."

There is even a difference between old and young teenage love. Says Marsha, seventeen, who's now engaged to her "dream man": "I was once in love when I was twelve or thirteen. At that age you think you're in love but it felt more like a crush than love. It's not like how I feel now. Now my fiancé and I are closer, can talk about anything, don't argue that much."

A crush: the best-kept secret

Oh, yes, the crush! It may begin as early as thirteen or as late as never; it may last a brief hour, or a heart-breaking year. It may descend upon us once in a lifetime or twenty times a month, hit like a bolt from the blue, or grow like a slow, steady flame. The only consistent thing about crushes is that they're kept a secret—especially from parents—and more often than not, come to a screeching, grinding halt once we force ourselves to face reality. "I have had only two crushes and each only lasted a short while until I realized that the guy was just human," says Dale. "At first, because I didn't know them, the guys seemed really up there. Then I had class with them and I couldn't believe how stupid they were. They were not Mr. Americas." Ruth catches crushes like others catch colds: "I've had crushes on my soccer coach, math teacher, and boys I didn't even know—just guys I've seen or heard about—sometimes as many as twenty in a month," she says. "They all seem like such gentlemen, especially at dances. Then I just realize that I've made them into something they aren't, and they just fade away. They're just whims."

Most crushes remain unrequited, because mustering up enough courage to approach them is difficult, even impossible. Sadie Hawkins dances (where girls ask boys) or "stranger parties" (where friends invite boys we've never seen before) are good excuses for breaking the ice, but most girls fear that what happened to Supersonic Dater Amanda, fourteen, a pretty Park Avenue "debutante" with a love of excitement and male models twice her age, will happen to them. "I thought I loved him," she says, with the blasé lock-jawed frown that only boarding school girls can perfect. "I was in sixth grade and he was in eighth. It was in New York. He was pretty unattractive but had the best personality. I was in a play with him and had a crush on him since he was Birdie in *Bye, Bye, Birdie*. My friends began to like him, too. It got around and someone told him that we liked him, so one day he came up to all three of us, kissed us on the cheek and said that he thought it was cute. I started to cry 'cause he thought we were all 'little girls.' It really bummed me out. Later when we sat down and talked, he said it wouldn't work 'cause he was going to boarding school and we had different friends, since he was in high school and I was in junior high. But he did come to a basketball game that I played in. Afterwards he walked me outside. I told him I loved him and he kissed me on the cheek. My crushes haven't really been a mutual thing yet; it's usually one-sided." Says Jennifer: "I can remember having a crush on a very close friend of mine named Cole. We were the best of friends and all my friends had a crush on him too. They told him how they felt about him, but I didn't so we remained really close and I was happy about that. I didn't tell him because I knew it would affect our relationship."

Even worse is a crush on a truly unattainable movie or rock star that can never be resolved and, as a result, often gets blown out of proportion. Though all of us dream of being Linda McCartney—she was a Beatles fan before nabbing Paul—most of us realize that the probability of landing Tom Cruise in this lifetime is not very high. Such was the conclusion that Rachel, a stocky, frizzy-haired girl who has a tendency to hang back from the social scene and dream of boys instead of date them, came to when her crush on Laurence Lau, the actor who plays Greg in *All My Children*, became so intense it began consuming her life.

"The first time I saw him I didn't think he was that good-looking but my sister got me into him," she says, straddling the stool in front of her home computer, where she's been beating her twin sister at Centipede. "Then late November last year I was coming home from school and we were talking about him, and when I looked up I saw his image and fell in love with him. I tried to find out everything I could about him. I got lots of pictures, watched the soaps, and wrote him ten letters that I didn't mail 'cause they were too corny. I started them with, 'Wait! Don't throw out this letter!' I didn't want him to think I was just another fan in love with him; he was an obsession.

"I liked him for a year, then over the summer didn't see *All My Children* but still loved him. Then I realized it was silly to be obsessed with someone I didn't have a chance with, so I dropped him. My friend Jennifer still thinks I'm in love with him but I'm not. Twenty-nine's too old; he's fifteen years my senior and doesn't even know I'm alive. Once I saw him in front of the studio but was too awed to say anything so my sister got his autograph and gave me the pen he touched.

"I think a lot of girls love him like 'girls,' but not many are obsessed. I made a wallet-sized picture of him to carry around and a button with his face on it that I could watch in class while everyone else was talking."

What were the traits that attracted her to Laurence? "He's smart. A straight-A student and graduate from Columbia. He's awesome-looking, a great actor, sensitive, sweet, kind, like God. No guys I know are like that. He's like apogee."

Love: the real thing

Compared with Rachel's dizzying affection for Laurence, real love seems mundane and steady—especially when it's become part of a long-term relationship. Though it may hit with crush-like impact and at as early an age, the big difference is that it's usually two-sided. "Love is just always wanting to be with him because we have so much fun together," says Virginia about her boyfriend, "and I know no one else could measure up." Says Alexis, eighteen, a Sweet Southern Belle from Seabrook, Texas: "Yes, I'm in love. It feels like the first time you go out with a guy and he's coming to pick you up and you get all dressed up and excited, with butterflies; it's still like that. I get all excited when Jack's about to come over. And he buys me things all the time. He bought me this ring"—she shows me a diamond chip—"this pearl necklace for Christmas, and a gold bracelet on my birthday. He spoils me. I love it. I have to be spoiled or else I'm not happy."

Love can also be less materialistic, more secure, warm, and tender. "I'm beginning to think this is true love because he's beginning to express his feelings toward me and really does love me," says Lisa (eighteen, Solon, Ohio, a Strong Individualist and nursing student at Marymount College in Virginia) about her boyfriend, a schoolteacher. "I've known him since June and we've dated more seriously in the past four months. I've never been in love before. It's a totally different feeling I have right now. In one way it's hard because he's back home. I know that whenever I have a problem he'll be there to talk to. And I can go without talking to him for a while, you know, a few weeks, whatever—we still correspond through letters. But even though I don't talk to him every day, or hear from him all the time, I still feel that he's there. We don't have to be together all the time to prove we really care about each other. A lot of girls say they can't go a day without seeing their boyfriends, that they're not going to make it without them. But I believe that you have to have your own being. Two people in love can be together and complement each other, but still live their own lives. I've seen it work for my parents, who are apart when they travel for jobs. But when they're together they love each other, and that's the way it is for us."

Girls who are about to be married are even more explicit. "I'm in love right now," says Barbara, a strapping blonde who works as a secretary for an insurance agency just outside of Boston. "His name is Richard and he's everything I've ever wanted—masculine yet sensitive, romantic, tall, dark, handsome, muscular, nice body, gets along with others and cares for me. He knows I love him, too. He told me first and my feelings came out. Then I told him. We've been going out for more than a year and are now engaged." Her friend Marsha expands: "I'm definitely in love—it's not like when I was younger. Now I'm just happy because I feel much more sure of myself. I wasn't as open with my crushes as I am with my fiancé, Tom. I wouldn't tell a crush my real feelings. Tom's very protective of me. If a guy looks at me he gets jealous; he makes me feel loved."

The "I'll never fall in love" syndrome

Why have some of us never been in love? The reasons range from being too intolerant of another person's shortcomings and doubting our own ability to love, to just not being in the right place at the right time. One girl, for instance, says she wants to fall in love with an English boy, a difficult task considering that she lives in Pennsylvania. "I've never been in love," says Pamela, "because every time I like a guy more and more, I always find things wrong with him. I can't picture myself loving someone and caring for him all the time, accepting his bad points. I think I'm just too picky, but that will change with time. (It has already eased up as I get older.) In junior high I used to only listen to my friends. Now, if I like a guy, I'll see him. If I want to go out with someone who they say isn't good enough, I'll say, 'If you don't like him, then keep it to yourselves.' Junior high was the worst time of my life, because everyone copied everyone. I felt a lot of peer pressure." Ironically, Pamela expects leniency from those who would reject *her:* "I still may not be ready to be less picky about boys, but I hope they'll accept me the way I am."

But for some, true-blue love on the teenage level simply doesn't exist. Says Carmen cynically: "As teenagers we're not ready to love because we haven't been exposed to enough. New feelings and emotions are yet to be experienced. Even if we think it's love, I don't believe it's so."

So is there only one Mr. Right for each of us? Does he live in our neighborhood? Go to our school? Sit next to us in English class? Or do the laws of probability say that some girls will have ten Mr. Rights while others will have none? "There's no one Mr. Right," says Vanessa with a shake of her head. "When some of my friends say they've been dating a boy since their sophomore year and are getting married, I just laugh 'cause I don't think that way. I know I'm going to date a lot of different boys; I know that just because I'm in love right now doesn't mean he's the person I'm going to marry." Others say he can't exist, because there's no such thing as a perfect person. "To an extent I believe in Mr. Right, but I also realize everyone has their flaws," says Roxanne. "If you put anybody on a pedestal you're going to eventually find out he's not Mr. Perfect. That happened to me with a guy I thought was my perfect dream. After going out with him for three or four weeks, I realized he wasn't all I'd pictured or planned. I found a lot of things I didn't like—like sexual pushiness and the way he treated other people badly. That turned me off. I guess I'd misinterpreted his personality to start with because I didn't know him all that well."

Girls who believe in only one true love also tend to believe that he can, for the most part, be chosen like a china pattern—by simply registering with fate ahead of time. Then they can tick off his "must-haves" like ingredients for a recipe. "I've always thought when I find the right person, I'm going to know it," says Audrey. "I picture a tall, six-foot-three guy with dark hair, brown eyes, kind of country, good, down to earth, natural, who likes the outdoors, has a good education but isn't an Einstein brainwise, someone who can deal with the world and economics, has a good personality, is considerate, caring, affectionate, open. (Being honest is important 'cause I can't hold things in.) He has to have good humor, want kids, and be a good provider since I'm the old-fashioned type. Even though I want equality—the other half of me is definitely not a women's libber."

Another girl thinks she knows him already: "Mr. Right would be someone who's gorgeous, like Gerald, this guy I know who has dark reddish hair, perfect features and is already in college. He's cool and a model-perfect guy. The only problem is that he's very conceited because his father died and left him all this money. Everyone loves him, so there's no chance at all with him really. But I'd want someone who's like him—well, maybe just a little less conceited."

12

The Dating Game

Noel is a well-heeled black fifteen-year-old from the Bronx, whom I've managed to corner for an interview. Her tight red pants, broad-shouldered jacket, and pointed shoes say she's an arbiter of style, one of many fast-paced cosmopolitan glitterati who have their fingers placed so firmly on the pulse of social change that they already accept boys who wear makeup à la Boy George! If there are any changes in the definition of "dating" I am confident that Noel will have them. "It's not really called dating anymore," she begins. "That's really an old expression. You just sort of 'see' someone or 'go out' with him. 'Seeing him' means the boy is usually 'going out' with another girl and you two are just fooling around on the side. 'Going out' is a younger term, one you use in sixth, seventh, and eighth grades. No one officially 'asks you out' anymore; you just sort of fall together. And as soon as you get into high school you don't even ask anymore, you just assume you're 'going together'—you know what I mean? Basically, first you 'see' each other, then you 'go out,' and if that works out then you become a pair."

Sounds complicated, doesn't it? Well, no need to worry. Dating by any other name would be the same—still the only surefire method we have today for getting together with a boy we like. Whether that means "going out" with him in a group or "seeing" him alone on the side, dating has been, and will always be, society's only prescribed method of mate selection.

In the Eighties, when we're caught in a period of transition between old Fifties stereotypes and reforms made in the Sixties and Seventies, the etiquette of dating can become even more complex. Just offering to split the bill at dinner can raise the question of equality; just opening your own car door can bring up old vs new values. When nuance and stereotype exist side by side, as they do today, we must choose what works best for us. And while it's nice to know that almost anything goes, it's also very frustrating to know that very little "goes" all by itself.

This period of transition explains why so many of us want to ask boys out but are afraid to pick up the phone; want equal pay, help with the housework and kids, but not a total role reversal or "househusband"; want sexual freedom but fear making the first moves. Many such paradoxes will be left for our children to untangle; many will remain forever as a price women pay for a newfound freedom. In any case, it's consoling to know that boys haven't figured it all out either. "I don't know if I should take this or not," a male friend said recently when I handed him money for a taxi ride from the airport. "These days some girls are insulted if I take it, others if I don't. I never know quite what to do."

"Well, Dan," I said, "neither do we."

Three's company

One thing we do know, however, is that we prefer, at least at younger ages, to date in groups where we can huddle together like little sheep and hope for safety in the crowd. If our date's a dud, we figure others in the group can save us; if he's a stud, we can check out group opinion, watch how he gets along with friends, raise our social status a bit. "Dating in groups is friendlier, more fun," explains one thirteen-year-old, "because things are less scary, less embarrassing with a bunch of people; even stupid accidents turn into jokes. It's like getting in trouble after school—if you all have to stay after, it isn't so bad." Groups also ease the anxiety we feel about meeting boys. "Being with girlfriends on a date makes me less nervous," says P.J., thirteen, Cresskill, New Jersey, a Strong Individualist with a squeaky voice, who was first in her group to get kissed—because *she* kissed *him*. "Once, I went with a group to the movies, and everyone left me and my date alone while they went to get popcorn. I was as stiff as a board and very uncomfortable until they got back."

As we get older, more secure about ourselves, about our ability to handle boys, one-on-one dating becomes the norm. "If I go on a date, I want to be alone with the guy so I can get to know him better," says Rita, sixteen, like most fast-paced daters in her category. "Groups are bothersome."

"Girls just wanna have fun"

Where we like to go depends on where we live. Large cities and suburbs often have discos or clubs we already frequent; in the boonies, we take trips to the beach, walks around the lagoon. Shopping malls, parties, school dances are acceptable hangouts, as long as they jibe with our budget—or that of our current boyfriend. And while every girl loves to be "wined and dined" at fancy restaurants, many say they actually get no closer than a Burger King Whaler.

Where *don't* we like to go? To loud parties or bars where it's impossible to talk and especially uncomfortable on first dates. To "his" house, where prying parents or overly curious sisters and friends can drop by unexpectedly and lay waste to an otherwise romantic, intimate evening. To his room, which for obvious reasons is off limits. "I like to go to parties and movies, sometimes just on walks to the waterfront," explains Helen. "But I don't like to go to suggestive places like his room! One guy said to me, 'Oh, I have to go pick up something at my house first and you can meet my mom and dad. Come to my room; let's hang out there.' I just said no; but I felt like saying, 'Why don't you just tell me you don't have any gas in the car and that we can't go anywhere but your room!"

Girls from small rural towns say that casual dating is hampered because there's nowhere exciting to go, nothing interesting to do. "In Galax we have a movie theater where a decent film comes every six months, and a disco you don't want to go to because it's a pick-up joint. That's it!" gripes Mickey. "A date usually means a guy coming over to my house to watch TV, going camping, or cruising up and down Main Street. Big deal! Parties only happen when somebody's parents go out of town. You can't really say that dating goes on in Galax, Virginia; it's more like relationships go on and everyone ends up going steady with somebody, just 'cause there's no other alternative."

13

Defining the New Social Etiquette

Who asks for the date?

Taped to the wall of her Marymount College study cubicle is a picture of a stud in Calvin Klein briefs with a hand-penciled balloon floating from his mouth. It reads: "Lisa, I want you!" A joke, no doubt, but one with an element of truth, because Lisa, a pleasant-looking, dark-haired girl, has what guys want, girls envy—Lisa has guts! Guts enough to ask a perfect stranger for a date—not to some socially acceptable girls-ask-the-boys affair, like a senior prom, but for an intimate dinner at home or an evening at the movies. She also knows how to handle the disappointments and elations that come from being one of the rare female "Askers" in a world of female "Askees."

When we meet she is wearing jeans, a pink and white acrylic sweater and she exudes the kind of warm, smiling confidence that makes you glad she's a nursing student. "If a guy apears to be interesting," she begins, "I may think about it a while, I may hesitate at first, but eventually I'll do it! Once I met a guy named Bob at a mixer by saying, 'I've been looking at you from back over there, would you like to dance?' He said, 'Sure!' so we talked and got along great. Then I asked if he would like to go out the following weekend and he said okay. We had dinner at his house, which he cooked—a nice change 'cause usually it's the girl who cooks dinner for the guy. Then we saw a movie. Unfortunately, Bob didn't work out too well. We saw each other at another mixer, danced all night, but he never called back. He just kind of gave me the runaround. But I'll try it again."

What went wrong? "I think he was just afraid of something new." She grins calmly, balancing her chair on two legs against the wall. "There are a lot of guys out there who like to be dominant, like to ask the girl out and pay. Bob was probably one of them. That's also what most girls are accustomed to, so they get too shy or don't have enough self-confidence to ask guys out. But that's okay. I see myself as having a lot of self-confidence in other areas, so it rolls over into my social life."

Lisa *does* have exceptional confidence. At eighteen she talks like a thirty-year-old about "sharing" and "communication"—what she calls the most important aspects of a relationship. When she argues with her home-town honey, Steve, she says winning means little—compromising means more. And, if her nursing degree means earning more money than his teaching certificate—then that's all right, too.

Her tips for asking boys out? "Do it casually. Don't come on real strong or throw yourself at him. Just be friendly and say, 'Hi, how are you doing?' Don't commit yourself too soon either because sometimes after talking to him you'll get a totally different picture and you won't want to go out with him. Also, do it in person because facial expressions reveal what he's really thinking. He may say yes, but you might 'see' apprehension; he may say 'no' but still look interested. And, keep a good perspective. The time I asked Bob out, my friends were saying, 'Aren't you all excited?' I said, 'Yeah, I'm excited, but only to a degree because I don't want to set myself up to be hurt or let down. We're friendly; I just met him. I'll have to work on it.' "

About calling boys: "I think it's open territory. My father is really negative about it. He told me, 'It's not your place, not your role; it's up to the boy to call you.' I disagree. If I have something that I want to share with a boy, I should be able to call. When we first started going out, my boyfriend said, 'If you ever have to call, do it; there are no rules around here about a girl calling a guy.' "

To ask nor not to ask?
That is the question of the Eighties!

Believe it or not, asking a boy out may be the dating dilemma of the Eighties! It's the single most important privilege of the dating system that every girl I interviewed wants (see Chapter 39), something that 64 percent of all girls in the *TeenAge* Relationships Survey long to do, yet only 47 percent have mustered up enough courage to try! What hesitation in an era when 75 percent say things are "liberated enough" to allow it!

What sets the "Askers" apart from the "Non-Askers"? A strong ego, like that of the Twentieth-Century Fast Tracker or Supersonic Dater, which is more tolerant of role reversals and can buck the conventional wisdom that it's "embarrassing or unromantic to ask a boy for the first date." Askers are also more likely to be sixteen or older and in the company of boys already (73 percent are currently dating, more than half of them just one boy), which obviously makes asking easier. They're also more liberal and are more likely to have had sex or to feel that premarital sex is acceptable. Just as many girls I interviewed assumed, Askers are also slightly more "fast lane" than Non-Askers! They are 22 percent more likely to smoke cigarettes, 32 percent more likely to drink, and less likely to feel a boy must make the first moves with kissing or making out. Ironically, however, they're just as confused as Non-Askers about whether or not to pay for that date!

Perhaps that's why the majority of girls feel that asking a boy to anything more than the movies as "a friend" is totally out of the question. Asking him to go steady is declassé. "Boys have to ask us," snaps one Modern Traditionalist. "I would feel cheap and pushy if *I* did it, so I wouldn't. I know a girl who's done it several times and been successful, but it seems like she's aggressive and easy." Another agrees: "I can't stand a girl asking a boy out! It's just not right. We should be able to earn the same amount of money as men but not ask them out; we're not that equal. I can't picture myself calling a guy and asking him for a date. It just isn't done."

Askers vs. Non-Askers: Who Are They?

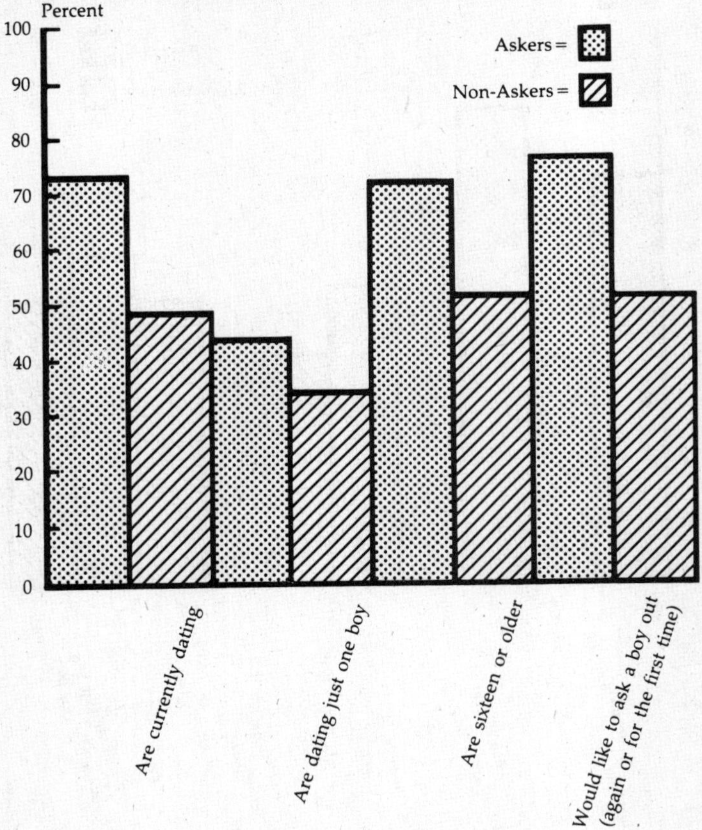

"Askers," girls who have already asked a boy out for a date, tend to be older and more socially advanced than non-askers. Seventy-three percent of askers are currently dating compared with only 48% of non-askers; and 44% of askers say they are dating just one boy—which obviously makes it easier to ask him for a date. Non-askers come in at only 34%. Also, 72% of askers are sixteen or older, compared to only 52% of non-askers. Of those who've asked a boy out, 77% say they would do it again. Fifty-two percent of non-askers say they would like to try it some day.

Askers vs. Non-Askers: Their Ability to Buck Convention

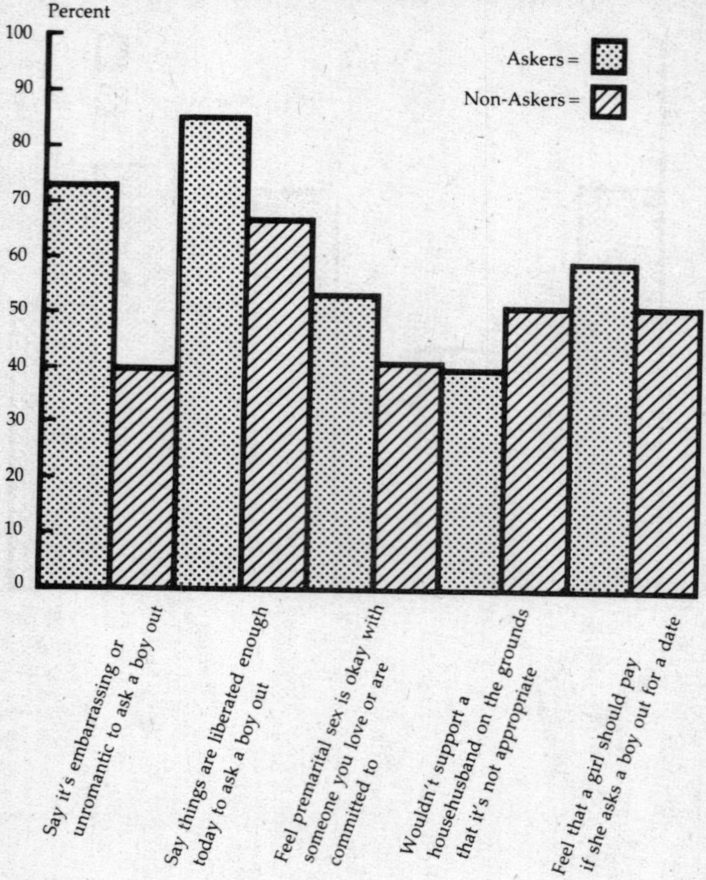

The TeenAge *Relationships Survey shows that girls who have asked a boy out seem to be more willing to buck social and sexual conventions than those who haven't. Seventy-three percent of askers say it's not embarrassing or unromantic to ask a boy out while only 40% of non-askers agree; 85% of askers say things are liberated enough today to do it, while only 67% of non-askers agree. Askers are also more sexually tolerant: 53% say premarital sex is okay with someone you love or are committed to while only 41% of non-askers agree. And, they are more liberated: only 40% say they wouldn't support a househusband on the grounds that it's not appropriate while 51% of others say the same thing. But here comes the big dilemma of the eighties: though 47% of all girls say they have asked a boy out to some kind of social affair before, only 59% of them felt that they should have paid!*

Still others say asking a boy out is only permissible "if you know him well," "know he likes you and there's a good chance he'll say yes," "know he's shy," or you are "both drunk." In an ironic twist, many girls go on to cite relationships that work out well once the girl has taken the initiative. "My brother is shy and not too good-looking," explains one. "Once this gorgeous girl asked him out and now they've been going out for two years; it never would have happened if she hadn't done it."

Still the only totally acceptable way to "snag" a date remains dropping hints, which according to Didi, a master of the game, "is not very hard to do. I just figure that if I see something I like, the only way I'll be sure to get it is to go after it myself. If I'm talking to a guy, I simply say I'd like to get together for dinner. It's not really set up as 'a date,' just as a continuation of good times. The guy always says yes.

"Once a friend and I had lunch and decided the waiter was good-looking. We also wanted another beer but didn't have enough money for it. So I wrote him a check for the tip, put my name and phone number on it. Sure enough, he called. I knew he would. But it was an easy way to cover my tracks—it could have been totally innocent."

But all the scheming in the world can backfire, says sixteen-year-old Casey, a sweet-faced Supersonic Dater from New York, with a halo of frizzy brown hair, an off-the-shoulder sweatshirt, and jeans: "Once I asked this boy Phil out because I was pressured into it. I thought he was cute and I guess my friends could tell 'cause of the look on my face whenever he was around. His friend found out through them and kept prodding me to try it. In the lunchroom one day he said, 'Hey, Phil, what would you do if a certain person asked you out?' Phil said, 'I might say yes.' But when I asked him, he said no. It was really embarrassing."

That is exactly the kind of embarrassment most girls would rather avoid. "I wouldn't ask a boy out 'cause I wouldn't want to get rejected," concedes Pamela. "A lot of girls do and end up going steady with them, but a few get rejected and laughed at by their friends. Then all the other guys think they're hard-up or can't get asked out so their status gets lowered and no one will ask them out later."

(I must confess that for all my liberated talk, up until a year ago my palms still sweated and my heart still raced when I had to call a male crush—even if I had a perfectly legitimate excuse. Only after a few flight checks with friends could I get "all systems go" with my ego. Even then I'd ring a few times and hang up and try again. One friend avoids the conflict completely by calling a boy she likes when she knows he won't be there—at lunchtime, early in the morning, during art class—so that he'll have to call her back—which makes it seem, at least in her traditional mind, more acceptable!)

14

Who Pays the Piper

No doubt you've heard your mother say, "Never discuss religion or money at the dinner table." Well, perhaps there's a good reason: money, like religion, can for some be a very sensitive subject. And when it comes to doling out dollars for a date, it can be even more touchy. Though the Census Bureau reports that in 1982 alone, teenage girls earned nearly as much independent income as boys ($1,698 to their $1,786); and a 1983 survey called "The Mood of American Youth" by the National Association of Secondary School Principals (NASSP) showed that girls, on the average, were given larger allowances than boys ($9.60 to their $8)—largely to make up for that discrepancy—girls still say they expect boys to pay for a date!

"I never even bring money on a date! If a boy asks me out, then he's the one who should pay for everything; it's tradition," says April, seventeen, a Sweet Southern Belle from Pike County, Kentucky. "I wouldn't pay my boyfriend's way and we've been dating for ten months. It's just not the way I've been brought up! If a guy said, 'Well, this time you can buy dinner,' I would say, 'I will not—we just won't go out!' I'd feel he was a tightwad or that he really didn't care about me; even going Dutch would make me feel terrible. Besides it would look strange for me to pay his way into a theater! I've never had to pay for a date and I never will."

Tradition then, not financial status, is the deciding factor for many girls. "Some of the richest girls go out with guys who don't have any money—and they still don't pay," says one observer. "It's stupid for a guy to have to work hard and do without something he really needs just to take his girlfriend out. So I don't think he should always pay. The only problem is that in my high school any girl who paid for herself might not get asked out again. If she was a slut, it would be expected; if she wasn't sleazy, they'd think she was strange because she'd be breaking the stereotype."

The few who do manage to break the old rules find it leads to just that kind of confusion. "Because of equal rights, a girl can *occasionally* pay." Marsha hesitates. "I once did, but gave the guy money ahead of time so as not to embarrass him in front of the waiter. It still didn't make me feel real comfortable." Says Carmen: "I did it once and it felt great! It just shows that women are not incompetent people, that we can do *almost* anything they can. But I am *not* a feminist! If we were all exactly equal (and I quote from my mother), then we'd only have one restroom. Obviously we're not equal. Women will remain one step behind. We know there are lots of things that contrast." And yet some Twentieth-Century Fast Trackers (who are more likely than any other group to pay) call this monetary tango the hypocritical dance it is: "Today girls are saying, 'Pay for my meal, pay for my gas, open the car door for me, treat me to a nice time, but treat me as an equal,' " expands Charlotte. "It isn't logical; we're sending boys two very conflicting messages."

Girls who *do* split dates (only 49 percent in the *TeenAge* Relationships Survey) call it "sharing," "helping out financially," "showing independence," "strength," or just "not wanting to owe a guy anything after a date." "If the guy insists on paying one time, then I say, 'Let me make the plans next time,' or, 'Let us make the plans and let me pay for it,' " says one true egalitarian. "I do it now with my boyfriend and I like it. I enjoy doing things for him. It makes me feel like I'm giving, too." Devon agrees: "When I go out on a date, I'm really money-conscious, because I feel bad, you know, because he has to pay for everything. I mean,

I'm an able person. Why can't I pay for some of it? I'm a cashier at K-Mart; I work, too, and I like to help out."

Amazingly, only 55 percent of girls in the *TeenAge* Relationships Survey say that if we ask a boy out we'd better expect to pay! Says one Texan, "The confusion's good because girls are just getting a taste of what guys have to go through all the time. Maybe now we'll be able to sympathize a little more with why boys do what they do."

(Raised with a strong sense of financial independence, I too have been caught more than once in the web of "who pays" confusion. On some dates, my nerves would be knotted like the napkin in my lap, until the boy I was with waved aside gropes at my pocketbook or slapped enough money for two on the table. Even though I wanted to pay for myself, and knew a girl should, I always felt bad about asserting it. I was a terrible hypocrite: if he indeed accepted the offer (as he should have), then I wondered if he really liked me! Somewhere my upbringing, like that of many girls I talked to, had confused his money with his respect.

One other comment: I will never cease to be amazed at girls (some of them friends) who exploit the financial leverage we have over boys, who think that an extra X-chromosome entitles us to a free ride anywhere, anytime, for any reason. One Sweet Southern Belle I know still expects male "friends" to pick up her dinner tab, while another accepts dinner and travel invitations from boys she couldn't care less about, simply because the food and airfare are free! It's too bad that our society encourages women to "use" boys financially; it's even sadder that boys are raised to think their masculinity lies between the sections of their billfold.

Unfortunately, little will change in the social system until women's economic positions change, until girls begin to establish themselves as financially independent—and are proud of it—from the teen years on. Then the whole notion of who pays for a date will no longer be obscured by role playing, symbolism, and hidden meanings and will become instead what it should have always been—an indication of pure pleasure, a measure of who would like to "treat" the other, one of the nicest, most common, gift-giving events life has to offer.)

15

"All the Right Moves" —But Who Makes Them?

Along with questions about asking boys out and paying come questions about who should make the first "moves." We read articles, watch TV shows, hear boys testify that they'd love to have sexually liberated girls "put the moves on them." But deep inside we wonder—what would they *really* think? We know rumor and grapevine gossip don't treat some "sexually assertive" girls with kindness and admiration. And yet we all run into that special guy whom we like just a little bit more than he likes us, whom we'd like to kiss, to hold hands with—or at least show we're interested in. But dare we? The road to sexual equality is riddled with potholes; daring to cross them, even in our minds, may involve putting our reputations, all our ideas about the role girls play, on the line.

Perhaps that's why most girls say they don't want sexual equality and don't want to deal with the confusing stakes at hand. The fear of being called "easy" makes even the toughest equality nuts crack just a little. "I wouldn't make the first moves because tradition says it's the man's role," says Mickey, who claims otherwise to hate being thought of as "the second sex." "I'd be afraid of being called a sleaze. Around where I come from, guys are very kiss-and-tell and everyone would know in a period of thirty minutes what happened on our date. If I went out with somebody and *I* kissed *him* good night, the next day my best friend would be on the phone saying, 'Oh, I hear *you* kissed *him* good night on the first date!' " Says Pamela, echoing the same general sentiment: "A boy should make the first moves, otherwise you'll look like a sex maniac. It's only okay if you're going steady."

Ironically, we don't mind rejecting *his* advances and certainly don't consider him "sleazy" for trying. (Some girls even wonder what's wrong with him if he doesn't try something!) Yet *we* don't want to take the risks. "The boy should make the first moves because I would never know if he wanted to kiss or not and would be embarrassed if I found out he didn't," says Kate, revealing the unexpected quirk in the nature of most Supersonic Daters. "But I wouldn't mind if *he* made the mistake. I might even be flattered."

When a girl does make the first moves it's usually within the context of a relationship in which she feels safe enough to be herself. "If you feel comfortable and the boy is not offended, then it's okay for you to express desire," says Dale. "I once did it. I'd been going out with this boy for six months and he never did anything. One night at the movies I simply put my arm around him and he smiled. He wasn't really surprised. Then I drove him home in his car and he took over from there. He just needed a little encouragement. That was after being in a relationship, though, not on the first date."

Shy boys, who are unlikely to brag about us "making a pass" at them, seem fair prey as well. "Whenever I've made the first move it's been great," says Didi. "I kind of know when they want me to because they act shy. I let them know I'm shy too, that I'm not going to attack them, and simply reach over, give them a little kiss. They make the next move. I've never been truly thwarted. In fact, I've been very lucky. Once when a guy didn't respond, it felt like I was being rejected but it was really only a clear indication of what was going on in the relationship anyway."

Such are the dangers of being a rule-breaker. "I know a girl who mistakenly put the moves on someone else's boyfriend," says Rachel. "He *did* mind because he wasn't into it. But then again, that's what boys go through all the time. If he puts the moves on me, there's always the possibility that I don't want it either."

16

How to Get a Date Without Even Trying

Many dating problems have little or nothing at all to do with the changes society makes in male/female sex roles and everything to do with how we relate to boys on a personal basis. They are problems our mothers and grandmothers dealt with, problems our children will struggle with as well. They have been the themes of great novels, love songs, plays, ballets, and operas; have caused wars and ended them, led young lovers like Romeo and Juliet to suicide. The clash of the sexes fuels gossip sheets, magazines, epic nighttime soaps; conflict is what modern romance is made of. And while every solution must be considered within the uniqueness of each relationship, there are some general words of advice that friends who've been there before can give about the most common.

Getting him interested

First and most important, of course, is catching his eye, which may be as simple as a wink, a smile, a well-timed touch of the wrist, or as strategic as "running into him a lot," "being super friendly," "showing lots of interest in everything he does," "offering to help with his homework." It can even require some tactical planning. "I try talking to him a lot, joke around," says Kim, eighteen, a Strong Individualist from Huntington, New York. "If we're at a party where there's dancing, I get him out on the floor. Once I went up to this guy I thought looked cute and nice and started talking to him about his likes and dislikes. Later we danced. By the end of the evening, he asked for my phone number."

Or it can be coy. "I don't flirt, because I'm an old-fashioned girl and like to let nature take its course," says Audrey. "Usually I find that being my naturally friendly self works just fine. I've had my eye on a guy before but never actually tried to 'go for it,' like some of my friends. Though they often succeed, I don't think they've done any better than I have."

Going blind

Another way to meet boys or get to know a "crush" is by going on a date that's been set up by friends. "Blind dates are fun," says Marsha, who's been on three. "I did it to meet different people. If the guy had turned out to be ugly or if he thought I was, I would have just chalked one up to experience." Her last semi-blind date—one with a guy she'd admired at the local roller rink—turned out to be her last; she and Dave are now engaged to be married.

For others, blind dates are as repulsive as anchovies on ice cream. "My friend Bridget was going out with this really cute guy in tenth grade and I wasn't dating anyone so she convinced me to try it," says Julie. "It was awful. We felt uncomfortable and just sat there not talking because we knew we didn't like each other. He was too quiet for me and not my type physically. Bridget wanted to stay out late and all I wanted to do was go home. It caused a lot of problems because I made such a scene."

Obviously, our attitude going into a date determines the outcome—because if we want to have a rotten time, we will. Being positive, remembering that a blind date doesn't mean we're hard-up, unpopular, or unattractive, is key, as is not expecting him to be Prince Charming; the guy can only be as human as we are. "It always works the same way," says Joan, who's gone on many blind dates, set up more. "It's usually a boy and a girl who've been out of circulation for some time, who want to get together with friends. It's just one way to do it." Joan set up a newly unengaged friend with her boyfriend's best friend. "They had a good time; they were always laughing. They didn't go park, but they did go to a movie later. It was up to them, not us, to get the romantic aspect going."

And being a good "blind date" means playing it cool. "I always feel tense because I don't know how to act around my friends and this new guy," says one Utah girl. "I'm never sure if I should sit next to him and if I should pay. But if I just treat it like we're all a bunch of good friends having a good time, it always works out well."

(If it's truly a blind date—where a friend just gives him your phone number—and you're worried about getting stuck all night at the movies with a real dud, tell him that you have to be in early to finish some homework. Then if you like him, you can always change your mind. And if not, it makes a quick getaway easy.)

He loves me/he loves me not

Once he's interested, we have to decide what kind of attention we want—friendship or something more. If we want "more" and he asks us out, our problems are solved; if he doesn't, we're left to wonder, in which case some girls prefer to take action. "For me, it's always worse being strung along, not knowing, thinking that there's a chance," says Kit (eighteen, Linn, Kansas), an attractive "upright" kind of Strong Individualist, whom you could never accuse of doing anything even close to "pushy." "So I ask him what he thinks. Or I get a friend, a guy or a girl who knows him on a platonic basis, to act as a mediator and feel him out. It's a good protective device for both people, because he doesn't have to give me an answer face to face and I don't have to see his face when he answers. It kind of softens the blow, and he can be really honest."

Other girls say it's better to lie low and wait quietly for more feedback. "I usually don't know if a guy likes me or not, but I certainly don't go asking his friends," warns one. "They might tell him who it was and I'd be mortified. If I get some idea that the results will be positive, I have my friends ask his friends and report back to me. If he likes me, then I tell his friends he should ask me out, who tell him!"

The shutout and clique pressure

Having been fortunate enough never to have been in this situation, my heart goes out to girls who are too gawky, shy, or unrefined to swing easily from vine to vine in the social system, girls who are shut out of the dating game right from the start because they cannot or will not "play along." I don't know what makes some of them shrink back into the woodwork, while others overcompensate by becoming class clown, athletic star, yearbook editor, but I do know that there's nothing more confusing or painful than feeling left out. Allison, seventeen, from Sycamore, Illinois, is a Twentieth-Century Fast Tracker, who's had to sharpen her wit and smarts so that when she leans up against the clique scene they are the ones who break. It's a subtle internal battle with a result so carefully planned to look like a matter of choice that it sometimes fools the duper.

Extremely bright and outspoken, Allison is the sort of girl who played with racing cars instead of dolls, who hung around with our brothers instead of with us. She has fiery green eyes, a head of untamed dirty blonde curls and a pasty, uneven complexion. Allison has made academics, politics, and basketball her priorities, all-consuming concerns that always come before boys and dating. As a result, she often feels like an outsider at her own school, where she says, "Most guys act like they're too good for you."

"Dating's real big at my school, especially before class when everybody's making out in the halls." She laughs, adjusting the wire-rimmed glasses on her nose. Allison is my first interview of the day and we're sitting in the musty gray conference room at Marymount College, where the Congressional Seminar meets. "If you're not dating somebody, you walk around saying, 'Oh, my God, what is this?' Everyone's really into cliques—with the football players and cheerleaders on top, the 'aggies'—the Future Farmers of America—in the middle, the burnouts—the druggies—at the bottom. Everybody wants to know who the quarterback is going out with this week; if it's not a cheerleader, it's like 'Oh-h-h-h-h-h! The Eleventh Commandment has been broken!' The drama club people go with the drama club people; the choir people with the choir people. If you're in a lot of things like me, then you can't be in any one clique and you just sort of float around. Then you end up dating boys from Dekalb—the neighboring school."

Growing up "horsing" and joking around with the boys at Sycamore made it difficult—or so she says—for Allison to take them seriously anyway. "I know a lot of them like brothers. But I prefer the boys at Dekalb, because they don't go into mass shock if I show up in a dress one day or do something out of character. They're also easier to talk to about everything—from religion to school work." As a result, her boyfriend Ron, whom she's been dating for three years, is a Dekalb graduate. "What I really like about him is that he hates cliques," she adds. "He's not a nonconformist; he's just not a conformist."

Athena, sixteen, a Modern Traditionalist from Grosse Point Shores, Michigan, finds that cross-clique dating in her school is difficult too—even if you *are* a cheerleader as she is. That's because at her school apathy's "in," involvement's "out." "Cheerleaders are not the elite group because we have to be really spirited down there on the field, screaming, yelling, dancing all the time. The 'in' people—very wealthy, disinterested kids who've known each other forever and wear the same kind of clothes—don't do that. They're not open to others and don't want to be. They don't go to dances because it's not 'cool' and they criticize everything."

Athena was part of the "in" crowd until their smothering exclusivity forced her to rebel. "I couldn't stand how they couldn't associate with other people. I like having other friends so I just kind of dropped out. I don't really hang around with any one person or group now. I just act like who I am."

Both Allison and Athena are individuals strong enough to buck the dating system and look for satisfaction in other friends. But some girls, especially those from age thirteen to fifteen, find it's just easier to give in. "We only date boys within our group," explains one New Jersey clique-captive. "It's not a restriction—a friendly or nice guy could break in—but it would take a while. Last year I was really surprised when a guy from a different group asked me out. Of course I said no. They have friends like them; we have friends like us."

(The clique pressure I experienced in college took the form of sororities and fraternities and was so strong that I realize now I should never have condoned it. The Betas only dated Tri Delts and Sigma Chis only dated Alpha Delta Pis, and I watched social discrimination and catty jealousy "shut out" my freshman-year roommate (who continued hopelessly to rush them through junior year), because she was a little too wild, a little too blonde and attractive for the competition to take. I can only imagine how much worse it must be at a co-ed high school where everyone's much younger, more vulnerable.)

The pressure to have a boyfriend

Another problem is the pressure we feel—usually unspoken—to have a boyfriend, the urge we get to scream with frustration when we discover all our friends are busy for the weekend, can only talk about their relationships and their plans for the prom. As a defense, many boyfriendless girls simply pretend they don't care—"Whenever boyfriends come up, I just change the subject"—while others feel the pressure so strongly that they round up a date just to be included. "I once ended up dating someone who was terrific-looking, but who I didn't like, just to be dating like my friends," admits one girl. "After about a week, I figured it was wrong and broke it up. I told my friends I just wasn't the type to get involved unless I really liked the guy."

One of my boarding-school friends used to prop a giant-size picture of whatever boy she was dating—or just hoped to date—in direct line with the doorway, so all passers-by would know she was "involved." In college, rumors went around that some girls were so embarrassed to be without a Saturday night date that they actually turned out their lights, turned off their stereos, and pretended they weren't home! The anguish of being a "have-not" in a world of "haves" is exceptionally difficult at any age, especially for sensitive fifteen-year-olds like Carol, a dancer-like blonde beauty and Strong Individualist from Memphis, Tennessee. "It's hard to break up with a guy I like or have a crush on because I want to have a boyfriend so much," she explains. "Some people like to be free, but I like to be tied down. Whenever Ted and I would break up, I felt like I had nobody to talk to, like nobody was there. When everyone else is just into their boyfriends, they don't really have time for a close, close girlfriend."

Joan, a girl equipped with an unusual, inspiring sense of optimism, has felt left out, too, but doesn't let it get her down. Unlike Carol, she expects to depend on friends. "I know exactly how it feels," she says. "All your girlfriends are going out and you end up feeling stupid because you don't have a date, so you sit home or something. But it really isn't all that bad if you rely on friends. This summer I went alone to a party with three couples and I drove. I had a great time, 'cause it was a standard shift and a real nice car. It didn't bother me that I didn't have a boyfriend because I was with them. I'll admit I would have had a better time with a boy, but we still joke about the time I played 'chauffeurette,' and how I just made the best of it.

"You can't feel bad if you don't have a date. It doesn't mean you're not a good person. You just have to be positive and know that there's bound to be some guy out there who's interested. Sometimes they're even thinking about you but can't show it for a long time because they're dating somebody else. I know, because I broke up with Kip many times to date other guys. Then I'd find out it wouldn't work and would be upset that the security of the relationship was gone. Then one day I just realized that I had to go ahead with my life and not worry about it. There are guys out there who are going to want to date me, and when they do, they'll ask me out. It all works out in the end."

Other solutions: find other unattached girlfriends and have a great time with them; cultivate innumerable male "friends" to go out with and just have fun—their friends might turn out to surprise you.

17

Weeding Out the "Dweebes"

Hooking the guy we're interested in—and not just anybody—means discouraging the "Dweebes"—the ones we don't like. And while it's flattering to be lavished with male attention, a guy who likes us more than we like him can be as nauseating as too much icing on a birthday cake. We slink through the halls to avoid him, dread every time the phone rings, every time we see him at a party. If he's persistent enough, we know a confrontation is brewing. "I had this good friend who liked me," recalls Devon. "It was an extremely difficult situation, because I didn't really like him as a boyfriend but wanted to stay friends. After he asked me out several times, I finally had to say, 'Eugene, we have to talk about our relationship; it's really bothering me. We're friends, nothing more, nothing less.' It was pretty difficult to see him after that, but he eventually got over it."

Some boys, however, take the slightest bit of rejection badly. "One kid asked me out ten times," says Emily. "I only said yes twice. Then he started saying he couldn't treat me just as a friend, that he wanted to be my boyfriend or nothing at all. When I said no, he called me up, told me off, put nasty notes in my locker. I think he really had problems. He really couldn't communicate with me. Funnily enough, he grew up over the summer and wrote me a letter of apology."

To avoid such reactions, many girls couch rejections in "little white lies" that convey disinterest, yet let the boy down gently. "I told one guy that I was dating someone away at college who was really mean," says one, "and that I didn't want to go out with him and risk a fight. Of course, none of it was true." Or they stress what a great "pal" or "friend" the pursuer is—too wonderful, of course, to forfeit to an unsteady romance! A few even excuse themselves with the oldest line in the book: "I'm not ready to get involved."

"The guy I went to homecomin' with was really nice but wanted to go out again and I didn't," says one gracious Sweet Southern Belle, who emphasizes being polite enough (and wise enough) not to close the door to future invitations. "So I just said I wanted to date around. He got the picture." Offers Dierdra, "Many boys are understanding if you can make them see they've been in the same situation before. Remind them of a time when a girl liked them more than they liked her; that helps heal the wound faster."

So right, but so out of reach

Of course, there's always the reverse situation—a boy we like more than he likes us. When this happens too frequently, it can signal a problem. "I have a friend who always picks someone she knows she could never go out with," explains Athena, "because he's either already going steady with someone else or is so far out of reach—like the captain of the football team who only associates with certain girls—that she could never have him. Then she idolizes him, pines away all day. When she finds someone she *can* have, she immediately loses interest and isn't happy until she's found another unattainable heartthrob."

Luckily, most girls know when to give up. "That's happened to me several times, and I believe that the only way around it is to try and forget about him, get out and meet new people, have fun and always look my best," says Bobbi. "Sometimes, though I may not *really* be trying, I turn his head after all." Says June, nineteen, a Strong Individualist from Huntington, New York: "If my friends know him, I ask them to put in a good word for me or arrange a meeting. If they can't or if all else fails, I forget him, because there are many more fish in the sea. My girlfriends do the same thing but some keep a small fire tucked away inside and hope that time will eventually bring them together."

The tug-of-war boyfriend

Another common problem: when two girls like the same guy. "One of my friends was interested in this guy and asked me if she should end her nine-month relationship with her boyfriend Danny to go out with him," says Bobbi. "Since I'd never met him I said, 'No, stay with your boyfriend.' But when I finally caught a glimpse of him I about died! He was beautiful! He told me he wished we'd met instead and that he was sorry Ellen was breaking up with Danny to date him. I felt so guilty!—especially when the relationship lasted only two weeks and her boyfriend wouldn't take her back. I've had opportunities to see him but I won't chance it; we're both still too upset over what happened."

Not all girlfriends are so loyal. It appears many even enjoy a good fight to the finish. "When that happened to two friends of mine, they started talking behind each other's back, stopped doing things together because each wanted to be with him alone," says Athena. "They even compared notes like, 'Did he talk to you today? Well, he talked to me!' In the end, he didn't choose either of them and they ended up consoling each other. The whole thing was sad and stupid, because they worked against each other and it backfired."

To avoid such confrontations, many girls establish unofficial ground rules that circumvent competition. "My friends and I have a mutual understanding, that whoever gets the guy first, gets blessings from the rest," says June. "There's no point in fighting over a guy, because you can't force him to like you if he doesn't anyway." Or they feel no guy's worth a fight. "None of my friends would even flirt with a guy I like; it just wouldn't happen!" exclaims Christy. "Even if we just look at the same guy, we don't move in on him if the other one likes him more. I don't think anyone else has the relationship with their friends that I do. Certainly not boys, who steal each other's girlfriends just to impress each other. Girls respect each other's feelings, because they don't have anything to prove."

Falling in love with a friend

Another problem can occur when we start out "best friends" with a boy—sharing secrets, walks in the rain, all-night rap sessions—and accidentally "slip" into something more. Sometimes it works positively to free up underground emotions and cut down the sexual tension between us. Other times, especially if the boy is unwilling, it can set our friendship into an indefinite tailspin. Then risking love with our best friend means risking it all.

When "The Peace Train" pulled out of its last station in the Sixties, Denise, a fourteen-year-old Supersonic Dater from Paoli, Pennsylvania, should have been on it. An earthy type of tie-dye intellectual, she dreses in what she calls "flower child" clothes—Indian prints, long skirts, and workshirts—this time, an olive sweatshirt, jeans, suede booties that tie around the ankle. Perhaps because she lost her virginity at age twelve—"We were alone at his house; he was stronger than me"—she looks down on dating and has trouble getting anything more long-term than a crush off the ground. She is, right down to her music preferences (The Beatles, The Rolling Stones), an odd, yet ironically appropriate contrast to the prepped-up company she keeps. It was most likely that streak of individuality that led her into a relationship with her best friend Patrick, a black-eyed, black-haired boy who everyone at school agreed was good-looking, but she thought was "gorgeous."

"He had a nice body—really muscular but not too worked out, was about five-six—just the height for me," she points out in a surprisingly alto voice. "And he had a really great personality—sweet, considerate—all the things I look for. We started out as friends but I grew to like him even more. I was going out with someone else at the time, but when we broke up Patrick and I started seeing each other."

Being friends before getting romantically involved made their relationship progress quickly. "Dating was the same but just like being together a lot more. It was really great." A small smile creeps across her makeup-free face. Unfortunately, it started out with such a bang that it also started fading quickly. After a month he was already interested in another girl who was three years older, his age. When it ended they didn't hate each other, but Denise admits jealousy bubbled beneath her cool exterior, especially when she'd see them together; that made continuing their friendship impossible. "I let my jealousy pass undiscussed, because I sensed from knowing him there was nothing I could do. If I'd tried to confront him with it in the beginning, we might have ended up enemies."

Denise's story echoes others about teenage friendships that, once romanticized, go sour. Christy is still confounded by her next-door neighbor Hank, who keeps tugging at her string. Every time he comes home from school he says he doesn't want to see his old girlfriend Ann "because there's nothing there," and yet every time Christy is free to date him, he backs away. Fed up and hurt, Christy doesn't even want to be friends anymore. Explains Louisa, seventeen, a Strong Individualist from Los Alamitos, California: "My friend Pam and Wayne were best friends for three years before they started going out. They would always talk about their boyfriend/girlfriend problems and sometimes ended up together at parties or football games. But when they started dating, it ruined the friendship—especially for Pam, who felt it was getting serious too quickly. They talked it out and went back to being really good friends; but it was really difficult."

18

Dealing With Relationships: "Is Love a Battlefield?"

The long and the short of it

Once we're in a relationship we have to decide how serious it is, i.e., whether we want to date him casually—once every two weeks—or see him exclusively all the time. Though some of us are tempted to rush into relationships for the security they offer, most prefer light, easy, non-binding encounters that allow experimentation with different types of personalities. "There are kids in our school who have been going out for two and a half years," notes Holly, a bubbly, bright date-arounder. "I think that's getting a little heavy at our age. I don't want to marry the first guy I like because I don't know if he's what I want. I have to check out the field first."

Girls who've been going steady for a long time are, indeed, secretly curious about the fun they may be passing up. "I sometimes wonder what I'm missing out on by not dating around," confesses Gigi, whose three-year relationship with a popular quarterback, Ernie, has kept her out of circulation since junior high. "I like a relationship because of the trust it builds. But I've never had a chance to really meet a lot of guys. I really care for Ernie, but he's not necessarily the guy I'm going to marry. He'll go away to college and I'm going to stay home. Then I'll probably date other people just to see what it's like."

Girls from rural areas and small towns complain that because of the automatic intimacy imposed by a tightly knit community, "dating around" is difficult at best—at times nearly impossible. "In a small town, if a guy likes you and you like him, other boys back away and don't ask you out, so you're really almost automatically going steady," says Janice of Ryan, Oklahoma. "It can happen even if you've been seen together only once! You kinda go with one at a time, break it off, go with somebody else." Roxanne, from Belcourt, North Dakota, cites a similar problem. "There isn't a lot of casual dating at my school, not a lot of back and forth. If you're going with someone, you're more or less 'going steady.' I don't know why but everyone's into relationships. It's especially a problem when you're from a small high school like mine and don't get to meet thousands of different guys anyway."

The two-guy girl

What about relationships with a few boys at a time? Well, they have their ups and downs too, and can get particularly hairy when neither person knows exactly what's what. Carolyn, eighteen, a bright, pretty Strong Individualist with big blue eyes, dark wavy brown hair pulled back in little-girl barrettes, a purple sweater, and jeans, says her boyfriend, Peter—"very kind, considerate, athletic"— is "not [her] top priority," nor is she his. She also says they both like it that way. "I'm too young to get seriously involved," asserts the Marymount freshman from Floral Park, New York. "I watched my sister, now twenty-two, date the same boy since first grade. They're getting married, but I wonder how they know they're right for each other since they've never dated anyone else! To me that's crazy; you have to know a lot of different people before you can make a choice."

Carolyn uses Guy, really a casual weekend fling from Villanova, to keep Peter off balance. "Peter knows I've got another boyfriend I've been dating for a year, because he's seen Guy's picture on the wall," she says. "But if he gets jealous, he doesn't show it;

he's never come out and said anything. Besides, he has another relationship with an old girlfriend in Vermont. He says they're not romantically involved—but I know they are."

And last New Year's Eve her suspicions about Peter's other relationship were confirmed. "We'd agreed to celebrate together," she explains. "But it was tentative, I guess, since he'd just landed a job for break at the Dartmouth college book-store, near where his family lives. Since Dartmouth was going back early, he said he had to work New Year's Eve and that he couldn't come down to New York. When I called New Year's Day he seemed worn out, so I asked how his night was. He told me that he'd gone up to Vermont to visit Madeline who'd had a skiing accident. It was a last-minute thing and the family had called him because he was very close with them.

"He said I didn't have to worry, he'd spent most of the time with the family, not with her. But as much as I wanted to believe him, it still really broke my heart. I'd had such high hopes of seeing him—only to find he'd been with her! We discussed it, instead of fighting about it, and I told him I was jealous. He said he understood and would have felt the same way if it had happened to him." That didn't cure Carolyn's hurt, however. To this day she still wonders if she and Peter have a future together. The safety net she set up to protect herself from getting prematurely involved may in the end keep them forever separated.

Making a commitment

In high school, in college, in our reach for adulthood, we demand, often too soon, that our mates behave like adults and do the "adult thing"—like making a commitment. But those years are really a time for experimentation, a time for taste-testing the smorgasbord of boys available to us. Even though we want it, being forced into commitment too soon may cause us, like Ginger, to rebel. Then a relationship really becomes an excuse for misbehaving.

"I'm going out with this guy Cliff now, but I cheat on him all the time," she says mischievously and without a whole lot of guilt. "He doesn't know I see anyone else and would kill me if he did. I have some guys, some best friends, who come over to my house who I'm real flirty with, too. I've even been dating another guy while I'm visiting here in Washington. There are so many guys I'd like to go out with that I feel like it's cheating all day just in my mind."

Ginger says she likes the concept of a relationship but very few of the constraints. Like many teens, she's trying to behave like an adult without accepting any of the adultlike responsibility that comes along with it. Many boys "cheat" for similar reasons. That's why Joseph, "the best-looking football player in school," began to give Milly, fifteen, Gulnare, Kentucky, a hard time. So hard, in fact, that dating him became like trying to ride a roller coaster with both hands tied behind her back. "He was so good-looking that all the girls from Pikeville, our rival school, would come over to the ball games just to see him," she says with peevish delight. "They'd go wild over his Mexican looks. It would make the other boys so mad that he hardly had any friends at all."

Sweet and bouncy, with an oval face and punky fringes of black hair streaming down her neck and into her eyes, Milly, a little bit of a Pat Benatar look-alike, was the first in her school to nab Joseph, the mystery boy who'd just moved in from Texas—"nobody knew anything about him so he was extra exciting." Her sister, who'd met his family first, introduced them, and Milly discovered their lockers were next to each other. "I couldn't believe it." She smiles. "The relationship just went from there."

But going steady for several months also meant listening to the Pikeville girls cruise around town and report they'd seen Joseph with someone else. Milly, a Modern Traditionalist, was actually relieved when Joseph told her he wanted to "date around." It would be hard, she said, but at least better than hearing it from others. But the new arrangement made her nervous, anxious, unsure. She didn't know if she could rely on him or trust him to care. And then it devoured her confidence. "It made me so insecure that I felt like I had to look my best all the time, wear makeup and skirts—instead of my usual jeans—just to keep his interest. There was so much competition that one girl would even flirt with him right in front of me. I really didn't know if I could keep up."

She became suspicious, jealous, and distracted. "At a cheerleading competition in Texas, I stumbled upon Joseph and his 'old' girlfriend," she recalls. "I couldn't concentrate so I left the competition and went outside to talk with him before he left with her. I had to know if the gossip I'd been hearing was true—that the whole time we'd been going out, he'd also been seeing her secretly. But instead of giving me an answer, he just got mad at me for getting mad at him. It was so confusing; it was really too hard."

Milly's problem solved itself when Joseph moved back to Texas. "Once I knew he was leaving, I was relieved," she says solemnly. "If he hadn't, I wouldn't have let it continue that way. It made me too jealous." Realizing she was not the type for open-ended relationships, Milly set her sights on Joseph's best friend, Jeffrey, a cute, fun-loving boy who was eager to leap into the arms of the girl he'd coveted for so long. "I noticed he didn't ever go out with more than one girl at a time and I thought it might be more comfortable for me to go out with someone like him." She was right; today Milly and Jeffrey have been dating for three months.

"Whenever one person wants exclusivity and the other doesn't, there's jealousy," says Tish, eighteen, a Strong Individualist from New York, New York, who's all too familiar with the "can't-be-tied-down" boyfriend. "The best way to handle it is not to crowd him. As long as he sees you two or three times a week, let it go. But if he hasn't budged in a month, forget it."

Another solution that often gets results but keeps us from ever feeling really comfortable in a relationship is teaching him a lesson, something wheeling-dealing April seems to be a pro at. When her boyfriend Gil, a basketball player from a neighboring town, "wanted his freedom," she gave it to him—but good! "He said his parents were putting pressure on him because they were worried about him driving an hour at midnight over the mountains to see me," says the pretty, spunky seventeen-year-old with a turned-up nose, torrents of short dark brown curls. "So he said, 'Well, April, you know it's hard for me to see you anyway. Why don't we just call it off.' I said, 'You're lying! You just want to date other people.' Though he denied it, I agreed and cried like usual. Then I decided, well, I'll just make him so jealous that he'll want to come back to me no matter how far it is." She winks a turquoise eye at me. The next weekend she and her best friend's handsome brother ran into Gil's brother (an amazing coincidence!) at the local dance club. The next day Gil was back to dialing her number—and that was just a week ago.

"I think I've done a pretty good job of making him jealous," she says, slipping her orange sweater over her white polo shirt. "I haven't talked to him in two days now. I don't want to call him too soon. I don't want him to think he doesn't need to call me since I call him. It's not right for him to have me when he wants me. Maybe it'll draw him back to me. Maybe he'll eventually say, 'You know, I do miss her.' I love him to death, but there's a point when it has to get serious. Right now he says I love him more than he loves me. That's just because he's never really dated anyone seriously. He'll come around."

Barbara, on the other hand, found it was best to forgive and forget. "My boyfriend cheated on me," she says. "What's worse is I knew the girl. I got wicked emotional about it, and he started crying and couldn't look me in the eye. He said they didn't really do anything bad. He just picked her up in his truck and went four-wheeling. She made a pass at him, he kissed her and dropped her off. He felt really guilty. I'd never bring it up or use it against him. But I'd never do it myself."

19

The Games Girls Play

All of us like to play games because they're fun. And a good romance needs mystery and intrigue to keep the suspense going. But when the game-playing becomes our only way of keeping him, when it becomes an end in itself, we lose. Because then the games we play have begun to play us.

Russian roulette with jealousy

Alexis is well-practiced at the art of deception. So it's no accident that this tall beautiful Amazon with chiseled features, freckles, and shocking blue eyes was voted official "sweetheart" for every athletic team in her school. Nor is it surprising that she has her boyfriend Jack, the undisputed "star of the basketball team," twined carefully around her little finger. Self-adoring and power-hungry Alexis, who's swallowed the unfortunate notion that anything worth getting *has to be* difficult—even impossible—plays with Jack's affections as a child plays with a yo-yo, pushing him away when he gets too close, tugging him near when he moves too far. It's a game that keeps Jack interested and Alexis far from ever feeling comfortable.

"Anywhere I go Jack gets jealous," says the sandy-haired Scarlett O'Hara clad in bright yellow shorts, sweatshirt, and meshed football jersey. "He's wonderful and doesn't have any reason to be insecure, but he is. He doesn't even like anybody talking to me. He's told me that a couple of times when we've gotten into a fight, and once gave me a card saying he was afraid of losing me because he's never been in a relationship that lasted so long.

"He's said that when he sees me talking to a guy he gets jealous 'cause I flirt; but all cheerleaders flirt! I just happen to have a lot of guy friends. I could do without them but I think it's neat to have them. Besides, I like it when Jack's jealous; it's flattering. It keeps me sure that he still likes me. Then I'm never worried about losing him."

Alexis also likes the romance of making up. "After we have a fight about his jealousy, we sit down and talk about it or I send him a card and he apologizes. He's good at apologizing. I don't like it when a guy can't lower his ego to say he's sorry. A couple of times he sent me flowers, which changed my mind immediately. Then he apologized, saying, 'I know you're right.' Sometimes he'll even call me up and say, 'Be ready in an hour 'cause I'm taking you out to dinner.' I'll hang up the phone and say, 'All right! Got him again!' In every relationship somebody kisses butt more than the other person, but in this one it's pretty even. I love it. It's never been like this. It's always been me getting away with everything. But I know Jack won't stand for it."

Alexis also got more than she bargained for because Jack's jealousy eventually turned to anger. "When I told him I got a job as a cheerleading staff person this summer—the biggest thing that ever happened to me in my life—he got mad. I was so excited I started crying but he only said, 'Oh, great, you're going to be gone all summer while I'm home! You'll be flirting away with all those male cheerleaders, too!' I was about to break up 'cause that upset me real bad. I don't like it when he gets jealous of me spending too much time with my friends or mom. I'd love it if he could just get jealous without getting mad; it makes me feel so good."

So totally lost in the game of not being herself, Alexis at last reveals the meanest twist of all: "I guess every time I get jealous of him I get mad inside but it makes me like him more. It makes me worry and keeps me interested. But even if I saw him with another girl and it bothered me, I wouldn't let him know; I wouldn't want him to think *I* got jealous. Not everything in life comes easy, you know; it's not just a bowl of cherries. It's just a game people play. It has to be." Tragically, Alexis doesn't realize that love doesn't have to be *that* hard either. If she had the guts to chance it, maybe Jack would like her without her little games.

Luckily, most girls know when to stop. Like Athena, they know that a little manipulation brings a boy around, but too much risks losing him. "I was at a party recently with this guy Mac who was taking me out," says the beefy Michigan girl with long, flowing black hair, chipmunk cheeks. "And he was like, 'Let's go sit over here.' So we sat down and then he took off. He wandered around the house and left me there all alone. Since it was a party with all his friends I didn't know many people and ended up feeling really stupid 'cause I had nobody to talk to. So I got really angry at him and went over and started talking with this other guy I know from school who's got a reputation as a ladies' man, you know, a real gigolo. Mac suddenly decided, 'Oh, she's talking to him; well, I'd better get over there.' And so he started paying attention to me. I did it on purpose and it worked! But," she adds, "I wouldn't make a habit of it. For instance, I haven't been able to go out a lot because of exams and another guy has been asking me out so I have to keep saying no, which is the truth. But the way he keeps asking, I wonder if it makes him think, 'Oh, she's a pretty exclusive person; I'd better ask her out again.' I've never done it on purpose. I'd be afraid he'd say, 'Oh, forget it,' and walk away. Then I'd really feel like a jerk 'cause I really want to go out with him."

20

The Games Boys Play

The love-me-I-won't-love-you boy

Boys play games too, especially when they don't know what they want or wish to keep us off balance. Such is the story of Judy (sixteen, a Supersonic Dater from Clarksville, Tennessee), an effervescent blonde cheerleader who looks and acts like a cross between Doris Day and Sandra Dee, and Joe, a six-foot, great-looking quarterback, baseball, and basketball player, who tried hopelessly since seventh grade to win her affection until she finally out-and-out abandoned his friendship for another boy. "You're my only love," he told her. "I may go out with other girls, but I won't get really involved; you'll see." Now that Judy's decided she wants him back, however (any wonder girls are considered fickle?), he shies away and won't go for anything more than a platonic relationship. "He says we're supposed to be best friends—but we're not!" She laughs nervously as we sit by the pool in Florida. "We've gone a lot further than that! We go out together and do stuff all the time, and our obvious mental connection's already ruined two other relationships of mine. Every time I tell a guy that Joe and I are just friends, they never believe me.

"But now that I'm ready to date him, he says we're just supposed to be friends! I hate it! It's so unfair! He sits there and tells me how much he likes me and all that bull but says we're not really going out. Recently I even heard he told other people, 'Oh, she's so hooked on me that I can date her and anyone else I want and not worry about it.' That made me mad.

"And if we're just friends, why does he act so moody around me? The other night he called me up and I went over to his house to watch TV, when all of a sudden he sat up, got mad, and said, 'You don't care about me, so I'm going to take you home.' When we got there I asked, 'What's your problem?' 'Nothing,' he said, 'just get out of the car.' The next day he didn't call and when I saw him in school he pretended like nothing at all had happened. I just don't get it. He wants me when he can't have me and not when he can. The problem is that he's always on my mind when I'm dating someone else. I don't know if I love him; he's kind of a jerk but I guess I like him anyway, because he fits all the things I want—someone to have fun with, do things with, share things with."

Once burned, Joe's game is to keep Judy forever unsure of his intentions. Even though he had to suffer to get there, he's managed to have his cake and eat it too. Chances are Judy's persistence will eventually bring Joe around, but it's only one example of the many back and forth movements many relationships make before they get off the ground. It's also an example of how games can keep both of us from ever getting what we really want.

The prestige-seeker

Another frequent game-player is the boy who dates girls the way others dance the Virginia reel, dosey-doeing from one Ms. Popularity to the other, until they've elevated their status enough to have a meaningful relationship. The number of broken hearts they leave along the way is irrelevant; winning the girl, and therefore the game, means more. "I hate guys who switch from girl to girl just to see how many they can get, guys who move up the ladder, depending on who's popular this week, hanging on to her, then dropping her the next day," says Dierdra. "It really bothers me."

It also bothered her when Andrew, the dynamic class hunk who dated only homecoming queens, suddenly appeared on her doorstep the day she became the new cheerleader. "We were a lot alike and had a great time just being together," she says but admits that before Andrew she'd hardly dated at all. "Then I was voted junior prom queen and he became even more attentive. Later in the year, a sophomore girl was voted into one of the royalty dances and within minutes Andrew dropped me and headed straight for her. In fact, the second anyone at school started 'being noticed,' he was dating her." Though hurt and disappointed Dierdra knows that what went wrong had more to do with his hangups than hers. "I think he thought it was prestigious," she surmises. "Prestige seems to be especially important for guys like Andrew, who can get anyone they want, because it's the only thing they can still 'go for' that will impress their friends."

The prestige-seeker is a phenomenon many girls have experienced. "I know lots of guys in our school who don't like the girls they date at all but go out with them because they're really popular or pretty," says Anita (sixteen, a Sweet Southern Belle from Grosse Point Woods, Michigan). "They even tell their best friends, 'I don't really like her,' but do it anyway. If that girl goes away with her parents or friends for the weekend, you suddenly see him at another party, hanging all over some other prestigious girl. I think guys like that are just insecure and feel they have to keep up an image."

Dierdra and Anita are right. "Prestige-seekers" are a little like "star-gazers" and "fashion victims" who have so little identity of their own that they have to "get," "wear" or "be" near the latest, greatest, most shining star around in order to feel worthwhile. Like girls who feel uncomfortable dating anyone but the most popular boy, they believe that being with a popular girl makes them popular too. Also in high school and junior high when we're still "testing" our skills—academic, athletic, and social—many boys view dating as a competition. Each time they ask a girl out they're only trying to break a previous record. Some never grow out of the need for a social tally sheet and end up as dissatisfied adults, who, like hamsters in a wheel, are always trying to get to the top but never really make it.

The come-on

While there are occasional louts who like to leave a battlefield strewn with love's destruction, most guys actually lead girls on in innocence—either because they're confused about what they want or because they don't know how to say no. Some may even view girls like racing cars, test-driving many, investing in few. Unfortunately, such hit-and-run behavior leaves us wondering what we did wrong, when in fact *we* probably had nothing to do with it at all.

Such was an incident that left Liza, a robust, dark-haired Venezuelan Modern Traditionalist (now living in California), dazed and in a quandary when a Don Juan, who gave her all the right I-like-you signals, simply cut out. "I hate guys who lead you on, then suddenly don't call you again," she says, her many-braceleted arms jingling like change in a bank as she sits down in my crowded living room, where I had invited myriad teens for brunch. She is picking politely at a chocolate-chip scone, while I can tell she'd rather gorge on it. "You get all wrapped up in liking him, but then don't know what happened. For instance, last New Year's Eve I fooled around with a guy I've had a crush on since ninth grade. His name is Miguel, and he is tall, slim, really cute, with kind of hazel eyes, dirty blond hair. I'd never really considered him before 'cause I never thought I could have him. But this time it was great. We made out and he called me the next day and we saw a movie. We kept in touch for two months while I was away at school, and when I got home on vacation I went to see him in a school play. I told him I wanted to go out with him and he said 'Yeah.' But nothing ever came of it." She shakes her head in confusion. "It might have been the distance. But I really don't know what happened."

No one but Miguel knows for sure, but it's easy to assume that though he liked Liza, he probably liked staying unattached better. In such cases, girls, who are brought up to look for relationships and attachments, present boys, who are brought up to do just the opposite, with a dilemma that has no easy way out. Either he squirms out of it politely or simply pretends it never happened (which is sometimes easier). Liza will probably experience many other disappointments like Miguel until she meets someone who has the courage and desire to work for a relationship.

Boys can also seem to be leading us on when we like them more than they like us. Then, in our quest for a relationship, we may actually misread their intentions and attribute to them more meaning than they began with.

"This guy was a real tease," says one girl who slipped into the "see-what-you-want" trap. "He didn't actually take me out but if we were together he brought me to parties and football games. It was casual but he was always really nice. He'd even drop over to my house three times a week. And when I went on vacation with my parents for two weeks he told me to write, which I did. But when I got back I found out he was going out with this other girl already. It really hurt 'cause I felt like it meant he just didn't care. I mean if he was so interested in me, why was he going out with her? When I saw him he acted like nothing at all had happened between us, like he didn't even really care, you know? I was too embarrassed to talk to him about it. I wasn't about to go up to him and say, 'You liked me! What are you doing with somebody else?' 'Cause I felt like he'd say, 'I never liked you. Where did you get that idea?' And I just felt stupid about it, too embarrassed to say anything, so I forgot it."

This girl is afraid to approach her friend with what went wrong because she suspects deep down that she may have over-reacted to his overtures in the first place. Recognizing who is at fault will not mend her broken heart, but it will help her avoid making the same mistake over again.

21

Breaking Up Is Hard to Do

It was the spring of ninth grade, and she had just landed the part of the drunken tart Gay Wellington in their school's rendition of *You Can't Take It With You.* Terry C., the most gorgeous, dashing sophomore boy around—they called him "Casanova C." behind his back—had been cast as the lead. Both of them were staying up late to paint sets, when all of a sudden her foot ended up in the paint tray. Before she knew what was happening, he swept her off her feet and rushed her into the bathroom. In the dank green light he washed her foot and kissed her gently. It was her first encounter with Mr. Wonderful, something she'd thought would never happen to her. It was, without a doubt, true love.

The next week in assembly he passed her a love poem copied from his Latin primer, one the great Latin poet Catullus had written to his beloved Lesbia—which was appropriate, she supposed, only because her name began with the same three letters. She had no earthly idea what it said or meant; nor did she care. This was romance Hollywood style and reality had no place in her script. Her world began and ended within his arm's reach, and when he gave her a braided silver ring, she knew nothing could surpass life at fourteen.

And then . . . she stumbled upon him kissing another girl in the tennis club lounge. And then . . . she yanked off his ring, threw at him, and stormed off in tears. Though they saw each other again, she knew the bond had been forever broken. In one short fleeting moment Terry had taken love from its most soaring heights to its most crashing depths. Thunder rolled; lightning flashed. The Latin gods no doubt were angry. As the forces of destruction threatened to squash her like a mortal pea between their evil fingers, she vowed never to fall in love again. That is, until tenth grade—when she met Peter.

That was me in ninth grade, but it could have been any girl in love. Obviously, the worst part of any relationship, and the very reason why some of us don't get involved in the first place, is the breakup, which can take love as sweet and soft as bubble gum and turn it into a hard unappealing lump that sticks to the back of our throats. Yet breakups, in all their appalling meanness, are necessary evils, because even though each love seems like the last, unless we plan on marrying the first boy we meet or date, we know there have got to be others. For that reason our hearts are resilient, and each time around we learn something more about what we like and hate about boys.

The beauty of breakups is that they come in so many different shapes and sizes; they never get boring. They can be quick, fiery explosions, like when he forgets the plans we made for the weekend or starts flirting with and dating another girl, or continuous confrontations, when we disagree about everything from food to families. They can be earth-shattering revelations, when we catch him with another girl, or gradual painful realizations, as we get weary of the day-in and day-out spats. They can even be long, silent drifts apart, in which we both agree that there's nothing left to date for, or triumphant surges of elation, when we finally break free of something that has been tying us down.

Why can't we be friends again?

In any case, the most difficult thing to do, and ironically the thing that girls desire most, is to remain friends, to tie up the loose ends of the relationship into a neat, clean package that can be stashed away in our memory so we can begin afresh. But being friends is difficult, because chances are one or both of us harbors too much anger, guilt, or resentment to ever just forgive and forget. That is unfortunately what Fatima discovered when Roberto (see Chapter 4) broke up with her a little over a year later to go out with his grammar-school flame, Jarmaine. Since he accused Fatima of spreading terrible rumors about her rival but never gave her a chance to show that they were all in Jarmaine's imagination, Fatima was left dangling. "I never felt I could date another guy, because I never felt it was resolved with Roberto," she confesses. "It always bugged me that we couldn't be friends after we'd been so close for over a year."

Even when they bumped into each other on the street, he would pretend to be running for a bus. "It made me feel sad that we couldn't even say hello," she adds. "Then the following Thanksgiving at a football game he refused contact again, but I persisted. I just kept staring at him until he smiled, then laughed. As we were leaving I said, 'Happy Thanksgiving,' but he ignored me. Then all at once he turned around, you know, like he'd just remembered something he'd forgotten, and gave me a big hug and a kiss on the cheek. It was one of the happiest moments of my life, because it really cleared the air. Then he went right out of my mind! I realized we could be friends and it was great."

Remaining friends, of course, is always easier if *we* do the breaking up; then we can be magnanimous enough to help pick the thorns out of his side. "By the end of the school year Rick and I weren't talking as much and had stopped doing things on weekends," says Heidi. "And I guess there was this expression on my face—like a 'let's break up' look. So I ended it. The next year at the first eighth-grade dance we got together again though. At first I thought we could go out again and that he'd changed over the summer, but in the end I realized I was only remembering how much fun it had been before. It quickly ended up getting boring. I said, 'You know, Rick, things aren't going well and we're not talking. I think one of the best things to do is break up. I'm not saying we shouldn't be friends or anything, 'cause I really like you a lot but I just don't think we should be going out! Now he calls me every once in a while and I call him. His locker's next to mine. We talk. It's nice. We're closer now as friends than we were as boyfriend and girlfriend."

Many girls say it's the boy's macho attitude that makes amends difficult. "Most guys don't want to be friends after a breakup," complains Milly. "They might want to but they say, 'It's over, let's go on,' like okay, goodbye, forget it—no matter how much fun we've had together, it's over. I think that's dumb. I don't understand that. My old boyfriend and I still date; we still go out to the movies and stuff. But it's just as friends, both paying. It helps me a lot to know I can talk to him. He tells me how to handle my new boyfriend and vice versa."

Saving face

Remaining friends is the last thing on our minds, however, if the breakup is lopsided. Then all our energy goes toward salvaging our ego. Or so says Lara, who spent six months trying unsuccessfully to lasso the class stud until he finally just pushed her too far. "He thought I was at a play that night but I decided to go by this party at intermission to check out what he was doing anyway," she says. "I kinda knew something was going on, because my friends had been telling me. They'd been pressuring me to break up with him for months. But when I actually saw him with another girl that did it. I just passed by nonchalantly and pretended that it didn't bother me though, 'cause I didn't want to look stupid; that was my main concern. Even though it really did hurt me, I didn't want anyone to know, because I was afraid it would get back to him. I wanted him to think I could just blow it off. So when anybody asked me what happened, I said, 'It's no big deal, we're not serious or anything.' When he called me at home that night to apologize, I said, 'Okay, whatever. It's no big deal.' But I knew it was over—even though I really liked him."

Grace agrees. "The way I am, every boy I meet, if I date him, you know, I think I'm in love. As soon as we break up, I hate him; he's terrible. I say, 'How could I have liked him?' Sometimes I say it and don't mean it. Sometimes I'll say, 'I'm glad we broke up; I didn't like him anyway,' just so people won't feel sorry for me."

22

Looking for Ms. Popularity

It's late February and we're poolside at a hotel in Orlando, Florida, during a cold snap. I'm laid out on a chaise longue in jeans, lace-up shoes, and a full-length down coat. But the sun is strong, and a smattering of glistening pink "nymphets" are lined up around the pool like giant shrimps around a dip bowl. Enormous stereo radios compete for my audio attention, as quivering houses of human cards compete on the lawn nearby for the best "pyramid." It's a teenage boy's paradise, a national cheerleading competition, the place where, I've been told, I can find *the* most popular girls in America.

And I am not disappointed. As I soon learn, there are more homecoming queens, more bathing beauties, and pep-squad leaders here than in any American high school in the country. The girl I've just been talking with is so model-perfect—long brown hair, hazel eyes, exquisite features—that a man she doesn't even know asks to take her picture. I am surprised, however, when she tells me what I hear again and again from these girls, that she doesn't consider herself popular, that even though she has been elected to "the court" every year, she is not as adorable, as charming, as NutraSweet as Ms. Popularity.

"I don't know what the difference between me and the most popular girl is," she says. "Maybe she's just sweeter. She's real quiet and never says anything. She's super sweet . . . she never really does anything or goes anywhere. And I guess you could say she's real uncontroversial. She may not have dated the best-looking guy in the school, like I did, because it made a lot of girls jealous. She doesn't even have a boyfriend and only just started dating somebody—her first date all year—two weeks ago.

"Being pretty definitely helps," she continues. "If kids don't know you or you're the new person at school, nobody's going to talk to you if you're ugly. After they get to know you, looks still matter—you can't say they don't because they always do—but very shortly thereafter personality becomes everything. At least I think so. A bad personality can change your looks and your popularity very quickly."

Another semi-beauty queen says she's too shy and modest to consider herself popular. "I have a lot of friends and have a good time but I'm not popular like Farrah over there," says Randy (sixteen, a Strong Individualist from Ashland, Kentucky), pointing to a tall, unspectacular, round-figured girl in a blue and white flowered bikini. "She's real nice and pretty. She doesn't hate anybody, not even somebody who's treated her badly. The guy she's dating is really nice too, really funny, really good at basketball and they get along really well. She has everything—good looks, personality. Some guys look for personality first, but most guys would do anything to date Farrah, because she's pretty, built real good, and nice."

Bobbi describes her vision of Ms. Popularity in a similar way. "I don't think I'm popular, at least not like Heather. There's nobody that doesn't like Heather. She's got a great personality. In the beginning if you don't know her, she's quiet and shy. But when she warms up, she's crazy and fun. She's very beautiful, too. Everybody likes her." I examine Heather from afar. She's cute but not incredible-looking, with short blonde curls tucked up under a white visor. She even seems a bit plain and square around the jaw. Her only real appeal is the motherly way in which she tends her younger-looking brood—a trait my male friends tell me later is very appealing to young boys, especially those who doubt their masculinity.

Even more revealing is the fact that I'm unable to land an interview with either Farrah or Heather, who keep putting me off with sweet, gentle "a little laters." Though I'm not offended by their lack of interest, I am quite convinced about how they remain so uncontroversial. And in the end I'm left with the indelible impression that popular girls are a little like Jell-O—sweet, bouncy, pretty, but with very little substance. Everything they do is wholesome and good-natured—but very, very boring. (My apologies to those popular girls who are none of the above.)

Looks won't get you everything

And their physical plainness shows that looks have less to do with popularity than we might think! "There are a lot of pretty girls in our school that really get around—if you know what I mean," sneers Alexis. "But their looks don't mean anything, because the guys don't like them. One of the prettiest girls I know fooled around with every guy; she won't sleep with them but she'll do everything else—and it doesn't even bug her. It's her personality that makes her unattractive. Another can be mediocre-looking and it's her personality that makes her cute. It's like the guy I dated last year; I thought he was the most gorgeous thing in the world until we broke up. Then I didn't think so anymore. His personality made him seem good-looking while I liked him."

But not every popular girl is unanimously well-liked. "I'm popular," says April assuredly. "A lot of people know me because I'm a cheerleader and stuff. They see me at ball games and around town. I can walk up to a stranger and just talk to them. But I'm not the most popular girl in town. At our school that's the homecoming queen. She's not a cheerleader but the president of a lot of clubs and all that bull. The whole senior class votes for her and, you know, she got all the things she was nominated for, including most pretty in the class. It made me sick. I guess it has to be jealousy. I don't know what she's got but I don't like her and neither do my friends. She's got a group of friends that you'd think are her best friends, but all she does is talk about them behind their backs. She's really two-faced and I just can't buy that. She's in my homeroom but we've had differences. Once she wrote this dirty letter to her boyfriend and blamed me for sending it to her mother. I said, 'I wish I had. If you do something like that again, then you're asking for it.' "

Does being a cheerleader help? All non-cheerleaders think so, but cheerleaders say it's really "being involved"—in sports, in school government, in clubs, in action groups—that matters, that lets guys know you're fun, energetic, and open-minded. It also gives them something to talk to you about. Being a cheerleader, some say, can even hinder your chances because others get jealous. "Cheerleaders are not the most popular girls," exclaims Gigi. "Sometimes it hurts because people think you're just a showoff and don't like you 'cause they're jealous of you. I know lots of girls who are jealous. One even called me up and said she didn't like me but couldn't give a reason. It made me feel real bad, 'cause I couldn't think of anything I'd done to hurt her. Some other mean, tough troublemakers gave my friend, a cheerleader, a real hard time once 'cause she accidentally stepped on this girl's foot. She was just walking down the hall and she stepped on the girl's foot and turned around and apologized. But ever since then the girl's wanted to fight her. It was weird. It was awful. They just wanted to make her look bad."

What boys really hate—about girls

So what do girls think turns boys off? "The way she acts, how do you say it—like a little slut?" ventures April. "I just hate girls like that who just don't care who it is. They fool around with any guy 'cause he's good-looking or prestigious. Some will even come up to you and say, 'See that boy? Let me tell you what we did!' They just flaunt it, especially if he's good-looking."

Or being a tease: "That really hacks guys off," says Lara. "If you just say hi and then tease them and go back on your word, it's not fair at all. If you're going to offer something, then you have to go through with it. You hear that a lot about the kind of girls that tease. I guess it's just like boys who tease—I hate them."

Or being shy: "If I were a guy I wouldn't like a girl who's real shy," says Alexis. "Some girls think shy's cute. But I like outgoing people, ones who always talk. I don't like girls or guys who are real quiet."

Or being selfish: "I know a lot of pretty girls and none of the guys like them, 'cause of how selfish they are," says Jean. "One talks about herself all the time. I think it would be kind of a drag—it was for me when I dated a self-centered guy. It's not that she's boring but self-centered."

Or snobbish: "If she's shy, guys think she's snobby and won't talk to people for that reason," says Grace. "That's happened to me before. I'm not nearly as shy as I used to be but in junior high people used to say, 'You can't talk to her, she's such a big snob. She doesn't talk to anybody.' It was just because I couldn't go up to people I didn't know and start a conversation. If guys didn't know me they thought I was a snob too, 'cause I couldn't make the first moves; I'd always wait until they said something."

Some claim striking girls are not popular simply because their beauty scares boys away. "What happens to a gorgeous girl sometimes is that the guys think, 'Oh, she's a goddess,' " speculates Noel. "But usually she knows she's good-looking, expects people to like her and gets conceited and neglects her personality. Gorgeous girls always get the first bit of attention because all the guys say, 'Oh, I want to go out with her,' but after a while, they realize she isn't that great, because she doesn't have a personality. In rare cases a few good-looking girls are also nice. They're the ones that go right to the top."

Kendal, a true beauty in every physical sense of the word, explains: "I think boys consider looks first when picking a date but they look for personality too. I don't want to sound conceited, but I consider myself popular because I'm well-liked and well-respected. But being too pretty can have its moments. I used to wonder if it was causing problems, because I went through a phase when guys were scared to ask me out. Our basketball coach once told me, 'I just think everyone's scared to ask you out. They all say you won't go.'

"I'm sure it frightens some guys away. The guy I'm dating now nearly never asked me out because he was scared to call. Luckily, I ran into him at the mall, when he was with my girlfriend, and had a chance to sit down and talk with him. Even so, he had a friend call me first and check out my answer. When I said yes, Ralph called."

(One girl I knew at college was so adorable—she looked exactly like a Barbie Doll—that even girls couldn't take their eyes off her. She was also a well-liked cheerleader but when she walked into the lunchroom some boys who knew they'd never have a chance to date her would call out abusive names. It was the worst case of male jealousy I'd ever seen.)

The growing de-emphasis on looks, plus the increasing awareness that personality "makes" the person, explains why many less than attractive girls are popular too. Or it may be that physically unattractive girls compensate by "having excellent personalities to make up for their looks." Or it may be that "guys think they have a better chance of getting a date with 'them' than with gorgeous girls and therefore ask more of 'them' out." Or according to one cynic: "In my group some of the most unattractive girls seem popular because they sacrifice their morals for a date; something we gorgeous girls won't do!"

Yet remarkably, popularity for some means nothing at all. "I don't think popularity is so important," says Bobbi. " 'Cause after high school who's going to care? Right now it's fun to go around and be a cheerleader and be popular and have all your friends and go to parties, but that's not going to matter in your adult life. In real life, you don't have to be popular, beautiful, or well-liked to be somebody and have a good life and be happy. I'm not real popular—but I am having fun."

Daters vs non-daters

Obviously, popularity is not a special chemical equation but a combination of ingredients that work well for some, better for others. Contrary to popular opinion, the "right stuff" may not be rare, unusual, or hard to find; it may instead be very ordinary. And what makes someone popular among boys may have nothing to do with what makes her popular among girls.

Though it's not possible to say why some girls date and others don't, the *TeenAge* Relationships Survey does reveal that daters (girls who were dating at the time they filled in the questionnaire, or 60 percent, 100 percent among Supersonic daters—dating was part of the group criteria—and only 46 percent among Strong Individualists) and non-daters have some very different dating

Daters vs. Non-Daters: Dating Attitudes

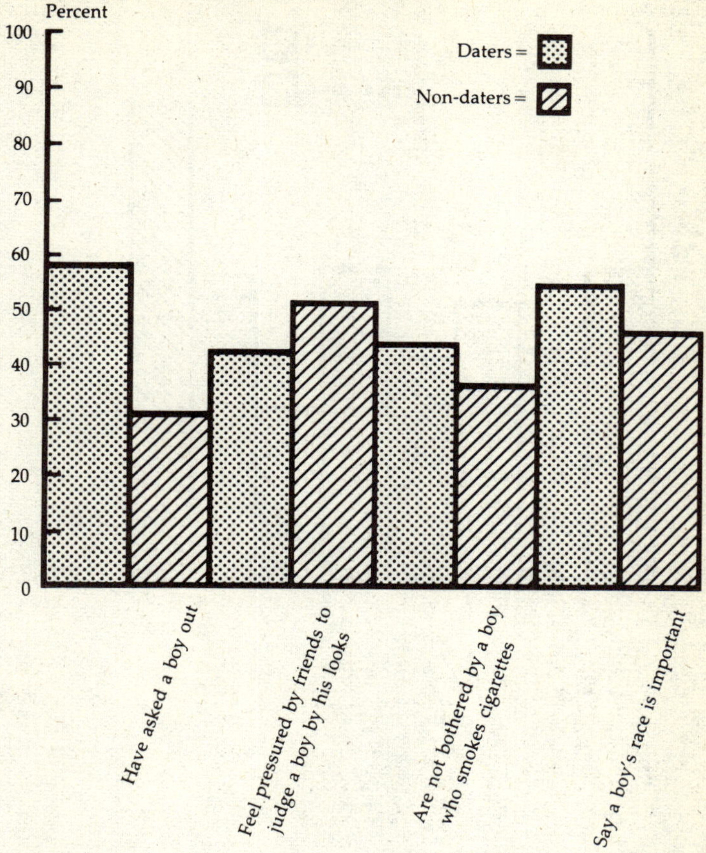

The TeenAge *Relationships Survey suggests that non-daters feel more hemmed in by social convention and outward appearances, and are less independent in their decisions about boys, than daters. For instance, 52% of non-daters say they feel pressured by friends to judge a boy by his looks while only 43% of daters say the same; and only 31% have asked a boy out for a date, while 58% of daters have. Non-daters are also less willing to overlook a boy's nasty personal habits—like cigarette smoking: only 37% of non-daters say they will put up with a boy who smokes compared with 44% of daters who say the same. Conversely, daters seem to be more race conscious than non-daters. Probably because they have to "bring him home to mom and dad," 55% of daters say a boy's race is important, while only 47% of non-daters feel the same way.*

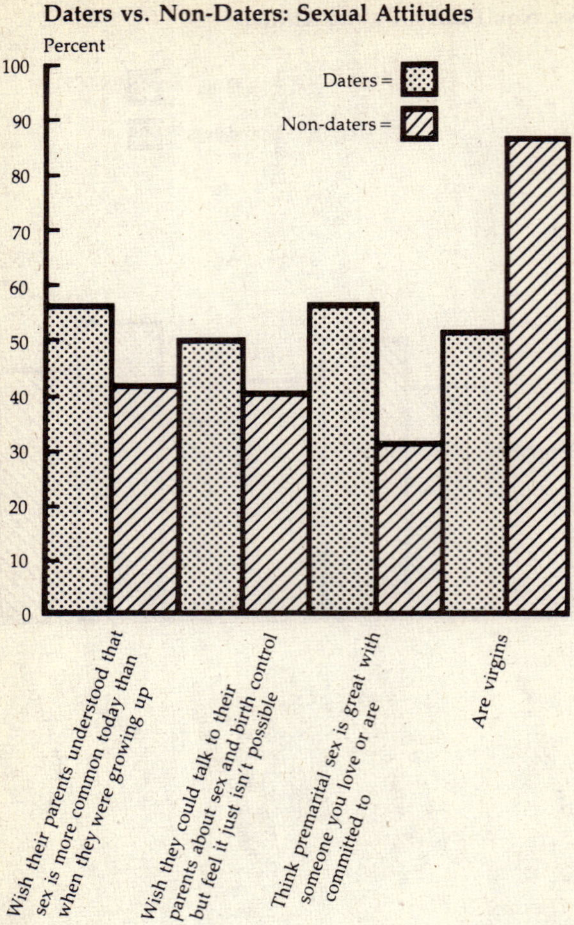

As one might expect, the TeenAge *Relationships Survey points out that daters are more exposed to sex and must make more serious decisions about sex than non-daters. Perhaps for that reason, daters have more liberal attitudes about sex than non-daters. For instance, 57% of daters think premarital sex is great with someone you love or are committed to, while only 32% of non-daters say the same.*

When it comes to dealing with parents, daters seem to want the most contact: 57% wish their parents better understood the new sexual mores (43% of non-daters feel the same way) and exactly 50% wish they could talk to their parents about sex and birth control but feel it just isn't possible! It's even more disconcerting to discover that almost the same number of non-daters (41%) feel the same way!

attitudes. Daters seem to be more independent, less idealistic, more willing to compromise their ideals than their non-dating peers; they are more likely to be older (often sixteen plus), to feel less pressured by friends to pick a boy for his looks, and are more likely to feel it's okay to ask a boy out and to have done it. Perhaps because of the age difference, they are also more likely to be smokers and drinkers. Because daters have more liberal outlooks on sex, they are much more likely than non-daters to accept premarital sex, not be virgins themselves, to wish their parents understood that sex is more common now than when their parents were growing up, and to wish they could talk to their parents about sexual problems.

Section Three

Sex, Birth Control, and Pregnancy

23

Great Sexpectations

On the TV series *Dallas,* J.R. blackmails his wife, Sue Ellen, to get her back into bed with him; on *Falcon Crest,* Melissa and Cole fight over their illegitimate son Joseph, even though they're married to different people; on daytime soaps, gorgeous men and women hop in and out of bed like fleas in heat. And that's just the video message. Print ads suggest our sex lives will improve if we wear designer jeans, drive sporty cars, use toothpaste gels. On the radio, one singer croons, "Tonight's the night," while another moans that "A woman has the right [to sleep around] just like [men] do." No question. Society's attitude toward sex has warmed considerably since the Sixties and Seventies, when *That Girl* gingerly pecked Donald good night on the cheek, since the Beatles pleaded, "I Wanna Hold Your Hand."

"It's a world of great sexual expectations," says Alfred F. Moran, executive director of Planned Parenthood, New York City. "The message is that being sexually active is an adult standard to aspire to, that if teens want to be 'with it,' sex is the thing to do."

And he's right. The movie industry capitalizes on the new sexual message with films like *Little Darlings,* in which Kristy McNichol and Tatum O'Neal compete to lose their virginity; *The Blue Lagoon*, in which Brooke Shields and Christopher Atkins lust together on a deserted island; *Risky Business*, in which Tom Cruise loses his virginity to a teenage call girl and uses profits from a teen prostitution ring to replace the family Porsche. The publishing industry exploits it by revamping magazines to cater to a more "liberated" crowd, by running cover lines about "The Big O," and by dressing teen models like succulent semi-adults or "Lolitas."

Sex has become the ice cream of the Eighties, something teens say seems "incredible and wonderful to try"; virginity has become like baby teeth, "something to lose before graduation." Is it any wonder that by age nineteen half of us in urban areas will have had sexual intercourse, double the rate just fifteen years ago? Is it any wonder that girl after girl complains of feeling pressured—even for the quintessential good-night kiss? Every TV show, commercial, movie plot you see is based on sexual contact," says Noel, who recently gave in to an undesirable good-night kiss. "So you picture in your mind what you're supposed to do, feel pressured, and end up doing it."

The problem is not society's unfettered attitude toward sex, but the fact that it sends teens a conflicting message. "Society condones sex in movies, popular books, magazines, television ads, but says nothing about contraception," says Planned Parenthood's Moran. "Or when the subject comes up, parents yell and scream about how controversial it is. As a result they give teens the impression that sex is great but that being responsible about it is not. Adult ambivalence about birth control has abandoned sex education to the advertisers who teach them only about the marketable side of sex, not how to hold out or be careful." The result: a nationwide teen pregnancy rate for girls under age twenty that is now 1.1 million—the highest ever.

To wit, Moran asserts that many television stations refuse to run contraceptive ads because they "are too controversial or not profitable enough"; that sex-education courses, featured in only 25 percent of U.S. schools, are spotty and rarely deal with the emotional issues at stake. We also have a President, he says, who has an anachronistic attitude toward women, one that would make girls less likely than ever to say no to sexually aggressive boys, and who supports a "squeal law" that requires family-planning centers to report teen visits to parents.

These conflicts may help explain why a study by the National Association of Secondary School Principals calls the Eighties a time of "unprecedented . . . teenage pregnancy," a problem that Moran says "cuts across all economic and class barriers, and is growing among youngest teenagers twelve to fifteen years old." Opines Holly: "The Sixties had drugs, the Seventies had the 'Me generation,' maybe we're just the 'Sex generation.'" She is, unfortunately, most probably right.

24

What Girls Like and Hate (and Never Tell Boys) About Sex

It's one of those rare balmy days in September when the air is white with haze that's just rolled in off the Hudson. On the quad in front of me, boys and girls loll in the grass, intermittently fighting with each other like brothers and sisters trapped in the back of a station wagon during a long trip to the seashore. All at once a girl lobs a pen at the boy across from her; suddenly, he's up, grabbing her shoe, dunking it like an ill-shaped basketball into the trash can across the quad. Everyone laughs as she gets up—frowning—to retrieve it.

Behind them, in front of the beautiful old gothic high-school building, another girl heads toward the giant oak doors of the main hall. Two boys in denim jackets accost her, blocking her way to the entrance; one even spread-eagles himself across it like a giant human latch. Smiling, she grasps the big brass handle anyway and tries to pull it open. Cheeky grins creep across their faces as she folds her arms, taps her foot impatiently. All at once, the boy drops his arms, twirls around like a courtesan begging her pardon, offers her the door. Moving quickly through it—and without a word—she is gone.

I laugh to myself from my perch on the steps of the adjacent building, where I'm waiting for my next interview. The male/female mating dance is still the same old pas de deux my generation rehearsed in high school, rebelled against in college, accepted as we entered the "real" world. It's still as precise, as complex, as unwritten as a bee's. And in the unconscious actions of these flirtatious girls, I see myself, my friends, every woman I know, working her wiles on the male ego. I am more convinced than ever now that love, sex, and relationships change very little over time or with age.

When the girl reappears she is flanked by two prim, proper beauties, and they move menacingly toward me like a female panzer division. Delighted, I realize they are the girls I've come to interview—the *only* girls I've managed to find who'll talk openly to me about sex. Unlike the majority of teens who hem and haw in my presence (most have undoubtedly been taught not to "talk dirty" in front of adults), these Supersonic Daters claim they'll lay it on the line. They've even secured a classroom from the principal, they say, for our discussion about "girls, boys, and education." We all laugh sheepishly: what do men know about girls anyway? They bubble with enthusiasm as we head inside to begin.

What do girls really want—sex or affection?

"Guys are mostly interested in sex," begins Jerry, a very pretty, sophisticated fifteen-year-old from Palisades, New York, with dirty blonde hair, a white button-down shirt with a Ralph Lauren polo horse galloping across the pocket, a long, black and white striped oxford skirt. The crow's-feet around her eyes make her, at moments, look twenty. "I mean, if a guy sees a girl walking down the street he's not going to think, 'Oh what a mind!' " She giggles self-consciously, scanning the faces around the room for approval. "He'll look at her body and think, 'Oh, wow, I'd like to—' "

"But you'd do the same thing!" accuses Priscilla, seventeen, from Piermont, New York. Clearly the leader of the group, it's the way she dresses—in a man's white and yellow striped shirt, gray pants, turquoise and silver jewelry dropped like tinsel about her neck and wrists—that gives her that same prematurely sophisticated look; only her soft brown eyes, flushed cheeks, and freckles betray her youth. "You're first attracted to a guy by what he looks like. I guess that might be subconsciously related to sex but we don't really think of it that way. We think oh, he's so cute, he's so adorable—not about whether we can make out or get down to it with him. Anyway, making out with a guy, or fooling around to a certain point, really isn't considered sex. Sex is making love. Fooling around is different; it's sort of acceptable. . . . But not all sex is acceptable. Like if you had a new boyfriend and really didn't know him and all of a sudden you started getting down to the nitty gritty—it wouldn't be acceptable."

"Yeah," affirms Donna (sixteen, Congers, New York), a shy, almost perfect-looking white-blonde with creamy skin, and an intriguing front tooth that protrudes when she smiles. "There's nothing wrong with sex, but it's best to work your way into it. You take it slowly. It has to begin with affection—like kissing." (If given the choice, nearly all the girls I talk to prefer emotionally-fulfilling affection to just physically-fulfilling sex.)

"Making out is simply a way to relate to a guy, a way to get to know him better," says Priscilla. "For that reason a bad kisser—especially someone who bites your lip—is a turnoff."

"I'm an affectionate person," Jerry says. "So it's hard to get to know a guy who doesn't kiss well. If a guy won't kiss and moves too fast, if on the first date he's all over me, it's a turnoff."

"You just want to get away from him, 'cause it seems like all he wants to do is have sex," adds Priscilla. "It feels like that's all you're there for. Like my boyfriend now, who's in the next room. He won't come near me at school, but he'll take me downstairs to the basement and kiss me hello and goodbye. it bugs me that he won't show any affection. It upsets me so much that I begin wondering why I bother with him at all. People tell me that he likes me, but he's not affectionate so I'm never sure. When you have sex without affection, you really don't get much out of it. My old boyfriend, Danny, was that way. All he wanted was sex all the time."

"You can tell if a boy wants sex or affection, because affection-oriented guys are all huggy, kissy, and cuddly," Jerry explains. "Guys who just want sex are like, 'Okay, let's get down to it.' "

"Yeah, I can just never get enough affection," says Donna.

"I could O.D. on affection!" says Priscilla. "I could go with a guy just for affection, no sex, for just kissing and being close. I could do that forever. And affection can be sexy. For instance, when I'm about to fall asleep and I want to have nice dreams I think about a nice-looking guy wearing good-fitting jeans. His back is tan, V-shaped. He holds me and kisses me on the neck, the cheeks, and sort of cuddles. One thing leads to another and it gets more passionate. . . . I also like guys to rub my back when we're making out, to touch my hair, my thighs, my stomach. I love it when they kiss my shoulders, gentle kisses."

"Sometimes not doing anything sexual at all—just having the guy lying on top of you so you can just feel his body, even if your clothes are on—is really sexy," says Donna.

"Hugs are great, too," says Priscilla. "I always ask boys for hugs. I love having a guy hold me completely; I like having my face in his neck." Donna sighs. "The first thing I say to a guy is, 'I need a hug so bad.' "

"Yeah. Sometimes I could just hug for hours. But some guys totally miss the point—"

"I love it," says Priscilla, "when you're driving in the car, and a guy's just holding you. Or when you're watching television and you're sort of schlopped down on the couch and he just sort of holds you or kisses the top of your head."

"I'd be more satisfied with that than any kind of sex," says Donna. "Making out or having them blow in your ear or kiss your neck is great."

"The only problem is that guys do what they like the best," says Priscilla, "so you have to sort of start it with them so they know how it feels. Or you have to tell them. Or you have to show them. Danny didn't know what I liked at all. Once I did it to him, then he did it back to me. You have to share with them if they don't do it on their own. Then they get the hint."

"My new boyfriend and I haven't even kissed yet!" exclaims Donna. "I love just being near him, touching him, just standing shoulder to shoulder. I love it. Sometimes he just puts his arm around me and it makes me crazy."

"That's truly romantic!"

"When we're driving somewhere, my boyfriend will lean over and say, 'Just give me a kiss,' " says Jerry. "And so I kiss his cheek, his neck. And he says, 'You need love.' It's weird, 'cause his father said to me, 'I know what type of person you are. You're affectionate and need a lot of love. If you get that love, you don't care about sex or money.' That's true. I don't care about looks, money, or anything like love; I just need somebody to care for me and love me."

"That's what I loved about Charles, my marine," says Priscilla. "He'd walk over to me and say, 'Can I give you a kiss?' and softly kiss me. Or he'd come up behind me and put his arms around me. He was affectionate; it was so nice. Then you kind of want to explore more, but at first it's nice."

"When I started going out with this new guy, Priscilla, who'd dated him before, told me he doesn't give out a lot sexually," says Donna, her deep-blue eyes lighting up, like a child savoring a favorite dish. "I thought that was so great. That's just what I was looking for. I have the greatest time with him, just talking to him. I love every second of it."

And affection is not important only before getting into bed—but also afterwards—another point many boys seem to miss.

"I hate it when guys just get up after sex and go about their business," says Jerry. "They're like, 'Okay, let's roll.' And I'm like, 'Okay, let's not.' I like it when they cuddle afterwards."

"Yeah," agrees Priscilla. "Like one night I was with Danny and when we were done, he just got up and walked into the bathroom. He didn't want to come near me after sex! I just started crying 'cause I felt so lonely. I really felt alone! It would make sex so much better if guys could add a little bit of closeness by giving a little affection before and after. After's when you really need it.

"It's important for a girl to know there's feeling and compassion with sex," she continues. "There's no point in fooling around with someone you won't talk to again! The big challenge is to get close mentally and affectionately; that's what's so important. Besides, when you're confident with a guy you can have better sex. That means being sure of his caring for you, of his attitudes, his feelings. You have to be able to talk to him, too. Otherwise you feel so inhibited that you can't do anything."

Postponing sex means keeping the electricity going longer.

"Girls need a sexual challenge," says Priscilla, turning to Donna. "Like, you keep asking me, 'I wonder how he kisses?' He could be amazing or terrible. But you don't know. And that keeps you interested."

Donna nods agreement. "Up until now, it's been the same with all my boyfriends. I meet 'em. We fool around. And we keep fooling around until I get bored with it, 'cause there's no affection. But this new guy I just met is really different: he hasn't even kissed me yet! I like that a lot! I don't know why. I just feel great around him; it's fun. We don't have to kiss; we don't have to fool around or anything. In the past I think I fooled around a lot just because that's what I thought I was supposed to do."

"Yeah, when you're going out with someone and you have sex for the first time, it's special," Priscilla says. "The next time it's special, too. But after you're going steady, every time you see him you have sex; you make love. After a while it gets tedious. That's not to say that you don't want it. But maybe less of it. It would be better if it wasn't so expected, so standardized."

All three say yes. "The problem is that if you're with a guy, and you don't feel like it, he acts like, 'What's the matter with you?' " Donna says, flushing. "They just don't understand."

Jerry grips the edge of the desktop and stares at the gold bracelets on her wrist. "That's why I always sort of give in to them."

"Me too," says Donna. "At least a few times! But then I get so moody sometimes that no one can touch me!" She laughs, then looks around inquisitively. "I just don't understand why we have to have sex every time we're together. Why can't guys just sit and talk, or watch TV with us?"

"One of my friends didn't make love for eight months, which is a very long time," Jerry announces. "That's how she knew the guy really loved her. I give in a lot because guys say they can't handle not having sex. I even asked one, 'What if I didn't give in? What would you have done?' And he said, 'I probably would have dumped you.' " She laughs, disguising her emotion. "I think it might have been true with Danny." (She and Priscilla went out with the same boy at different times.)

"What about with Willy?" Priscilla asks.

"No, because . . ."

"No, because he really was in love with you! That's the difference!" Priscilla exclaims. "He really *was* in love. But you sort of fell in love while you were having sex. If you hadn't had sex in the beginning, maybe he would have said, 'Oh, forget it. She's a prude.' "

Jerry agrees. "I said no for—was it two months?" She glances again at Priscilla, who seems to have been more involved in her relationship than she was. "Maybe a little longer. But finally I just had to get closer to him, to know what he was really like, to know he wouldn't just leave me after we had sex. I had to know if that was all he wanted. After sex you feel closer, like you know the person better. It's like they become a part of you." She blushes and giggles like a ten-year-old. "Literally!"

"The problem is that after you do it over and over again, you feel like you're doing all the giving and they're doing all the taking," says Donna. "The first time I do it, if I really care for the guy, and he really cares for me, I feel satisfied emotionally—"

"—never physically—"

"—yeah, never, never." Everyone laughs.

"Sometimes you can picture yourself being with a guy," Jerry ventures, "but it's never to the physical extent. Girls just aren't like guys; they don't *need* to get—'laid.' "

"Though I know a girl who does—with my boyfriend, too!" Priscilla cuts in. "She was my friend at one point." She grins. "You see she's young, maybe sixteen now, and had a relationship with a guy she really liked. But when he went away to camp, they broke up and she went wild. All she wanted to do was have sex, to physically use guys. She's still confused and doesn't know where she's going so she uses sex to compensate."

(I am surprised to hear what some might think of as pots calling kettles black; clearly "sleazy" is a subjective word.)

"She doesn't even care what girls think about her," claims Jerry self-righteously. "All she cares about is that guys like her. She thinks she'll have a guy to be with day and night." Then suddenly she sympathizes. "Well, sometimes when you get close to a guy you feel that even if your best girlfriend leaves you you really have somebody. Girlfriends can just leave you flat, like she did to Priscilla. You never feel like a guy you sleep with is going to dump you, straight out flat."

Indeed! All three say the sexual bond transcends any friendship—any day. "Yet if all you have is sex, you lose the emotion and the bond evaporates," says Priscilla. "The key is finding a really caring person, someone you can talk to and have sex with on an equal basis—that is, when you want it and not when you don't want it; then you're really linked. If you don't have both, or if he wants more sex or emotion than you want, then it falls apart. Needing that balance makes it hard these days to find a relationship that lasts for a long time."

"When I first started dating, I used to be looser than I am now, because I liked to experiment," concedes Donna. "But after the same thing happened over and over again—I got into a relationship; I really liked the person; he really liked me; we had sex—I just got bored." Because, she says, the emotional bond didn't hold out.

"The first couple of times I had sex with my old boyfriend Danny it was really new; we were sort of reaching out in new directions, doing new things and fun stuff," says Priscilla. "But after a while, o-o-o-o-o-o-h-h-h-h it was boring! A lot of the time I would just lie there. It kind of satisfied me that I was making him happy but it wasn't really much else. That's not to say sex is never good; sometimes it is. But a lot of the time it's just boring."

"For that reason, I find that the longer I hold out, the longer the relationship lasts," Donna says.

"That's always true," pipes Jerry, " 'cause you have to give a guy a challenge. If you say, 'I'm not going to make love to you right away,' they say, 'Okay,' but keep on trying. Virgin or not, in order to have some control over the relationship, you have to keep them guessing. If guys think you'll do everything they want, they think they have you wrapped around their finger. They'll say, 'Go wash my car.' And you'll say, 'Okay, okay!' " Giving in on sex, she implies, is the bottom line.

Sexual power plays: Who gets whom?

"Once you have sex," says Donna, who claims her attitude is more like a boy's than a girl's, "there's nothing really left. You know what I mean? If you haven't done it yet, there's always something to hang on for; and I love that little bit of intrigue. But afterwards you think, 'What else is there for us to do?' After a while it feels like something's gone." She hesitates for a minute, shifts uneasily in the hard wooden chair. Though her pale blue jeans, white sandals, blue striped shirt, and heavy New York accent make her seem less sophisticated than her peers, there seems to be something deeper brewing behind her eyes. She leans closer into the group and calls forth a daemon in many girls' hearts. "You know, I feel used a lot afterwards—even though I know I wasn't ever used—and even if we really cared for each other, I still feel used. This society is so unfair. Boys are expected to do it just 'cause they're boys; girls are put down for it."

Jerry gets angry. "Yeah! If a girl makes love to a guy one night and it gets around the school, no one looks at him like a sleaze. They think he's macho! . . . The worst is when a guy knows you're not a virgin and he gives you a guilt trip about how he would have liked to have been the first one," she continues. "My current boyfriend did that. He said, 'I've only made love to one other girl.' I knew that was bullshit because he'd slept with my friend Brenda before. He said that wasn't making love. I said, 'What would you call it?' He said, 'Good sex!' " Everyone laughs. "He said some girls you make love to and others you just have sex with and there's nothing between you." She reconsiders. "I call it making love when you really care about the person and there's a bond between you."

Is it love or is it sex?

One of the major points of contention, one that might be partially blamed for the high pregnancy rate, is the difficulty of seeing sex as sex. Girl after girl, especially those here, claim that having sex and making love are two different matters.

"Well, one time I was with my boyfriend and we were making love and the phone rang and it was his friend," says Priscilla with a daring look in her eye. "And he goes, 'You're calling me at a bad time.' His friend must have asked 'Why?' because he said, 'Because I'm fucking her!' I pushed him off and said, 'No, that's not what you're doing! If it is, I don't want to have any part of it!' I didn't care that he told this guy we were making love because he already knew exactly what was going on in our relationship. But the fact that he considered it fucking—or just having sex and not making love—seemed so vulgar."

"It wasn't sex," Jerry laughs. "You were just celebrating your love."

"Yeah." A raspy laugh. "Celebrating our love!" She turns to me. "We've tried to think of new definitions because we don't like the words 'having sex.' And since sometimes we aren't making love, the idea of 'celebrating' something or other seems better."

"I like that." Jerry giggles. "There once was this fad in school when people were going around asking, 'Which do you prefer? Celebrating your love? Getting laid? Getting fucked? Having sex? Or making love? Most people preferred 'making love.' You never hear anyone say, 'We celebrated our love last night.' I mean, that sounds stupid."

"Yeah, we also made up two new euphemisms," offers Priscilla with a punkish grin. " 'Make.' Which is sort of short for 'making love' or 'making sex.' No one knows what you're talking about, because no one has put a definition to it and there's no emotion in it at all. It's just 'make.' It can be anything you want. It's mainly for girl talk though. Like if guys are around, I can say to Jerry, 'What were you doing?' and she can say, 'Putting.' That's another word. 'Put.' Not putting out. That's sort of more vulgar. Just 'put.' To 'put.' It's a nickname, sort of. We should think of a new word, that would be really neat. . . . Most guys call sex . . . fucking," she continues, "but know that if they say 'Let's fuck,' a girl is going to say no, so they ask to make love instead. But the first time they don't even bring it up; they just sort of let it happen."

"No they don't," quips Jerry.

"Oh really?" Priscilla's eyebrows raise.

"Well, from all my experience," she excuses herself jokingly, "the great many— I find that guys ask you. They don't say 'Are you a virgin?' They just find out by asking, 'Do you want to make love?' They just kind of whisper it sexily and hope you get all excited about it."

"Actually, they don't ask," Priscilla corrects. "They just *tell* you, 'Oh, I'd really like to make love to you. I'd really L-O-V-E to make love to you!' " She is half mimicking, half mocking boys. "It's a proposition. I've had it a couple of times—more than a couple of times."

"I've only had one guy in my life that didn't ask at all," says Donna. "He just started in and it *completely* turned me off. I just wanted to get away from him; I didn't like that at all—"

" 'Cause then you feel they've spent the whole night thinking about having sex with you," adds Jerry. "Finally, you get to the end of the night and you have five minutes left and he's like, 'Here we go!' "

"Exactly. I get so turned off by that, 'cause I feel like every time you make love you're giving something of yourself; the least they can do is ask! I've heard a lot of girls say guys just force themselves on them."

"Yeah. After you've been with a guy for a while, they don't even bother asking anymore. They figure—"

"We've got ten minutes; let's go upstairs—"

"And you know exactly what that means—"

"You just say no—unless you're in the mood. You just have to say, 'No, forget it. If that's all you want from me!' "

Where has all the foreplay gone?

Another problem girls mention is foreplay or, rather, the lack of it. "In the beginning there's a lot of foreplay," Priscilla says. "But after a while he gives up. He just realizes foreplay was the little link to getting you into bed. Once he has you, he realizes there's no point." Her brows knot. "But there always is a point for girls, because foreplay is what gets a girl going and turns her on. She doesn't have the urges that guys have. I mean, guys see a good-looking girl walk by and they're turned on. Girls aren't like that. Girls have romantic fantasies and foreplay is part of it. But after a while guys are like, 'We know this but why do we have to go through this?' "

"When they skip foreplay and just get down to it," says Donna, "I find myself just lying there, thinking of other things—"

"Like, 'How am I going to get home tonight?' "

"Or 'Did my dog die today, I can't remember!' " Jerry laughs. "You just lie there and they're not even looking at you; they're just doing it and you're lying there dead and they're like, 'Oh-h-h-h-h-h, this is great!' Then they look at you like, 'What's wrong?' 'Oh, nothing. I'm just thinking about my homework!' "

A feeling of *déjà vu* sweeps over me and I hear my own teenage thoughts spoken, I hear endless women complain. And yet there's something terribly shocking about teenagers so jaded by sex. I wonder how much of it is really anger—anger at all the giving in, the unequal role-playing so many girls feel they must accept.

"I remember one time Danny and I were having sex in my bedroom," says Priscilla, now on a roll. "Jerry's rabbit had run away that morning and I'm thinking, 'I wonder where that rabbit's gone? I feel so bad!' "

Everyone cracks up at the vision of some poor guy going at it with a limp body and a mind that's miles away. And yet their laughter is not unbridled; there's something scary about having *this* last laugh. "And when he's done, he's like, 'How was it?' and I'm like, 'How was what?' "

"How was what?" Jerry and Donna echo, leaning over laughing.

"After a while I just pray for the phone to ring so this guy can get off of me," explains Jerry, taking the female chauvinist posturing one step further. "I pretend like I'm psychic. I play games thinking, 'The phone's going to ring now! One. Two. Three.' And it never rings. I just think about the weirdest things."

"I wish there was a way you could contact guys and say let's do something more interesting," says Priscilla. "It's just too hard to tell them. Like in the beginning with Danny it was so great. We went skinny-dipping, we made love in the pool, in the shower. It was great. Once I was with two guys and it was great because I learned a lot. We were all in bed, really being open with each other, asking which parts of the body we liked. Finding out what each of us liked—like being massaged on the thighs, being kissed all the way down the body, on the earlobes. I even found out guys love to have you gently nibble on their ears and breathe into them."

Just then the classroom door swings open and Patty, a tall, dark-skinned girl in an orange dress and white plastic pumps, who's been desperately trying to get an appointment for a pregnancy test, hurries in. She's two weeks overdue and she's in hysterics—but calm enough to do the interview. She says it's happened before and turned out to be only nerves.

(I wonder how many other girls at that moment must be worrying about the exact same thing. I wonder if these girls are "fast"—like the ones my prudish high-school friends sneered at in study hall. Or are others, were we, simply "slow"? How many other "sweet young things" think these thoughts but never venture to say them?)

"The thing I didn't like about our relationship," says Priscilla as we resume, an accusatory tone sliding into her voice, "is that Danny just used me for sex so that he could come!" Everyone agrees. "And he would say, 'If we're not going to have sex, if we're not going to fuck—then I want you to give me a blow job or a hand job!' " Anger wells in her voice. "That's the ultimate thing! We'll have sex, and if there isn't that much time then he's just going to do it wham-bam until he comes! And that's it! And after that he doesn't give me any affection!"

Everyone agrees again. (This is becoming, I think, a monkey court.)

"One time he came over to my house," she continues, "and said, 'Let's have sex.' I said no. So he looked at his watch and said, 'I've got ten minutes; just give me a hand job.' I started laughing at him. I said, 'You are just incredible!' And that was the last time I saw or talked to him. Sex for most boys is 'to come.' I've had guys who don't feel that way, but it annoys me when it is! You don't get anything out of it."

"My old boyfriend and I were fooling around one night," says Jerry, "and he asked me to do the same thing and I said, fine 'cause I was into it. Afterward he got up and said, 'Okay, I'm leaving.' I said, 'I really feel like a whore. I feel like you're using me.' And he got really upset by that. He said, 'Why did you say that? Why did you do it if you didn't want to? I never forced you.' "

"And that's such a lie!"

"It's true; they coerce you all the time," says Patty. "You feel like killing them and if you say something they give you this, 'I didn't force you. I'm so sorry! How can you say that, that's so mean' bit."

"They say, 'You wanted to!' " says Priscilla. "And it's not that you were forced but you've been through it before and you know that if you say something there'll be an argument. He'll say, 'Fine, I do things to please you and you won't do this to please me.' It's bullshit. I want to say, 'You did force me to do it.' "

"My boyfriend doesn't think of it that way," Jerry protests. "We'll get into sex and because he's worried that the protection's not great he'll be careful. He'll even stop."

"But isn't he the one who likes to do it without protection?" Patty asks calmly.

"Yes, because he thinks it's more natural. But I think it sucks."

"I think I should walk out of the room," Priscilla says. "You haven't gone along with it, have you?"

"Well, um—" Jerry stammers.

"You don't! You don't! Do you? I want to hear the honest truth!"

"No, I don't! I don't!" She lies, her eyes glazing in a way I'm sure her mother has seen many times.

"I know a lot of people who've done it," Patty leaps in. "There's a girl on the school bus who wasn't using anything for two years and she slept with about fifteen guys. She kept saying, 'I'm just not going to get pregnant.' And then she got pregnant. And now she's on the Pill, which is stupid because she smokes, but it's better than nothing."

"Well, remember that guy I said tried to force himself on me?" asks Donna. "He was doing it without any protection. I said to him, 'I'm not into getting pregnant.' "

"And they say, 'Oh, I'll pull out—' "

" 'I'll be careful—' "

"No way. I know that line. I've had it before. It's never true and it's always dangerous. You can still get pregnant."

Sex: The good, the bad, and the great!

Part of the anger I hear, part of the resentment over sex, seems to be the fact that few girls are actually physically satisfied. Be it for emotional or physical reasons, many girls just don't understand what all the push, so to speak, is about.

"I've never had an orgasm in my life!" declares Donna. "I've talked to a lot of guys about it and I've asked them what it feels like. They say it just feels like you can't feel anything around you, and you're just totally, totally in paradise, completely satisfied. And I was like, 'Wow!' I mean, I've fooled around with a lot of guys. I've made love a lot of times but I've never come out of it completely satisfied. I don't know why. If Don Juan made love to me, I don't know if I'd come. Though if I had one of the Chippendale's guys make love to me, I might." She laughs.

"I don't know either," says Priscilla, "because I've never ever had one. Sometimes I've been really satisfied, or really gotten into it a lot, but I've never really had the feeling like all of a sudden—wow! It felt good, and it was over. But I've never had an all-of-a-sudden 'Oh boy!' "

"I did," volunteers Patty. "But it wasn't until after four or five months of fooling around. And for a long time it was only when

I was fooling around, not when I was having sex. Sometimes sex is really, really, really good. And sometimes it's just not. I don't even know what makes it so good sometimes. Sometimes if I'm really into it and I don't come, then I'm upset and I tell him."

"I lie," says Donna sheepishly. "I have lied. The way they ask you is like, 'Am I good?' And I'm the type of person who can't say, 'No, I didn't get anything out of it.' "

Feeling a little left out, Jerry says she can count the times she's come on one finger—she thinks. "Sometimes I don't know what I'm going to do," she says. "I get out of control. Guys moan and groan but I just sit there scared. I don't want to start screaming, 'cause I'm afraid of what the guy might think."

"Like the girl in *Porky's*, when she starts wailing—"

"Yeah, every time I think of that girl—I just don't want to sound like her. No way. Besides it takes longer for a girl; guys usually come before a girl has a chance to."

"I think it takes less," counters Patty. "If we're fooling around and we can't have sex, I can just," she snaps her fingers, "—quick—much quicker than he can."

"If I'm really in the mood for it, and I really like the guy and I'm really satisfied, then it doesn't really matter if I do or not," says Priscilla. "But since I never have, maybe I don't know what I'm missing. But it doesn't really bother me. If I was really in need of physical satisfaction, then I would be frustrated. But like if I was worked up now, I'd be in the mood for any kind of contact; coming wouldn't really make a difference."

"I haven't come but my face one night got totally tingly," says Jerry. "It wouldn't go away. Hours afterwards when we went out, I'm sitting at this party and Louis is saying how cute and funny my face looks. He's asking, 'What did I do to you?' One kinky guy I know said his girlfriend had such a huge orgasm that she lost the nerves in her arm for a week!" She laughs, sounding more and more like the gullible fifteen-year-old she is.

"In the beginning Howie turned me on so badly without having sex," says Priscilla, "that a couple of times I almost hyperventilated." She pants aloud. "And I felt really faint."

"Yeah, it makes you shaky. So many times I've had sex in the middle of school—not at school!"—Donna breaks up laughing—"but with a boyfriend who lived close by. For lunch I'd go to his house.

I'd come back and have to sit through chemistry class, trying to write and concentrate with my legs all shaky. I felt really—"

"Positive—"

"Yeah."

"Sometimes I really have an urge for sex," says Jerry, "and I feel sometimes that my urges are more than a boy's. That's really weird." She pauses. "No, it's not weird! But guys can't handle it. Once I told Willy, 'I think I have a greater sex urge than you' and he started laughing. 'That's bullshit,' he said, 'I'm horny all the time. I want to fuck you every day.' I don't think that's true at all. Sometimes girls have a higher sex urge than guys."

"Maybe I haven't had very good experiences, but I don't agree," says Donna. "Maybe it's 'cause I've never done it in any romantic places. I've done it in the back of cars, on couches, floors, in kitchens, the woods, you name it. They weren't my idea of romantic places; I just didn't get anything out of it."

"I think part of the problem is that at our age it's so rushed," says Patty. "There's such a lack of time and opportunity. There's always someone around. You can't go home 'cause your mom's home, you can't go to his house 'cause his parents are home. Where can you go? When your parents aren't home it's like big-time neurosis. I'm always worried."

"One time we were making love and I thought I heard my parents come in," says Priscilla. "I was rushed for time, so I didn't get into it at all. I kept listening for my parents' footsteps, or the car coming up the driveway. He kept trying to hurry up. So then when my parents went away the next weekend, I felt like I had to have sex. Even though I wasn't in the mood."

"I think that's a big part of it. It just feels so stupid in the back seat of a car. It's like you say, 'Let's make this real quick, five minutes and go.' You feel so dumb. It's terrible."

"I used to sneak out of my house every single night to see my boyfriend," reveals Donna. "School nights, every single night. We'd meet about one, go into his car, have sex, then go back home. It got quite boring."

ARE BOYS ONLY AFTER SEX?

Another common complaint is that boys only want girls for sex. How much truth there is in this revelation, how often it serves as an excuse for sex-hungry girls, is hard to tell.

"I found out two weeks ago, after my old boyfriend and I had broken up, that all he was out for was sex," says Priscilla. "I knew because he came over after we'd broken up and I said, 'I just don't want to fool around with you while we're not going out because I don't want to be used.' He said okay, but started forcing himself on me. I pushed him off and we wrestled for a little while. So he said, 'Okay, I can understand your position. Listen, I have five minutes before I leave, just give me a hand job.' Then after that I found out he'd fooled around with my former best friend. Wouldn't you say that Danny was just out for sex?" She turns to Jerry.

"No. I don't think so. He cared a lot about you. He was open about his sex and wanted it really badly. But he did care. I think guys are worried about getting a girl pregnant so they have to care somewhat."

"He broke up with me the day I was supposed to find out if I was pregnant!" Priscilla cries. "He broke up with me before I got my results back! I think that's kind of douchy."

"Yeah, but if you were, I'm sure he would have come back and helped you. He wouldn't leave you like that. Guys don't do that."

Priscilla ponders Jerry's naiveté. Like a lawyer, she prepares her case. "Would you sleep with someone you didn't like?" she inquires suddenly.

"No," says everyone.

"Would you sleep with Mitch?" she asks Patty.

"No. Mitch would like to sleep with all of us even though he doesn't like us, it's true," says Patty. "So I guess some guys are just out for sex. But I don't think they get into relationships for it. They have one-night stands just for sex. Though guys at this school will fuck your brains out on Sunday, not talk to you on Monday morning."

"Well, Dawson was so sweet because I said, 'Listen, I don't want to go that fast; I want to take it kind of easy,' " says Priscilla. "He said, 'I wasn't planning on going fast because I know you just got out of a bad relationship and I don't want to hurt you.' That just seemed so special to me. He knew that I wanted a relationship."

"I've been Priscilla's friend for the past two years and we've gone through a lot of boys with her," says Jerry, turning to me like a mother explaining a problem child to the teacher. "I've talked to a lot of her boyfriends before they've gotten really serious and said, 'Listen, Priscilla's been hurt by guys.' There's something about her, I'm not saying this is bad, but that guys do hurt her. And this guy Danny said, 'I will never hurt her, she's too special.' "

"And he's the one who hurt me most of all! And I'm really getting to the point where I don't care anymore," says Priscilla, her voice lowering an octave. "And that's kind of—beat. I don't really get attached to guys anymore. I get bummed out when Dawson douches on me like he did today, but if we were to break up, then that would be that. And I never used to be that way. I've gotten kind of numb"—she laughs ironically—"over the years." She considers. "I think part of the reason Danny stayed with me was because I was there and he could have sex with me and go out and have sex with other girls. I think he held on to me for that, but I don't think he'd hold onto a one-on-one serious relationship just for sex, because he could go out and get it from someone else and not have the commitment."

"Yeah, but what about George?" asks Jerry. "You don't know this but we were seeing each other and he told me he loved me, and I have no idea if he did or he didn't. I just thought he was really special. And he said to me one night, 'You're the best person I've ever slept with. You've taught me a lot. Both physically and mentally.' It got me. I was pleased. It flattered me"—she laughs—" 'cause I didn't know what I did. And at the time he was seeing four other girls so I had no idea why he was holding onto me. We used to get into fights all the time and he was never wrong; he blamed everything on me. And then I just left him. I went away for a month; he went away for summer college. He said we'd date when we got back but all I heard from his friends was about all these girls he was with. I said, 'I don't need this. It's never going to stop.' I said forget it. But when I talked to him a few weeks ago he said, 'You just kind of left me; you didn't give me any warning. You hurt me, Jerry.' I didn't even think he cared. I like guys that are open and he never told me this stuff."

Fantasies

At first these four girls say they don't have sexual fantasies. But gradually, as we return to the subject again and again, we discover many. Usually, they have to do with taking emotion and society's censorship out of sex, or involve having sex in classic movie-style romantic settings.

"I think it would be fascinating," says Priscilla, "if just one night I could have a really cute guy—whose face I'd never seen before, whose personality I didn't know—to experiment with. It would be wild. Emotions make sex seem good or bad. If I could have sex with a perfect stranger, and not be scared, I think I could have a good time."

"That's what I'm doing now," says Patty. "Jake and I have been going out for so long, and now that he's at a different school we've decided to see other people; I just can't wait till someone decent comes along. I mean here it's impossible, the school is so small. Most of the guys aren't interesting and it spreads so fast. I mean these walls are probably listening."

"But when you're on vacation, like on a deserted island like Antigua," says Jerry. "You'll be there and meet this gorgeous hunk with a tan. You know you'll never see him again so it doesn't matter—"

"Yeah. If I was in Bermuda and I met this guy and he was gorgeous," says Priscilla. "If he had a good body, a clear complexion, a tan, nice eyes, well-done hair, if it was just some guy I met one night, we got drunk and we went back to my house and I never knew his name—if I had no ties with him—I would do it."

There's a chorus of agreement.

"One of my fantasies is to have sex outdoors in the wilderness," says Jerry. "This weekend my boyfriend said, 'Let's get a bottle of champagne and go out to the cliffs.' I said okay. My brother came along but we sent him to get pizza. It was just great; it was my fantasy. We did it on the cliff and I was afraid I was going to fall off. Even though we couldn't get champagne and had to settle for a six-pack, it was really romantic."

"I'd like to do it under the stars, up in the Adirondacks," says Priscilla. "You're in the dark, all alone, on the top of this meadow. The stars are bright up there because there's no city. Everything glows. It's the kind of lighting where you can just sort of see his outline. It'd be so romantic, so passionate. I did it on my boat a couple of times. It's a sailboat with a very small cabin but a big bed. We were all alone and rocking; we could hear the water slapping up against the boat. It was so great. It's the only thing I'd love to do again." She pauses and her face lights. "Waterbeds are great, too. The first time I had sex was on a waterbed. Oh, it was great! Being on the water, having the motion of the water and the two of you . . ."

"I had sex on my boyfriend's speedboat," says Jerry, "a big cigarette in the middle of Long Island Sound. Other speedboats were passing us but we were down in the cabin. There were mirrors all around the bed, everywhere. I love mirrors, 'cause you can see the guy. Now I can be in the middle of dinner with my parents and imagine his shoulder blades close together while we're making love. And there were stars out—it was fun. . . . I like it when guys are open about their fantasies, when they tell you what they want to do. Like my boyfriend's fantasy—he's conceited about his richness— is to do it on top of his Ferrari," she continues. "I think that's great. Now it's one of my fantasies, too."

Laments

One common fantasy I get from non-virgins who felt pressured into sex is to be a virgin again. Even though they seem to be having fun, they also, at moments, seem to mourn the passing of their innocence. For they know that they've made the passage into adulthood, even if they're not emotionally ready for it.

"I've been forced emotionally into many things, including sex," says Donna. "Like with my first boyfriend. I thought he was the world. We walked about marriage. I was fourteen and really didn't want to do it. But he kept saying to me, 'You know you love me; you know we're going to get married. What difference does it make?' After hearing that over and over and over—"

"—even though you know it's not true—"

"—I gave in. I was young and really believed it. I was pressured into it and I was really mad at myself afterwards. To this day, I think it's great that some girls don't do it till they get married—"

"I wish I was a virgin," says Patty. "I said that to Jake."

"Yeah, it would be really special to wait till you're married—"

"Or at least nineteen—"

"I look at girls who haven't had sex and I'm jealous. It's like they control themselves, they can say no."

"But the thought of waiting till marriage is kind of—"

"Prudish—"

"Not prudish. But I look at virgins and think it would be great to do it for the first time again. I don't wish I'd waited. Like my goal this year is to do it with a virgin guy." Patty squeals. "I think it would be great. I fooled around with this guy this summer who was really gorgeous and I know he's a virgin. I thought it would be fun. Not to teach him things but it would make me feel kind of new, kind of in control—"

" 'Cause then they wouldn't have already had the experience," says Priscilla. "And then you could be sure they're not doing it just for the physical pleasure. That you're really there to please each other."

"How do you know they don't think *you're* into it just for the pleasure?" I ask.

" 'Cause you wouldn't force them into anything—"

"O-o-o-h! But wouldn't that be great?" Patty giggles mischievously.

"My fantasy has always been to wait to have sex until my honeymoon and have it on one of those huge beds with nice sheets," says Donna. "Or in one of those baths with lots of bubbles. I think it's great to do it for the first time with your husband. My fantasy is to have waited."

"But then think of all the fun you're having now . . ."

"Well, I don't really regret it," she lies. "But I think it would be so nice."

"I don't feel that way at all. I think virgins are just as envious of us," says Jerry.

"I don't know what you guys mean by that!" Priscilla exclaims. "I've only had sex with two different guys. Both boyfriends. And I remember everything about it. So it's not like I've lost touch with where I am and what's going on. I don't feel like I would rather be a virgin. I'm glad I'm not. I know what there is for me. I'm not scared anymore. I still have the thrill of it being new. With any guy it's all new."

"And every time you learn something—believe it or not—about the other person."

Parents and sex: The conflicting messages they send

Another difficult situation arises with parents—especially with those who disapprove of teenage sex.

"You have to hide everything from parents," says Jerry. "Parents can ruin your sex life!"

"My mom knows because my sister told on me," offers Priscilla. "She got mad at me when I was living with her. But I told her four years ago, 'Mom, I'm ready to have sex with Lang.' She didn't like that at all. I'd die to be able to tell her face to face. But she's fifty and was brought up with different rules. She comes from a Russian background, a very stiff family. If I had a mother like yours, Patty, who seems like she'd ask me about that, I would seriously open up and just tell her."

"The thing is she can talk to anyone except when it comes to her own children," Patty counters. "Then everything changes. For instance, if I am pregnant I'm going to tell her and I'm not looking forward to it at all. It's going to be big-time guilt and crying. She won't try and make me feel bad, she'll just be so hurt, I know it."

"It's hard, because my mother says everything is bad—pot is terrible, you'll never do it, you should never have sex," says Jerry, "because she's from another generation. But she's also a psychologist, so she should know what it's like. She went through adolescence! Yet when I try talking to her, everything's a sin. She works with drug and sexual abuse; she knows a lot. But she can't picture it with me because I'm her little baby."

"Yeah!" cries Patty. "Remember the time we got caught for smoking pot? I know I told mom in the car that I'd tried it before. And she's walked into my room when Jake and I have been in bed; we weren't having sex but we were in a compromising position. Yet if I talk to her a few weeks later she'll say things like, 'I know you haven't ever tried pot; I know you haven't had sex; I know you're not going to.' I know she knows but doesn't want to say or admit it."

"I hear from my mother: 'Oh, it's wonderful when you do it with a man you love—whom you're married to—' " laughs Donna.

" 'When you're doing it to have children—' "

"I never heard anything about it's good or bad," Donna continues. "It's just 'Don't until you're married.' "

"My mom's really open about it," Jerry says. "She says, 'Your father and I only have sex on Christmas and Easter.' I'm like, 'Sure, mom.' So we went on vacation once and I walked into the hotel room and found something." She giggles. "It's like, 'Hi, how are you doing?' Every time they go off to take a nap my mom looks at me and starts laughing. . . . She wanted me to break up with this boyfriend I've had for nine months, because she didn't want me getting into sex. I'm sure a lot of mothers do that. They're worried. Like you get really close and you really want to have sex. I'm sure she'll find out."

"I really think they know!" says Patty. "I've been dating Jake for a year and eight months. We went to Key West and we were in an apartment alone and my mother was staying around the block. When she's away she's told me he can sleep over. But she says to me, 'I know you won't have sex for a while,' but it seems so dumb, because how can she not know?"

"I've never seen my parents naked, ever," says Priscilla, who's almost off in her own world. "I've never seen them affectionate. Wait—I saw them kiss at my sister's wedding—"

"My mom walks around in front of my boyfriends in bras," says Jerry. "I'm like, 'Mom!' "

"My mom does that, too!" says Patty. "She'll come in to my room and Jake will be there and she's trying on these little things asking how she looks. She's ridiculous."

"Guys' parents are more open about sex," says Jerry. "It's a boy. They'll give him condoms—"

"Like my brother's twelve and my mom treats him totally different. When girls start calling him I know she won't even think twice. She won't even wonder. It makes me furious!"

"But there are more dangers for girls—"

"Not if your brother gets a girl pregnant! That's the same thing!" exclaims Patty. "I do think some boys' parents get upset. Like Jake's mother found condoms in the car and it bothered her a lot. Now she accepts it and doesn't care. She likes me so it doesn't matter."

"Louis's father doesn't know we've had sex but assumes it because *his* boy is a man now," Jerry says. "And we were driving somewhere alone once and he said, 'You can keep doing it without protection but some day it's going to hit. If you ever have a problem come to me; I won't tell your parents. I'll help you get an abortion.' "

"Oh, that's *so* nice . . ."

"He's such a sweetheart! He talks to me about drugs saying, 'I'm sure you've tried pot. Just don't get hooked.' He said, 'If Louis ever does anything bad to you please tell me.' Louis himself said, 'Jerry, if I ever hurt you physically or emotionally please tell me.' He cares a lot. His father says Louis loves me; he's never acted this way toward a girl. If you get close to the parents I think that's great. Imagine if your parents didn't like your boyfriend or his didn't like you. It would make things really hard. You wouldn't be able to see each other."

"Like two we know," says Patty. "She has a lot of money and she's the baby. Her father will do anything for her. And she was going out with this guy, who was so gorgeous and well-endowed that they called him 'Tripod.' They were going out for a year and her parents found out they were having sex and she's not allowed to see him. She was banned from him. It must have been really awful."

25

Sex and the Sweet Sixteen-Year-Old

It can be seen from the previous discussion that despite the high pregnancy rate we are not, as one might expect, promiscuous. In fact, sex is ensconced in a complexly woven web of rules and regulations that governs how, when, and why we'll have it—and whether we'll have it at all. Attitudes, while more relaxed than in the Fifties, still have structure: sex is rarely casual, rarely without meaning, sometimes not even without marriage (or at least a decent relationship) in the offing. "It's important to 'go to bed' at least once before you are married," argues Liza, "because what if you're terrified about it? You shouldn't make your mate suffer because of it. But I would only go to bed with a guy if I knew that marriage was on its way. I don't believe in one-night stands." Reason many like her: "What difference does one night or a few weeks make if you're going to get married anyway?"

We would also like to be "in love" with the boy we sleep with, or at least feel the emotion is formulating. "A girl can make love when she feels she is ready and can handle it," explains Jennifer. "She should care deeply, maybe even love the guy first. Then it's right whether she's a teenager or already married." Expands Helen,

"It's not important to be a virgin when you marry. Sometimes you can experience a deep enough emotion with someone that you want to share and experience everything with. Often that happens before both or either of you are ready to marry. Then sex is fine. If you're a virgin, great; if not that's fine, too. Sex doesn't make you any greater or less of a person."

Those of us who watched the marriages of our parents' generation crumble under the weight of sexual dissatisfaction feel premarital sex will actually increase our chances of success. "Nobody is a virgin when she marries; sex is a big factor in marriage and girls should be able to compare, to shop around," says Rachel. "Suppose you marry someone who doesn't make love well? Then what?" Exclaims Mickey: "I think being a virgin until you get married is just plain stupid! My gosh, if you marry a guy who isn't sexually satisfying then that marriage is going to go right down the drain!"

And for many more, our growing interest in college, careers, and marriage at a later date means that remaining a virgin until wedding bells ring just isn't practical. "It would be nice to be a virgin when I marry, but I don't intend to get married all that early, maybe not at all," says Kate, "and I don't intend to miss out on anything until then!" Noel agrees: "I won't be a virgin when I get married because that may be a long time from now. I want to go to college, establish a career first. I heard about a lot of people not wanting to have premarital sex a long time ago, but I really can't understand it. Things are looser, freer, now; virginity has become less and less important."

The new sexual etiquette

Even though more and more girls are losing their virginity at younger and younger ages, most say losing it too early is—in their own reorganized morality—tacky. "Lots of girls do it to prove something or to make people think better of them," offers Norma. "That's silly and immature. A girl in our sophomore class slept around and everyone heard about it and thought she was easy because she lost it too early; maybe eighteen would have been a more respectable age." Carmen seconds the motion. "It's better to lose your virginity after you're eighteen or nineteen because you'll know your morals and values better then. There's a lot of feeling involved and you have to handle it emotionally, not just do it to be the first in your crowd or because it looks good."

Because sex is not meant to be random or arbitrary, just "sleeping around" is not encouraged; if it happens, we make darn sure a relationship follows—at least for appearances' sake. "Sex is more accepted today but it's not casual at all," says Julie. "I wouldn't go to bed with a guy on the first date, neither would my friends. If a girl did, it would be because a relationship was developing. People would look down on her if she was with a different guy every weekend. One girl I know went upstairs at a party to fool around with her boyfriend. When he got up to go to the bathroom, another guy got into bed with her. When her boyfriend came back, they had a little threesome. She bragged about it because the guys were really good-looking and she was an insecure Plain Jane. That was pretty sleazy."

So are one-night stands: "In my grade, in my school, everyone's saving their virginity until eleventh grade," affirms Noel. "I was shocked to find out that fifteen-year-old girls in another school were having a contest to lose it before New Year's! I'm not old-fashioned, but I've seen many girls regret it, because the guy uses them and goes off to find somebody else. I just think it's a waste to lose it in a one-night stand just to be cool." Some girls can even speak from firsthand experience: "Sex at the right time with the right person is great," says Rita. "Sex with a total stranger makes you feel cheap and selfish."

In the South, ironically, "sleazy" has little to do with your actual amount of sexual experience and everything to do with how much you talk about it. "The ones that sleep around with everyone, tell everyone about it, and have abortions are sleazy," affirms Ginger. "I know this one girl who had three abortions and dated this gross football player who would go to bed with anybody. She came to school one day, sat down at the lunch table and told me—a perfect stranger—all about it, using the most vulgar language possible. She didn't care what I thought. If you don't let anybody know you're sleeping around, you're not sleazy. Like I'm one of the non-sleazy ones; I've slept around (only with one guy) but no one knows about it. The difference is that *I* don't want to be sleazy."

Others accuse cheerleaders, those cute, rosy-cheeked keepers of the school spirit, of being the worst offenders. But cheerleaders say it's not so. "A lot of people think that cheerleaders try to play so innocent when they're not," defends Jean, "but it's really just that we like to live our lives privately. We don't like to advertise what we do. Other girls will sit down and tell you everything that happened to them the night before; they just blast it around. We're just not like that."

Of course, there is still a strong battalion of sexual conservatives (most of them Modern Traditionalists) who "bah-humbug" the new mores (two-thirds of the girls in the *TeenAge* Relationships Survey said they were virgins). "I want to be a virgin when I marry because I would feel guilty otherwise," explains Laura. "And we, as a group, think it's absolutely necessary! If someone went to our school and wasn't a virgin, we'd think very badly of her. With our kind of families and backgrounds, anything else is just not accepted or right." Sarah agrees: "Virginity is important; it goes unsaid that everyone should be a virgin when married."

For many, it has religious meaning, and sex becomes "the crowning glory" of a wedding night. "There's a strong Christian background in my family that's played a large part in my decision to stay a virgin," says Kendal. "I want my husband to be the only one I sleep with because I'm the best gift I could ever give him." Audrey agrees. "Premarital sex is wrong. I'm Catholic and it's against my religion. Sex is something sacred—something very emotional and spiritual as well; it's the ultimate way to express love and be close to somebody; not something to be flaunted. I want to save myself for the one special person in my life—my husband."

Will attitudes ease with age? Yes, say most girls who expect more conservative friends to "loosen up." But a few, like those in the previous chapter, have actually moved in the opposite direction. "I'm not a virgin, and now that I've found the man I want to spend the rest of my life with, I wish I were," says Lisa regretfully. "He's a virgin so we've talked about it and he accepts that I'm not. We've decided not to have sex until after we're married and are comfortable with that decision."

Virgins vs non-virgins

It is of course not possible to say why some of us rush out and try to get rid of our virginity like a bad cold, while others cherish it like a priceless family heirloom; the psychological and social reasons vary with each girl. But the *TeenAge* Relationships Survey does show that on the whole Supersonic Daters are more likely to be non-virgins (70 percent) and Modern Traditionalists the least likely (22 percent). Non-virgins also have a more liberal, fast-lane attitude toward dating and relationships, girls who probably begin their teenage years with a predilection for experimentation, rebellion, and risk taking. They are much more likely to be drinkers, twice as likely to be cigarette smokers, slightly more likely to smoke pot, and show a greater tolerance for "wild boys" who have "experimented" as well. Their go-getter streak means they are much more likely to be dating and to have chanced asking boys out.

The obvious difference in sexual views also means non-virgins are nearly four times more likely than virgins to view sex as "acceptable" and "fun," to approve of premarital sex, and to have less of an interest in marrying a male virgin. And non-virgins are more likely than virgins to feel pressured into sex by a boy, and to want to talk to parents about sexual problems but find it's not possible. They are not, as myth would have it, unusually sexually aggressive. The same amount of virgins and non-virgins feel that a boy should make the first moves in kissing and making out!

The last American male virgin

Ironically, when it comes to male virgins very few girls expect to marry one because they question whether one still exists. But given a hypothetical choice, half the girls I talked to and 41 percent of virgins in the *TeenAge* Relationships Survey want a novice who "won't know if [they're] bad in bed" and so sex can also be "something to share." The other half seem to accept the double-edged notion of an experienced man/inexperienced woman.

More non-virgins, however, want an experienced man because he's more likely "to like sex" and "be good in bed," but exclaim like virgins—he can't be too experienced! "I don't want a man who's fooled around with every girl he goes out with," says Esme, sixteen, a Strong Individualist from Metier, Louisiana. "That would be scummy!"

Non-Virgins vs. Virgins: Social Attitudes

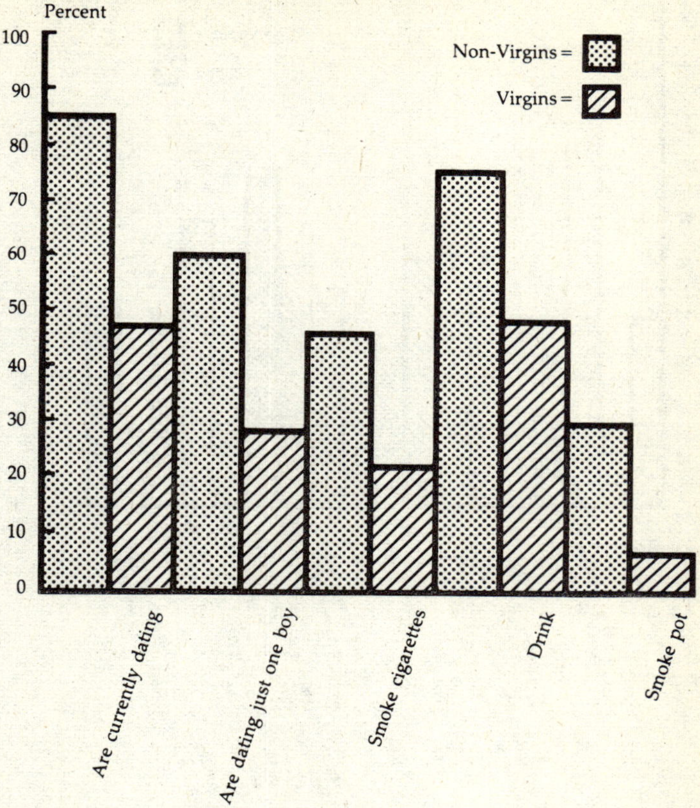

According to the TeenAge *Relationships Survey, non-virgins have more active social lives and more steady relationships than virgins. Eighty-five percent of non-virgins are dating while only 47% of virgins date, and 60% date just one boy while only 28% of virgins do. Non-virgins also seem to have picked up more bad social habits than virgins: 46% of non-virgins smoke cigarettes compared with only 22% of virgins; and 76% of non-virgins drink compared with only 48% of virgins. And 30% of non-virgins smoke pot compared with 12% of virgins. This of course does not mean that all non-virgins smoke, drink and have tried pot, nor that all girls who drink, smoke and have tried pot will lose their virginity. It only implies that non-virgins are exposed to, and have given in to, more social pressures than virgins.*

Non-Virgins vs. Virgins: Sexual Attitudes

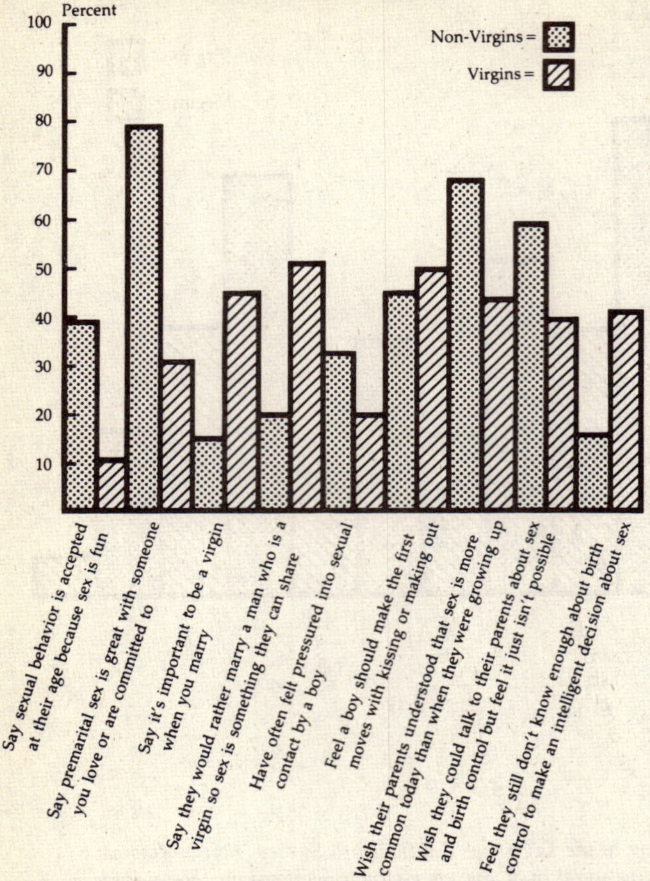

Non-virgins, 32% of those surveyed, are more tolerant of the new, relaxed sexual mores than virgins. Fewer non-virgins, 15%, feel it's important to be a virgin at marriage than virgins—45%; and fewer are interested in marrying a male virgin—by a ratio of 20% to 51%. Not surprisingly, 33% of non-virgins also report feeling pressured into sexual contact by a boy, while only 20% of virgins say the same thing, and say by a margin of 68% to 44% that they wish their parents understood the new sexual mores. Fifty-nine percent of non-virgins also wish they could talk to their parents about sex and birth control—but feel it just isn't possible, while 40% of virgins feel the same way.

But the survey does dispel one myth: non-virgins are NOT *more sexually "aggressive" than virgins. Almost the same amount of non-virgins (45%) and virgins (50%) feel that a boy should make the first moves with kissing or making out!*

26

Sexual Pressure and Dealing With It

We're in the pink and white bedroom of a well-to-do suburb just outside of Philadelphia. Heidi, fourteen, a white-blonde prepped-out version of her older sister—a seventeen-year-old non-virgin who likes romance in the fast lane—describes what she feels is pressure to lose her virginity. "Now it's looked down upon to be a virgin," she says confidentially. "A lot of my close friends have had sex and the ones who haven't are like, 'Oh, I'd better do it; everyone else has.' Most of the time it's been within a relationship, but other times the girl just gets really drunk and the guy takes advantage of her; she really doesn't know what's going on." She pauses. "Well, maybe subconsciously she wants it to happen."

As we wander off onto other easier subjects—careers, marriage—Heidi relaxes, putting her mind on defrost. Eventually, we end up discussing virginity again. "No one has ever tried to pressure me into it," she protests. "Except"—she pauses—"maybe one time when I was at a party at the shore and one guy was saying, 'Hey, girls, you want some beers?' So we went and got really drunk. I can't really remember but I think I got sick. He was pressuring me and pressuring me and I was like, 'No, no.' I think I fended him off okay though. I hardly remember anything about that night."

Indeed! Heidi can't remember because she wants to leave our impression of her open-ended. If we assume from her tale that she did fend the boy off, then fine—being a virgin is "good" and we'll be impressed with her character. On the other hand, if we assume she's not a virgin, then that's okay too because it's "cool and daring." In fact, in the *TeenAge* Relationships Survey there were just as many scribbled-out "no" answers as "yes" under the question, "Are you a virgin?" Admitting either one, for some, seems to be a major problem. And for girls like Heidi, sex has become the status symbol of the Eighties; virginity, the ball and chain of innocence that must be cast off as soon (and as painlessly) as possible. "By the twelfth grade people are saying girls who are still virgins must be lezzies or something," observes Marsha. "So lots of girls lose it or lie about having lost it just to get away from the pressure." Gigi concurs: "There's a lot of pressure because—this sounds awful—but not being a virgin seems prestigious; people think it shows maturity. I don't think sex is right before you're married, but I can understand what everyone's feeling."

In an ideal world, in an ideal society, we should all be strong enough to resist such peer pressure, to resist buying the latest pair of jeans because "everyone's wearing them." But society is composed of few leaders and many followers. And every girl needs, like Heidi, to feel that she belongs, is accepted, is comfortable with her friends. And here's a surprise—girls who go farther with sex than they want to are not alone. A 1982 survey by Planned Parenthood reveals that 30 to 35 percent of all teens who have sex feel peers pressure them into it!

The problem with sexual peer pressure is that it's not easy to identify, not something devious or deliberate, dramatic or evil, that we can promise ourselves to avoid. It's not a friend hovering over us with a box of birth-control pills, daring us to try it, not always a boyfriend who threatens to leave if we don't give in. It's often a friendly taunt, a passing tease, a subtle suggestion, couched in the best intents. It's the good-natured way Julie, Heidi's older sister, hassles her virgin friends: "Most girls lose their virginity freshman year; but there's no pressure in our group," she says. "For us, because most of the kids in our group aren't virgins, virginity's just like a joke. There's this one girl Morgan who's never found anybody she wanted to go to bed with. We'll be talking about sex and she'll say, 'Gosh, you guys, it's really unfair.' But we don't make mean jokes about her virginity; she laughs too."

It's the unconscious way Didi influences those around her: "Each of my friends came to her own conclusions about virginity," she observes. "Some decided keeping it was the thing to do. There's one girl who's a virgin and we give her lots of ribbing, but we don't make her feel like an idiot or anything. When we went to see the movie *The Last American Virgin,* we said, 'Oh, Gloria, they made it just for you.' She just laughed."

Peer pressure can even create olympics of female prowess, to see who can "make the grade" first. Those that do, dole out sweet sexual tales to runners-up, like the reds from a bag of M&M's: "Virginity is the topic of all our conversations," says Ginger. "Two of us are virgins; two are not. The two virgins wish they weren't and so they love hearing gruesome stories about sex. We sit around all the time and tell them everything; they laugh and laugh. One girl's never even been in love and won't do it with anyone she doesn't love. Each of us has one thing left to do—one girl hasn't smoked pot; two haven't made love, and I haven't slept with more than one guy. So we're each just dying to do that one thing."

We can even internalize the pressure and make it our own desire to please a guy, to "get" someone new, to "keep" an older man. "Tom would try to make love but I would just back away," says Vanessa, who tried at first to convince me she didn't feel any sexual pressure dating a divorced man who was five years older. "We'd talk about it. But I told him I wasn't ready and he understood. Well," she blurts out later, "we did make love once. But I said, 'Look, this isn't something I want to do all the time, 'cause it's just not right. It's not one of those things we can do every weekend, every week, or every two weeks. I'm not ready for that. But I know that you're twenty-two years old and that if we go on seeing each other but never make love, you'll go out on me. [He'd already done it once.] You're just older and you're going to want more, I know. I understand." Vanessa's so uncomfortable with her decision to have sex, however, that she doesn't even discuss it with friends. "I wish I hadn't done it," she says pensively, "but it was something that just happened."

A few girls even try to palm off the idea that virginity or pressure to lose it has no importance at all. "Virginity per se is never really a big issue," skirts one. "Some girls will say jokingly that they aren't virgins but it doesn't really matter to me or my friends. We're more interested in each other than in our accomplishments. Guys don't come out and ask who is a virgin and who isn't. They just don't ask a girl out to get fucked. Otherwise we'd be asking them, 'Don't you have any self-respect?' And we'd be calling a lot of girls sluts."

How to say "No!"

The problem with the pressure to have sex is that some girls find it hard to say no. Not because they don't want to, but because they're afraid of looking stupid, sounding immature, feeling like come-ons and "cock-teasers." Others feel they can't turn down a boyfriend they've said yes to before. "My boyfriend was leaving in a week," recalls Rita. "The sex we had was not worth much because we did it under pressure and we really didn't care as deeply as we should have. Other times I've felt pressured into it because I just didn't want to say no; I was afraid of being called a tease. Once I get something started I feel I have to go through with it." Didi has similar sentiments: "I felt pressured into sex once because I cared a lot about a guy—but not as much as he cared for me. I didn't really want to fool around with him, but I did, 'cause I didn't want to hurt him. There are still times when I've been dating a guy for a while and he cares more than me, but since we're already involved, it's hard to say no."

What Didi, Rita, and others like them must realize is that relationships involve *two* people giving equally. That women today have a right to say no any time they like to anyone they like—even to their husbands. Any boy who tries to convince them otherwise is selfish and chauvinistic. Says Craig Snyder, marriage and family therapist at Syracuse University: " 'You would if you loved me,' is a classic, exploitative line boys use to seduce girls. It never reflects their real feelings about the girl. Girls should turn advances like that around by saying, 'Well, if you really loved me you wouldn't put pressure on me.' Unfortunately, a lot of girls have been taught to be passive and submissive and are often afraid to test a boy, to find out what would really happen if they said no." (Witness what Jerry's boyfriend said back in Chapter 24, when she asked him that very question.)

Luckily, the majority of girls I met, and especially the Twentieth-Century Fast Trackers, do have the unabashed force of will to say *"No!"*: "I don't want to," "I don't know you well enough," or "I just don't feel like it." Even: "If you don't like it—that's just too damn bad." One or two like to finesse their rejections by giving him other options. Says Carmen: "I am careful and attempt to be delicate. 'No' is never said. I go around it by saying, 'Are you sure you want to do this?' Or by proposing a few other things. I don't just say, 'Stop, let's sit around and watch TV,' because we can usually find something equally fun to do. Once, for instance, I was asked to give a guy a blow job. I didn't want to and was perfectly honest with him. For a while he was mad but he got over it. Honesty is a great quality and people usually respect it, as he did, and I appreciated it."

When a boy becomes too persistent, we may even have to be blunt. Says Helen: "I've felt pressured into sex, but I didn't go through with it. I simply put my foot down and held my ground. If I'd felt he understood, we would have continued at a slower pace. But since he didn't, he wasn't the one for me. I would have changed my mind only if that's what *I'd* wanted to do; not because he wanted me to. Other times I just explain I'm not ready for sex by saying: 'It's quite easy for you to never call or speak to me again, but I have to live with myself in the morning.' "

Of course, one way to avoid sexual pressure altogether, say some girls, is to remain a staunch virgin—an idea that seems to be supported by the *TeenAge* Relationships Survey, in which over twice as many non-virgins as virgins admit feeling pressured. "If you're a virgin, guys don't give you that much pressure," claims Devon. "They might try the first time, but once you put your fist in their face they won't try again. With a non-virgin, they figure, well, she's done it before, why won't she do it again?" Margaret agrees. "A lot of guys think that since I date a lot of athletes I must not be a virgin, but I am. For instance, the guy I went to the prom with was all over me until I had to tell him to stop. He said, 'I don't believe this! I don't believe you're a virgin! You did it with somebody else, but you won't with me!' I thought, *God, I'm so embarrassed*. I just opened the screen door and said, 'Will you please leave?' "

27

The Double Standard

Ever since the first caveman hunted food, while the first cavewoman tended children, Western culture has promoted a "double standard"—the ridiculous idea that says, among other things, that it's okay for men, but not for women, to have sexual experience—or in some cases to even enjoy sex at all. While feminists attack the double standard as a sexist way of keeping women "subservient" (how else will we know if our husbands are bad lovers unless we've had better?)—naturalists cite its biological roots, saying that for the survival of the species, men are required to fertilize as many women as possible, but women to carry only one child at a time. Whatever its origins, the "double standard" and the confusing message it sends us is at least partly responsible for our poor rate of contraceptive use, for boys who "dump on" girls they've slept with, for virgins who condemn all non-virgins as immoral and unworthy of respect. Though Planned Parenthood studies show that attitudes toward the double standard are changing noticeably among college-educated men, changes among others are minute. Most men and boys continue to reap their high-school sexual rewards and expect to marry virgins, too.

It's a problem that confronts virgins and non-virgins alike. Laments one New Yorker: "A boy can go out with as many girls as he wants, sleep with ten in a week and doesn't get a reputation for being a gigolo; he's just called 'horny' and thinks, 'Oh, cool. I have a girl for the night!' Yet a girl who does it gets blamed for being a slut." Claire, a Kentucky girl, wrote a paper for her "Male and Female Sex Roles" class and was surprised with the results. "I found out that almost all the guys in the class, especially the big Southern football players, want to marry virgins. Oh, gosh, they do! But I say, let's be realistic here! Those guys are also all sexually active in high school and the girls they're dating are, too. Where are all these virgins going to come from? Are they the girls who sit around, look cute, and don't have boyfriends now?"

In the South, the double standard may even divide girls into categories of virtue—those who have it and those who don't. "Oh, sure, there are girls in my school who sleep around," says Kendal. "The difference between them and me is the way they get treated by guys. Guys act differently around them, tell dirty jokes, say crude things without apologizing. I've even heard guys say they don't respect girls who sleep around because they're too easy. I know they respect me 'cause I don't, and that's important."

Some girls, however, secretly thumb their nose at the establishment. "All my best friends have done just about everything, but no one knows about it," confesses Ginger. "We have this group called the Hustlers, four of us who once went over to this guy's house to read his *Hustler* magazines. We laughed the whole time and he told everyone at school about it. So we just made it into a club that gets together, reads dirty magazines, does things people wouldn't expect us to do. (It's great doing the unexpected.) We also go to The Drag, where there are a lot of diners and everyone sits in their cars and talks. We smoke cigarettes—even though we hate them—and duck if we see somebody. It's like we want to get caught but we don't.

"Once we went to my ex-boyfriend's house and put on a punk tape. Two girls wearing nothing but teddies and sleazy nightgowns danced on the couches and started taking their clothes off, while we sat on the floor and cheered them on. We were rolling on the floor hilariously because we knew the guys were looking in the window the whole time. We do stuff like that all the time because it's funny and different. Nobody thinks bad about us; no one knows."

Another more constructive way to counter the double standard is to use simple logic—which dictates that boys should practice what they preach. "It's really strange, because the guys want the girls to be virgins but they'll go around and do it," concludes one feisty Texan. "That's tacky for them to push the double standard! I don't like it! If it means that much to them, then they should be virgins, too!" Craig Snyder, a Syracuse University therapist, agrees: "Any man who says his wife should be a virgin, when he isn't, is a hypocrite. The double standard is the worst part of sexism, the worst part of the old idea that men should always be the sexual initiators and that women should always say yes."

How far to go on a date

So if sex is okay in a relationship, is it okay when we're just dating casually? Oddly enough, drastically eased sexual mores have left us with a void at the starting gate. Unlike the "good old days," when you could match the number of months with corresponding "bases" (excluding "home runs," of course), the amount of sexual contact each girl allows on a date today depends solely on the individual. "There's a place for everything," explains Marsha. "Making out on a first date is okay, as long as parents aren't present. But you shouldn't go any further until you get to know each other well. It's the quality of the relationship that really determines how far you go from there. If you see each other every night for three months, then sex is okay; if not, then it isn't." Colleen expands: "Among my good friends, if you date a guy for a while, it's okay to sleep with him. It's pretty much accepted. Most of the time the guy starts pushing. You hold off for a long time, but eventually give in. That's why I slept with my long-term boyfriend."

Nevertheless, some girls still believe that withholding sex will get a boy to do what she wants him to do or "respect her." But what used to mean holding out till after the wedding now means waiting a few dates. "If you wait a while," says Julie, "the guy respects you more—it's true. How long you wait depends on the depth of the relationship. It's not like you say, 'Okay, it's been a week, a month, a year, now we can do it.' It's just when you think it's time. You also have to think the relationship's going to go somewhere and really care about the person."

Yet for some the big area of contention still remains the good-night kiss. "On the first date, no, I'm not going to kiss him—no way," says Mickey in a bout of confusion. She is otherwise, a very forward-thinking girl who favors premarital sex and living together instead of marriage. "Some people go all the way on the first date! It's not really taboo. I just like to figure out if I like him or not, and I can't tell that early on. It's no big deal if you *do* kiss. Like I've been drunk at the disco and my date will kiss me and that's not bad. But I'm definitely not going to make out!"

28

Birth Control and the Conspiracy of Silence

"I don't think anyone really ever thinks it's going to happen to them," begins Julie, seventeen, a tall, thin, attractive blonde with a ragged ponytail, big blue eyes, and blemished skin that she tries unsuccessfully to conceal beneath too much makeup. "We all know the facts, because we're required to take health class. But I waited a year after I first went to bed with Don to do anything about birth control. He just withdrew or used a condom occasionally. I don't know why I didn't use anything; I knew it was dangerous. It really wasn't until my best friend Brooke got pregnant that I began to think it could happen to me." She laughs casually in between drags on her cigarette, then rests her back against the rocking chair in another friend's bedroom, where we are meeting.

"Don and I decided it was much smarter for me to go on the Pill than continue to worry about getting pregnant. I'd been planning on it for a while, you know, but never got around to it. When I went with Brooke to get her abortion, I went through counseling with her and talked about birth control. The funny part about it is that all I had to do was make a call to Planned

Parenthood. When I got there, the woman asked me what kind of birth control I wanted, gave me a ten-minute exam and handed me the pills." She flicks an ash into the ashtray. "It was no big deal; I only thought it would be (I was a nervous wreck) because I'd never had a gynecological examination before. My friends said I wouldn't like that kind of examination—but I was glad I did it in order to prevent something as serious as pregnancy.

"I have a friend who still isn't using anything. I talked to her about it because she and Brooke and I are best friends. But she refuses. I can't understand it."

Many girls across the country have sex without contraception, because they don't believe pregnancy will happen to them. "The idea of never getting pregnant is a common perception," says Janice. "I know many girls who've ended up pregnant just that way." Vanessa agrees: "A lot of girls could care less. Half the ones doing it don't use anything. A lot of friends tell me they don't use contraceptives and come to me a week later and say they think they're pregnant. They're just so ignorant. What's it going to hurt them or him to use something? Why ruin their life? I guess they think it ruins the moment or it's degrading or belittling. Or they think they can control it and nothing will happen. I don't agree."

The idea that sex, but not premeditated sex, is okay, is rampant. "Using birth control is premeditated," says Audrey. "If they don't use it, they say, 'It just kinda happened; it was our emotions; we couldn't possibly help ourselves.' When they see those birth-control methods, it's proof right there that they've been thinking about doing it ahead of time." Craig Snyder explains further: "If a girl reaches into her purse and pulls out a contraceptive, she fears the boy thinks she's easy; if he pulls a condom from his wallet, he fears she'll think, 'Who does this guy think he is—he expected it!' For that reason, teens think it's immoral to plan ahead for sex; there's almost a conspiracy of silence about birth control—especially the first time you have sex."

And we don't have to go very far to find out why. "Physically, a lot of kids are ready for sex, but mentally—no way!" adds Audrey. "I'm not mentally or emotionally ready to do it—because sex is the ultimate form of communication, the closest you can get with anybody. But a lot of teens just think it's sexual pleasure, having fun. It's like they say, 'We're having a good time, so who's it hurting?' But I think there's a lot more emotional stress involved."

Another obstacle to having responsible sex is that few contraceptive devices really answer the needs of teens. "The condom is not completely reliable," says Planned Parenthood director Moran. "The IUD is inappropriate for teens, and oral contraceptives require an extraordinary amount of foresight and commitment to using them each morning. Since teens live primarily in the here and now and believe in spontaneity, such planning ahead is close to impossible. While the diaphragm works, most teens don't have enough privacy at home to keep it without their parents discovering it. Even the newest method, the sponge, has a hitch because it requires you to be near fresh water to use it." As a result, 20 percent of girls not using contraceptives get pregnant in the first thirty days of sexual activity, one half in the first six months. "What comes first is sexual activity," Moran explains, "not the family planning center. In such a way it becomes not a question of birth control, but one of attitude. Girls have to believe it's their life, their future, and be increasingly informed and determined about it. They have to say to their boyfriends, 'If we're going to have sex, we'll have to do it my way—with protection or not at all!' There's nothing wrong with that. Both male and female partners must learn to be responsible; each person requires respect.

"Unfortunately, our society encourages women to defer to men's wishes," he continues. "We have just come out of an environment that praised assertive women and have actually begun to move backwards with leaders like Reagan and Jerry Falwell. They represent old attitudes, ones not in the best interests of today's teens."

The failure of sex education

Without doubt, sex education is one of the most hotly debated issues of this decade. While one side believes that teaching teens about birth control is like handing them drugs, needles, and a pat on the back, the other side looks to studies that clearly prove students who've never had sex ed continue to have just as much sex—but get pregnant more often.* In any case, most teens I talked with had little or no formal sex education at school or from their parents and culled most of their information from friends, books, magazines, TV, and locker-room gossip. Most of them trust what they hear, others just hope (and pray) it's reliable.

"I always wished my parents had sat down and told me everything," says Carmen, "but it just didn't work that way; my parents aren't like that. So there wasn't one specific source where I learned everything. I just got bits and pieces from all over. Imagine this: I found out how people had a baby when I was seven, when a kid who sat in back of me at school told me. I had to ask my older friend if it was true." Says Suzanne, like 34 percent of those in the *TeenAge* Relationships Survey who feel they don't know enough about birth control to make an intelligent decision about sex, "I'm kind of in the dark because I've never had a real sex ed class. I kind of wish I had. In the seventh grade they showed us movies but didn't make a big deal about it. I learned most of what I know from friends who just say something, then others add in, so you end up knowing a lot. I wouldn't dare talk to my parents about it—especially my stepmother. She can't even get used to me going out with boys. She's far too protective."

Many teens don't have a basic grounding in science to help comprehend the facts of life. "My science teacher said she didn't believe in evolution, so she was going to teach creation," says Marion. "But the only thing she managed to get across to the five already pregnant girls in the class was that the baby is not in the stomach (like everyone thought), where it can be digested by stomach juices, but in the uterus. After pounding it in all year long, one girl finally got the message."

And she goes on: "In junior high, one girl told me she'd gotten pregnant off a toilet seat! I don't think she knew anything about menstruation. We have sex ed (health) for only six months but it's often taught by gym teachers. Luckily, I have a pretty good idea of what to do and what not to do about sex. With all those diseases going around—herpes and AIDS—I'm definitely not ready for that yet."

* "New Insights into Teenage Pregnancy," *Family Planning Perspectives*, May/June 1982, pp. 116–26.

Many teens complain sex ed courses don't go after the emotional—the most important—side of sex. "What's sad," says Audrey, who claims she had good, extensive grounding in health, "is that they really don't discuss the emotional side. We hear only about the pleasure and how it's mechanically done but not about how we're going to feel afterward. We don't talk about the emotions we're going to experience. So a lot of kids end up thinking of sex as something physical and not emotional. They really don't know what they're getting into."

Then where do teens turn for emotional insight? Why, to friends or to television shows that present sex as a panacea for all our problems. "You turn on the television now and what's on? SEX. Every show. Sex. Drinking. But that's not a good place to learn it," Audrey adds. "Fortunately, my parents were open enough to talk about it. They taught me not to be embarrassed, that sex is not nasty, but something God gave to us to create with. Some kids feel they have to hide talk of sex behind closed doors; some parents aren't willing to say anything about it. That's too bad." (Ironically, all throughout lunch Audrey found it impossible to use the word "sex" in group conversations and would avoid it by adding, "you know. . . .")

For exactly that reason Planned Parenthood's Moran believes sex education "must begin in kindergarten and continue through twelfth grade. It must deal with interpersonal relationships and questions like 'Who am I?' 'How do I view myself?' 'How do I feel about parenting and kids?' For it to have any effect, it must be reinforced by encouraging, open, involved parents. Since adults can't be there to hold their kid's hand when they decide to have sex, responsibility has to be instilled in them."

I think it's a good idea. Not surprisingly, the most confident teens I talked to say their education came from both school and parents. "When I was eight my friend told me the basic facts of life and I said, 'Oh, gross!' and didn't believe her," admits Veronica, sixteen, a Strong Individualist from Metier, Louisiana. "So I asked my sister, a senior at the time, who explained things a little better. In fifth grade my mom gave me a book (still pretty basic); in grammar school my sister talked to me all the time. Freshman year, sex ed explained everything in detail, and biology gave us the scientific facts. I think I have enough information to say no if I want to." Says April: "My momma's really great. She sat me down and told me that if I was going to have sex, to come to her and she'd put me on the Pill. She'd rather I do that than take any risks. I said I would but I've never had the reason to do it."

The final question: whose responsibility is contraception? If we have sex with a boy, should he be thinking about preventing pregnancy too? Opinions are split. "The boy, unless he's really special and you have some kind of relationship going, doesn't really care," declares Julie. "It's not as big a thing to him because he's not the one who can get pregnant! Guys bring it up by asking, 'Are you safe?' And most girls tell them the truth. If they say, 'No, I'm not using anything,' he'll just assume he has to pull out." Luckily, the emerging modern attitude is that responsibility for contraception rests with both boys and girls. "It takes two to have a sexual relationship, so both should decide what kind of contraceptive to use," says Melanie, sixteen, a Strong Individualist from Lanahan, Maryland. "Boys are usually helpful because they don't want to become a parent either."

Should we tell our parents?

If we make the decision to have sex with a boyfriend, we may also decide not to tell our parents—or anyone for that matter—because we feel it's a private matter. If, however, our parents are not receptive to the new mores, we have to be prepared in case they accidentally find out, as Jean's did. "Just recently my mom discovered that my boyfriend and I had had sex," she explains. "I had a little calendar with a little star on it marking the day. I never should have written it down but I didn't think she'd read my diary. She's just nosy. She's always stressing, 'Please be my best friend; I want you to be able to tell me anything.' But I didn't want to tell her this. Since she knew I was hiding something, she read my diary.

"So we had to sit down and talk about it forever. I said I thought I'd made the right decision, that she had to let me live my own life. I said, 'Mom, where were you when you were seventeen?' She said, 'Married for two years.' I said, 'Okay.' I'd turned the tables. They really knew that I was grown up from there on in and she just accepted it." In many ways, Jean is like the criminal who longs to be discovered; like the majority of Supersonic Daters who wish they could talk to their parents about sex, Jean unconsciously wanted her mom to find out. Even though she says she hated discussing it, we can bet she felt better afterwards—especially knowing that she'd proved to her mom that she was "finally an adult."

Some teens really feel it's such a private decision—or fear their parents' negative reactions so much—that they actually lie about it. "My dad would die if he ever thought I'd had sex," surmises Ginger. "But then I think that maybe he knows. He used to be a policeman, so he suspects all teenagers want to try everything. In the back of his mind he's probably accepted it, but he doesn't really believe it. How did my mother find out? Well, my brother writes a lot of short stories in college and once rewrote some pages in his journal and threw the old ones in a trunk. My mother, who was cleaning up his room, accidentally read them. They were long descriptions of a conversation we'd had concerning my decision to have sex with Robbie. My mother and I are very close, but that's the one thing in the whole world I wouldn't tell her because I know it would hurt her a lot. I think she realizes I'm not a virgin now, but then I was just sixteen and she wasn't ready for it. When she asked me about what she'd read, I said, 'You know he's always writing fiction!' I think she wanted to believe me. Later I told her I would probably sleep with someone in college—before I get married. She said, 'I can handle that, but now you're just too young.' I think I'm too young too."

Others simply feel it's better just to bring the subject up and clear the air once and for all. "My mom lived in England until she was twenty-two," says Julie. "She was much more innocent than American girls are today; she was a virgin when she got married. Last year she found out I was sleeping with my boyfriend and flew off the handle, crying to me, saying, 'You're so young; you don't know what it's all about.' But she doesn't know how much I really *do* know. I also told her Don and I are involved. We were talking about sex and I said, 'Well, if you're going to worry about it you may as well know that I went on the Pill yesterday.' She said she was happy that at least I was being sensible about it. I guess it was shocking for her because they were still playing with dolls at fifteen in England."

Clearly, involving parents in our sex lives is a touchy subject. Some experts believe they shouldn't be involved with ours, just as we aren't involved with theirs. And we never really know how they're going to react. The most liberal parents may stiffen up the minute it comes to "their little daughter" talking about birth control; ultraconservatives may soften under the influence of reality. For instance, my friend's mother—a staunch Catholic—upon discovering Amy's birth-control device (she was fourteen at the time), didn't blow up as expected but simply said, "I wish you'd come to me so I could have taken you to my doctor."

The key is to tell them if you feel it's necessary—even if it won't get such a warm reception. Otherwise you don't have to.

29

Teen Pregnancy

More and more teens are getting pregnant at earlier ages, but fewer and fewer are carrying the pregnancy to term, says Planned Parenthood's Moran. "We've seen a 50 percent decline from fifteen years ago, which probably means more teens are terminating their pregnancies by abortion." Though it's still a divisive issue, the National Association of Secondary School Principals survey reveals that student attitudes about abortion have remained steady over the past ten years, with 52 percent favoring legalized abortion and 47 percent opposing it.

Fewer teenage mothers means fewer girls trapped in the downward spiral of never finishing high school, remaining financially dependent on welfare or family, decreased chances for a successful marriage. "I think it's stupid not to use contraceptives," says Jean. " 'Cause at my age I don't need a kid. Really, I'm just a kid myself. What would I do with a one-year-old kid? I couldn't handle it. If I got pregnant, I'd get an abortion. A lot of people think that's killing a child, but the way I look at it, it's not formed yet and it's going to ruin the rest of my life. One girl on the cheerleading squad got pregnant and had the baby when she was only fourteen.

Now she's fifteen years old and has a one-year-old to care for. It happened on her first date to the prom and it was the first time she'd ever had sex. It ruined the rest of her life.

"I can't understand that. Maybe she was just gullible. She was lucky that the guy married her. It's a wonder he didn't run off! Now she has to go back to high school while her mom keeps the baby."

Another girl formed her views on pregnancy because of her parents' mistakes. "I can talk about sex with my mom, because she got pregnant with me in high school," says Bobbi. "She told me about it when I was thirteen but I really didn't understand it then. Now I do. She just didn't know any better, didn't really think about it. She tells me not to ever let a guy trick me into sex without contraception, that if I'm going to do it, she'd rather I be safe so I don't ruin my life. She didn't tell me which kind to use but she gave me a book to read.

"When she was pregnant with me, her family wanted her to have an abortion, but she was against it—not for religious reasons, but because she's against all things like that—like capital punishment. She thinks that people are more cruel to little babies inside of you than they are to criminals and rapists. It's something moral inside her. Anyway, when she felt the life inside her, she couldn't do it. Dad married her. Though she was a real popular cheerleader in high school, that ended it. It was such an unfortunate scandal that people still talk about it."

Bobbi's lucky her mother escaped the odds that say that teens who are already parents by age eighteen or nineteen have a 30 percent chance of divorce; teens fourteen to seventeen have even higher odds. So why do girls even want to get pregnant in the first place? "Love," "to keep a boyfriend," or "get him to marry her," even rebellion. "There's probably forty girls out of a student body of four hundred at our school right now who've already had their babies," says Charlotte, perhaps exaggerating a bit for emphasis. "They're ignorant. If their parents don't like their boyfriend, they get pregnant so they can get married. Or it's just a one-night thing that was really fun and they haven't faced up to the consequences; they haven't taken any steps to control it. A lot of that happens—and it's basically a Mormon community; it's usually the bishop's daughter too." Others say girls who get pregnant are in pursuit of the mythological everlasting love. "Last year alone we had five girls who were belly-out pregnant. Every girl thought it was great that their friends were pregnant and going to have a baby to love," says Marion. "They think they're going to marry their high-school sweetheart at seventeen and have it last till seventy-eight. That goes for both black and white girls. That's crazy."

Section Four

Careers, Househusbands, and Marriage

30

Careers: Good-bye, Mrs. Cunningham

Goodbye, housewives, hello, careers! That's what teens of the Eighties and in particular the Twentieth-Century Fast Trackers are saying. Before even thinking of marriage and settling down, we want a livelihood that offers us our own sense of selfhood, our own reason for being. It's a desire so strong that it influences what we look for in boys we date today, in men we marry tomorrow. Boys and our new hunger to work are so inextricably linked that to talk about one without the other is almost impossible.

"A girl needs an identity," says Holly, who longs to be a television sports broadcaster. "I don't ever want to be known as 'Mr. Smith's wife.' I'm just not the type who could sit in the house waiting for him to come home and have dinner on the table. That's so unrealistic. I want to be able to go into the world on my own—not just go into the kitchen." Explains Roxanne, "A woman's interest in a career is probably the same as a man's. It's a part of you that you want to do; you need it. You need to make something of yourself, to feel like you're accomplishing something for more than just your family, that you can make an impression that lasts."

Others want to work because they "don't want to be idle," "would go crazy sitting around a house all day watching soap operas," or simply hate housework—"I'd work to have money to pay someone else to do it!" says one girl. A few who take the practical approach explain that if they've worked this hard to get where they are now, why blow it? "Everybody in college has a major and is working hard for it," says one for all, "so why let that degree go to waste?"

Not surprisingly in a success-oriented era, many of us view financial independence as the key to emotional independence, a way to be sure we're going to marry—unlike our mothers in many cases—for love and not security. "I'll never get married until I've established myself, you know, until I'm independent," says Bobbi, who's not yet sure what career she wants to pursue. "I want to be able to make my own decisions. Then if I want to get married, fine, great. If I want to have kids, I can. But I'll always have a career.

"I want to be independent and you can't be independent without money. I don't think most girls feel that way; most of my friends just want to get married and have babies. But I've thought about it for a long time. I've always wanted to be something. My parents sat me down and told me I should be independent before I get married. I should already be somebody. They want me to get more schooling, even after I've established myself. They want me to travel, to see the world, to do all the things that they never had a chance to do."

And for many, TV's old *Happy Days* image of a housewife like Mrs. Cunningham cajoling Mr. Cunningham out of fifty dollars every time she wants a new hat or a dress is not only archaic but demeaning. "I plan to work while I'm married," says more than one girl, "because I don't want to have to depend on my husband for money!"

In the twentieth century, the reality of economics has even put the squeeze on idealized love and tarnished the old adage that "we can live on love alone." "I was visiting my sister, who lives in North Carolina with her husband who's in the Marines," says Marion, who originally wanted to be a dancer until she found out she'd have to "starve a lot" and has now set her sights on a more lucrative law career. "And all we ate for three weeks was zucchini. Now I hate zucchini! When they got married they thought all that mattered was love, not money. Now they're finding out it's not true. I want a career so I don't have to worry about paying my mortgage, feeding my children, going on welfare."

Many even feel that new economic considerations have altered the definition of the "nuclear family." "It's no longer the mom staying home with the kids, the husband going out and bringing home the money," says Audrey, who originally wanted to be a surgeon, now plans to become an inspirational speaker or public-relations person."In today's traditional family, both parents work; maybe the mother works part-time. It's almost impossible for a couple to make it with just one income, unless one is doing exceptionally well. Gosh, the cost of living is so high! When you start out it's not easy."

Money as protection in divorce

Unfortunately, many girls I talked to (and 64 percent in the *TeenAge* Relationships Survey) also say that financial independence is important because they want to be able to support themselves in case of divorce. It's a hard lesson many have learned from their moms. "I'm not going to get married until I have my career launched, whatever that may be!" says Christy. "I don't want to be dependent on anybody; I won't let myself. The thought of it makes me sick. Why should I have to ask my husband for money to go buy something? That's dumb. I see what happened to my mom. She wanted to divorce my father ten years before she actually did, because she had to go back to school and get a job. I'm not going to live with a man ten years longer than I want to simply because I have no other choice! I'm just going to be ready to go. At this point I don't even know if I'll get married or have kids." Claire, who wants to go into medicine, agrees. "I've learned how important financial independence is from what my mom has had to go through since my parents were divorced. She stopped college when she met my dad and now she's going back. Throughout my marriage I want to support myself so that doesn't happen to me."

Yet for others a career is just part of the good old American process of moving up the ladder. "I want to have a career, make enough money so I can support myself," says Mickey, who aspires to political office some day. "To earn lots of money is a very important goal. It buys clothes and I'm a freak for clothes. I like money; it's fun. But it's not the most important thing in my life. The most important thing is to be happy, to have good relationships with people, and a career that makes me feel satisfied."

It also means the success of our children is guaranteed. "I think it would be nice if in a marriage my husband and I were equally successful," says Charlotte, who wants to get her law degree. "Then we could take a big stand in the community, be more accepted. It would give our kids a little bit of an extra incentive to be as successful as we were. I wouldn't hold them back, like my mom and dad did to me because they couldn't afford to send me to college."

I don't want to be a housewife!

If "I want a career" has become the Eighties' answer for everything from headaches to heartaches (even girls who really don't plan to do it, say it just to look "cool"), then "I want to be a housewife" has become the new no-no. Over 64 percent in the *TeenAge* Relationships Survey reject the idea and the girls I interviewed say it's just laughable. "If someone said, 'I want to be a housewife,' I'd probably crack up," says one New Yorker. "I'd think it was a joke." Another agrees: "I don't think anyone would look up to being a housewife these days. Everyone believes you have to have something of value to do, to devote your time to. Housewives would be considered lazy and boring. Also the science school I go to leads you to expect more of yourself than to be a housewife; you're almost expected to have a career." Sums up one for all: "It's terrible to say, but the feelings about a housewife are down now; it's not cool."

Those who disagree know they're in the minority. "I like the idea of being a housewife," says Athena. "I like the idea of working at home, of cleaning things and making everything neat. I don't know if I'd want to be a working mother with a kid; I think I'd like to be with my child more. I wouldn't want to leave a kid alone; it needs a mother. No one I know wants to be a housewife; they say, 'I'm going to work and don't care if my husband says I can't.' I'm just not like that."

Other girls, who don't necessarily want to be housewives themselves, say one should not berate it but view it as a kind of job instead. "A girl can either make it or break it being a housewife," hypothesizes aspiring dentist Anita. "She can say, 'I don't want to do this; I don't want to stay home.' Or she can say, 'This is my job and I'm going to make the best of it, make the house look nice, do the laundry, make the clothes look terrific.' A lot of girls are embarrassed to say they want to be a housewife when they shouldn't be. If I wanted to be one I wouldn't be afraid to say it."

It seems the new change in attitude has hit our boyfriends and mothers with confusion, too. "My mom gives me the hardest time about not wanting to be a housewife," says Jean, who hasn't decided what she'll do yet. "She doesn't think having a career's the right thing to do. My boyfriend also pressures me, not because he's a male chauvinist but because he thinks a woman should be in the home. Though he won't prohibit me from working, he'd rather I didn't. Still I want to carry both jobs."

31

The Rise and Fall of "Mr. Mom"

If more and more girls expect to work (fully 79 percent in the *TeenAge* Relationships Survey do) and few want to be full-time housewives, who's going to take care of the kids, cook the dinner, put the cat out? Why, the househusband of course! A new concept perhaps, but one that's now so universally accepted and used that *Webster's Ninth New Collegiate Dictionary* has added it to a list of evolving non-sexist terminology. And 47 percent of girls in the *Teenage* Relationships Survey (83 percent of the Twentieth-Century Fast Trackers) approve of a total role reversal, and say the idea of having someone to cook and clean for them is great. "If he'd support me emotionally," says one true egalitarian I interviewed, "I'd support us financially. I could at least try. He might be a better housewife than me anyway! I can't cook—that's for sure!" Another role-reverser agrees: "If it were my choice, yes, I would support him. I'd love him enough to do anything—this is not a sign of submission to the stronger sex. Of course, I'd let him stay home; I'd *make* him stay home and find out what it takes to look after children! I mean, come on, we all saw *Mr. Mom*."

The key to keeping a househusband happy? "Don't injure his

ego," "Don't let him sit home doing nothing all day," "Make sure it's a decision you both can live with." A few girls have even had role models. "I would support a househusband if he needed it 'cause I know he'd do the same for me," says Didi. "If he wanted to take care of the kids and it would make him happy, he could; my dad did it. My mom is a vice president at big department store. My father is an off-and-on publisher. He cooks and cleans, manages the money, pays the bills. I don't think he resents mom for being so successful, only for finding something she likes to do. He creates projects, gets halfway through them, and then drops them."

A slim majority, however, say no way—a man's place is out in the workplace, not in the home. They'd only support him in times of hardship or if he was an at-home worker. "I'd only do it if he couldn't work for one reason or another," says Marsha, who like most Modern Traditionalists won't go for it. "If he got fired or laid off, I'd work until he got another job because I'd want to help out. But if there was no reason not to work, I wouldn't want to support him. We could alternate staying home, but it wouldn't make me happy. If we got into a fight I'd always come back with, 'Well, I'm the one bringing in all the money!' "

Explains Marion: "If my husband just wanted to stay home and keep house, I'd say, 'No way!' But if he was an artist, he could work from home. It wouldn't be fair for him to just be a househusband; it's not fair for women to be housewives. Both have equal brains and both should go out and work. We may not be raised to think that way but I think it's true. Today most women are still expected to stay home, but because of inflation more have to go out and work. And no man should deny a woman that right to work."

The idea of supporting a man sits badly with others who fear it's too radical a break with tradition. "I'd chip in but I wouldn't do all the work," says Heidi warily. "I'd make him go out and get a job because they say it's a man's world, even though that's a sexist thing to say. I know it would be easier for him to get a job than for me. Or it would be easier if we both worked." Audrey, who had a househusband for a substitute teacher, says, "It was really odd. You hear about it but never really see it or talk to anybody who really does it. To be totally honest, I felt uncomfortable around him because I'm so traditional. Even though I'm so independent, if I found the right guy it wouldn't bother me to let him take over and be the breadwinner. A total role reversal is not really acceptable yet; it still feels strange. The man has always been the provider, the one who makes a woman feel secure. I certainly wouldn't want to support some guy who's loafing around the house; then, of course, he probably thinks I'm loafing while he's out; but it seems more acceptable that way."

The best solution, one that most girls go for, is also the most logical: a compromise and sharing of all financial and household responsibilities. Today girls talk of "alternating" days off, of treating household chores as "team work." Claire seems to tie it all up in one neat little package when she says: "A marriage should be set up so that both contribute as much as they can to make it function well. Each spouse contributes a percentage of what they earn and shares the household duties. It might be rough at first to make such changes, 'cause a lot of males don't have experience doing any household chores. Their parents probably made them take out the trash but certainly didn't expect them to do the dishes. But any guy I marry is going to learn real quick! We'll both do the dishes! If I work late two nights a week, he'll be responsible for dinner and cleaning up. That's how it works in my family now. My stepfather's home more of the time 'cause he writes at home, so he's responsible for dinner. Since my mom comes home from work and class frazzled, it works out well."

Of course, all this nouveau role-reversing can backfire when we suddenly find we'd rather have men do the dirty work after all. "Sometimes it happens the other way around and you expect a boy to do a man's job," laughs one girl. "Like when my father wants me to take out the garbage and I say that's a man's job! But he'll say there's no such thing anymore—so I have to take it out anyway."

32

Isn't It a Nice Day for a White Wedding!

With all of us heading off to our careers, who wants to get married? Everyone—including 97 percent in the *TeenAge* Relationships Survey—just a little later on, when we're "more established," more able to handle commitment, more likely to avoid making the naive mistakes many of our parents made. Perhaps for those reasons the average age of first marriage in the U.S. has slowly increased since the mid-Fifties, according to the Census Bureau, until it reached a new high in 1983 of 22.8 years for women, 25.4 years for men.

Truth is, many girls don't want to get married early because they don't want to give up their independence. "I want to get married but not until I've had a chance to make a life of my own," says Janice. "I want to go to college, have a career, have my own identity before I get involved with someone else. To make a marriage work, both people have to be strong themselves. When you get a job you have to face responsibility; going out on your own can be a scary thing. Getting married early, as I see it, is a way out. It's kind of like getting rid of responsibility for yourself."

Carmen agrees. "I want to get married in my late twenties

because I want to work and get settled before I look for or 'meet' someone. I want to have something extra to offer him, something that's all set up. I'm afraid that if I marry before my job's established I might be tempted to drop it. I'd rather build my marriage around my job than vice versa. Then once I'm married there'll be no surprises." Some even want to wait until they've carved a new life for themselves. "I'm from a small town where everyone expects you to grow up and get married right out of high school," says Ginger. "But I'm not like that. I want to go to college and not get married till I'm twenty-eight. I really have a lot of ambition and I'd like a political career. I want to do a lot of things first, like travel—go to Europe for a long period of time on my own. I want to have everything to myself before I get married. I want to be totally independent—have my own car, my own furniture, my own house. I would like to have a family, too! But not until I'm about twenty-nine."

Other girls (45 percent in the *TeenAge* Relationships Survey, 59 percent of Twentieth-Century Fast Trackers) simply want time off to "play the field." To them, getting married early means giving up dating and boys much too soon! "I have a girlfriend who's getting married as soon as she graduates," says a high-school senior. "It's great if that's what she wants and it makes her happy. But I and a lot of my friends think it's ridiculous, because she's going to give up so much and she's ending her youth too early. But what can you say if she's really in love and she's been dating him for years?"

Even though the National Center for Health statistics show that the number of divorces—currently three in five—has been dwindling since its peak in 1981, many girls, even those from happy homes, say the specter of a devastating breakup puts them off. "Chances are the girls who get married right out of high school change a lot as they get older and so do the guys," says one Midwesterner. "So they end up getting a divorce. Then the girls find themselves out in a world they know nothing about. They don't know where to start because they haven't had a job or a life of their own. I don't want to be caught in that position." Even girls from very happy families cite the statistics. "I couldn't see myself single for the rest of my life; I'd be in big trouble," says Carolyn, who insists she saw a minimum of divorce in her community. "But the national divorce rate scares me a lot. I'm aware of it, so I want to make sure that when I get married it's right. That's why I want to work for a couple of years before I do it. I hope our generation will be better equipped to handle it. We at least want to really, really make sure we're adequately prepared."

Explains Casey: "I don't want to get married until I'm twenty-nine or thirty. In fact, I'm not even sure if I want to make a long-term commitment. Right now I don't know if I could stay with someone that long without ever having desires for another guy. It seems too permanent! I get that idea because of all the divorce now. It's depressing. I look at all my friends' parents and see that the only thing holding their marriages together is the kids. There's no love there anymore. The man and woman just live together as friends." Mickey voices a similar fear: "I don't ever want to get married! I don't want to ever have kids! Marriage seems so boring—night after night with the same guy! We'd have nothing to talk about after the first few years! It's a great idea for some people but not for me. I like to go to parties and talk to everybody. If I was married, I'd have a husband tagging along all the time and he'd get jealous and bored. Then I'd get mad at him for cramping my style."

Living together

Any alternatives? "Cohabiting" gets some votes. "Living together is a great idea," Mickey quips. "That way if you split up you don't have to go through the red tape of divorce. If you want to get back together, great; it's no big deal. I'm not sour-graping, because my parents have been happily married for twenty-two years. But marriage would appeal to me more if I could find someone with my same views.

"For instance, my pet peeve is toothpaste in the sink. I hate it! I hate it! If I ever married somebody who left toothpaste in the sink, I'd just bug him about it forever and we'd end up fighting. I know he's never change his habit! It's things, little things, that can be worked out by living together with someone first. I've never actually seen it work before, because people just don't live together in Galax! Oh, my God, it's a sin. We're 90 percent Southern Baptists! My gosh! But it seems like a good idea."

Virginia, who wants to get married in her mid-twenties after taking a whirl at modeling, also gives living together high marks. "My boyfriend and I will live together first and see how it works. I think marriage is a risk. I wouldn't want to get married and divorced. Living together would at least prepare me for the daily type of compromises and problems we might encounter." Wrong! says Ginger—living together brings no guarantees! "It has all the disadvantages and none of the advantages of marriage," she proposes, "because there's absolutely no security. For me there'll only be security in marriage and I won't get married until I know it's right. I think—no—I know I can make it work."

While most girls I talked to still want to have children (73 percent in the *TeenAge* Relationships Survey), later marriage also means having fewer—usually one or two. "I want to have at the most only one child, which I might even adopt because of overpopulation," says Patty, an aspiring psychologist who wants to get married in her early thirties. "Kids are too much to worry about. They take up too much of your time. I baby-sit a lot now and can't imagine going through nine months of pregnancy, two years of diapers and crying! And four-year-olds are so annoying! I see women whose whole lives revolve around their kids and they end up duty-bound to them. That's not for me." Noel agrees: "Getting married is okay but having kids slows the whole pace of your life down. With kids you have to settle down, because you can't go anywhere without them. I don't want to buckle down until my thirties. But that's old enough. I don't want to be over the hill when my daughter or son is growing up."

Having kids too soon can put a strain on even the best relationship, says Janice: "I don't want kids right after I'm married—I want to wait for a while. If you rush into kids, you don't really have time to get to know each other and make your own adjustments. People date and see each other a lot before they get married, but they don't really have time to experience living with someone. I think that's important."

The majority of the girls I interviewed also praise the national trend of mothers returning to the workplace after they've had children. They believe it's now socially acceptable to try and do it all. "I'd like to have one or two kids because I really love them," says Charlotte. "But I don't want a lot because after they grow up I want my life with my husband back. I can't be someone who stays home all the time; I plan on having my own career. Having kids can wait for a while until I'm well established careerwise. A lot of people say that having kids and a career at the same time is wrong because you're depriving them of your presence. But I don't believe that. I can manage my time well enough to have room for kids and a career. I can do it all."

Section Five

What Girls Hate About Boys

33

Who Is Mr. Wrong?

If there's a Mr. Right, is there a Mr. Wrong? Yes. In fact, during these interviews, once we got onto the negative aspects of the male personality the answers came gushing forth. It's not that girls "bitch" any better than boys (I'm sure "their" locker-room raunch would cut through female sniping any day), but that we do it with such finesse, with such descriptive care and attention to detail. We may not know what we like about boys, but you can bet we know what we hate!

Gripes come in two flavors: those that signal a boy is "out of control"—too macho or flirtatious, into excessive drinking or drug-taking—and those that say he won't make it in the adult world—poor grooming, shyness, unreliability. While many of them have already been discussed in earlier chapters as foils to the characteristics we like, some are so out-and-out annoying that they deserve attention on their own.

Nobody wants a macho man

Surprising for girls I considered remarkably unradical, even conservative, is the first target area in the male character—macho—

which 79 percent of girls in the *TeenAge* Relationships Survey also reject. Though girl after girl I interviewed swears she doesn't want to break with tradition, doesn't want to pay for dates or support a family—she doesn't want a boy running her life either! In fact, many girls want the best of both the traditional and liberated worlds. But working out such a delicate balance is difficult.

Vanessa, for instance, likes the idea of dating an older man who's very traditional and dominant, who's ready to settle down and support her, to structure her life. But she's not willing to accept what he might see as the rest of the bargain—doing what he says. "I hate it when boys tell you what to do," she says woefully. "I can't stand it when they think you're supposed to do what they say just because they're men. I guess that's macho. The boy I'm dating now is like that and we broke up over it once. He'd tell me what to do but when I tried to tell him what to do he'd get mad. We got back together once we talked it out, but I told him he'd have to change or it'd never work out. I guess he just grew up in a family where the man's always boss and that's the way he expects it to be with us."

But Vanessa doesn't see it that way. "There's this place we go to dance on weekends called Gram's Station. Even though I've asked him not to, he'll go on Saturday nights when I'm not home. He'll tell me he didn't dance with anyone—and I believe him—but if I'd done the same thing the consequences would have been disastrous. He would have told me I'd been bad! I did it once anyway when he was gone for the weekend. He came back all mad, pouted for a week, and refused to talk to me. He's so stubborn he won't give into anything! We just clash. But we like each other so much that we decided to work it out and concluded that if he thinks it's right for him to go out without me, fine. If I think it's okay for me and I'm not doing anything devious, fine. Neither of us is allowed to leave with anybody—though I'd never even consider doing it. I suppose fighting it out is better than lying to each other about it. A lot of people go out with other people behind their lovers' backs, but we don't. He did it once when we were first dating, but he told me. He's just that way."

And when macho squares off against female chauvinism, it can bring thunder and lightning—but not the romantic kind. "I hate these macho guys like football players, like the guy I used to date who just made me sick!" cries Margaret, a strong-willed girl who won't take one ounce of male chauvinist lip from anyone. "He was all-state, all-everything, good-looking and muscular. He got trophies, money, and lots of scholarship offers. We had a pretty good relationship until all his success went to his head, and he began to think it should have gone to mine, too. I told him, 'I have my life and you have yours,' but he just couldn't handle it. He wanted me to be there for him all the time; I wasn't supposed to be Margaret, you know, just part of him.

"For instance, one day I went to the mall to shop for six hours. His mom told me later that he laid in bed all day and pretended to be sick because he was so mad at me for not being with him. He didn't want me to be a person on my own. He was really whacked. Of course, I was really happy for him when he got awards but I didn't like the way he felt I should hop whenever he said so. He wouldn't let me speak to other guys because he was supposed to be my whole world—like anybody outside of him was not real! Like when we went to eat—if I said hello to friends and started talking with them he'd get upset that I wasn't paying enough attention to him. That was just stupid."

Another true turnoff, which is sometimes associated with the manly or macho image, is dominance. "I really dislike dominant guys," says Lisa. "Some guys do things just for themselves and it really bugs me. They make plans and say, 'We're going to do this and that,' and don't even bother asking you what you want to do. They just make all the arrangements and expect you to go along. They seem to just be brought up to dominate and make the plans because they're paying for it.

"For example, a few years ago this guy I dated asked me out saying, 'We'll go see a movie and decide later what to do.' He said, 'We'll decide,' but when it came to actually going out it was, 'Oh, here, we're going to see this movie and out to eat afterwards.' In truth, I really would've preferred to stay in that evening because I felt like being quiet and low-key. I dated him one more time but that was it. I didn't need that kind of treatment. We tried to talk it out but it was useless. I don't understand why if you're both spending the evening together, the two of you can't decide what to do together."

It's a good point. But it seems that in groping for their masculine role many guys mistakenly overshoot the goal and try to overwhelm us with competence—which turns into dominance. And when he's as inflexible as Lisa's date, it's probably best to look elsewhere for a boy who doesn't feel so threatened by sharing the reins.

Another way the male image gets overdone: in guys who "lower their voices and talk real manly so they can impress you," who say "women can't make decisions or act responsibly," or have the impression that all women are bad drivers. "I know quite a few guys like that," says Helen. "They say they like to keep women barefoot and pregnant in the kitchen. We give them shit. They can do what they want; we'll do what we want. They're the ones in life who are going to have trouble dealing with it; it shows they have closed minds." Worse are guys who huff and puff and blow themselves up into peacocks to impress us. "I hate it when boys get 'with the guys' and sit in the corner and stick out their chests and flaunt their muscles," says Holly. "It's like they're saying, 'Yeah, look over here!' You see them at every party and watch how hard they try to get all the girls to look at them, because they're at an age when they care about their manliness and looks. It attracts some girls but not me. I like a guy who's just plain cute, who can stand there and talk to a girl like a normal person."

The real problem is that when macho gets too entrenched it can become an emotional barrier. "Macho really turns me off," says one Oklahoma girl. "There are a lot of cowboys where I come from, and they act like big tough guys; they won't let you get close enough to them to really talk. They always kind of stand away and put on a show. As a result, you never really know how they feel about anything." It's one element of the male mystique that can send girls like Fatima running for cover. "I hate it when boys put up a front to hide their feelings," she says. "When they're with their friends they act cool and macho, and then when you're alone with them act so sweet! I once met a guy like that named Walter at a high-school dance. He was a little into himself but I was able to break the ice and get him to talk to me by acting playful. He was standing against the wall with his arms crossed defensively, and I started imitating him until he laughed. He called me the next morning and we went out for three months. He was sweet but wouldn't let me get too close. If he noticed it happening, he'd back off. Once I asked him, 'Where do I stand?' And he said, 'Right now, I'd say you're standing about a foot in front of me!'

He'd always try and laugh it off and never address the problem.

"Though in private he was very warm and affectionate, when he was with the guys he was cool. If I walked by he just acted like he didn't know me! He wouldn't hold my hand or give me a little kiss in public. The thing is, I don't think his friends would have really ridiculed him even if he had. In fact, it was his best friend who came up to me once and said, 'Walter puts up a front—but inside he's a pussycat.' This guy had been Walter's friend for years and knew him well so he clearly saw through Walter's act! I don't think Walter knew they knew. If he had, he might have realized there was no use in fighting it. That act eventually broke us up."

Another macho type that girls attack is the braggart—a guy who is under the mistaken impression that we want to hear all about his latest sexual conquests, or worse, about ones he's dying to make! "I don't like guys who are all talk and no action, or who make up stories to turn girls on," says Nicole. "Some guys talk all about their sexual experience when they haven't really had any; they simply create stories. When you first hear it it's impressive, but when you find out the truth, it sheds a bad light on them." Suzanne agrees: "I hate it when everything in your relationship is known to everyone else because the guy talks to his friends. You know he talks because it gets back to you. Like last year it got back to me. It wasn't anything big but I knew he was talking. Some friends and I had gone over to a friend's house, and my boyfriend and some other guys snuck over and we were just messing around. The next day in school all his friends knew about it. Now I won't date him because of it. I really hate it."

Like macho, bragging can create an impenetrable wall between the sexes, even between friends. "The guys who brag about their sexual conquests get me really mad," confesses Colleen. "I've always gotten along with boys and had many as my best friends. But sometimes they'll sit there and start talking about girls and I'll get bright red and all upset. I say, 'Why do you talk about girls like they're dogs or something?' Guys are getting better about it as they get older, but they're not like the guys I knew when I was abroad in Denmark last year. When someone would ask them what they did with their girlfriend, they'd just say, 'Yeah, I was with her.' Here they brag about how far they got."

The masher

Just as big a turnoff as guys who are all talk and no action are those who are too much action! While it's fine when a boy we like shows affection through a handshake or a kiss, it's not fine to be mauled by boys we're not attracted to or to be left with the impression that all he really wanted to date was our body. "I know this girl who went out with this really cute guy but he kept pressuring her to do things sexually," says Heidi. "He wanted to have sex. She was only fourteen. That really pisses me off. That tells her that sex was the only reason he went out with her. She's very shy and doesn't speak up for herself that much. She kept telling me she didn't know what to say. I just said to say, 'Forget it! You're not worth it!' But he kept asking her to come over to his house when no one was there. It really makes me mad that guys would go out with girls just for that. That means they really don't care about the girl—if she has a good personality or has fun." (Amazingly, Heidi seems to have forgotten just how pressured she felt to have sex with such a boy in Chapter 26!)

Amanda found that Prince Charming quickly lost his charm when he tried to push her too far. "At the end of last summer I had a blind date in New York to see *WarGames* with a guy from Deerfield, who kept trying to make the moves on me all night so I gave him the cold shoulder," she says—and of all people, she could do it! "He was nice but I kept thinking, it's still the first date! The problem is that he tried to start a relationship in such a little jammed-up time of three days that it made me feel pressured, 'cause I had to leave for Maine where we have a summer house. Anyway, we went to a party that night and he asked me to go steady right there. So I said yes. We were supposed to go to a night club but ended up at another guy's house splitting up in couples. It was a Rockefeller house, and they had the nicest bedroom ever so we went up there. We fooled around a little and he kept asking me if I was a virgin and I said yes and asked why he was interested. He said, 'Are you ready to lose it now?' I said 'No!' He called me a few times after that and we did a lot of stupid stuff together. Then I got three million letters from him that summer but just decided I didn't like him. He called me four times a day no matter where he was—even if he was in Central Park he'd find a phone. He was being a jerk too, showing all that interest. He came to my house once drunk and said that I was his only love—but said it sarcastically. So I never called him back. At a school dance with Deerfield, I saw him and found out that he likes another girl now. It was great. It got him off my case." Amanda clearly liked Mr. Pushy, at least enough to go upstairs and make out with him in the first place, but when he got out of hand her interest switched off quicker than a light.

Says Liza, who had a similar experience: "The guys I have to deal with away at school are only out for one thing and I know it! So I just don't go to the dances. It's such a pain in the neck; it really bothers me. You meet them for one minute and they say, 'Let's go.' That's not what I want. I would rather be with them and have a chance for a relationship. They wouldn't push you into physical contact the first time you meet them if they were really interested in your feelings! Where I grew up in Venezuela, boys have a whole different attitude. They're not as pushy as in America and are taught by their parents to respect girls. That's a lot more than boys here do! If you make out with a Venezuelan, it's not as soon. Even if I dislike Latin boys for being sexist, I respect them a lot more."

Violence

Although it's not prevalent, violence, an aberration in the macho image, is worth bringing up because some girls mention it as a problem. It is without doubt a red warning light signaling that a boy has serious problems—the kind that should be handled by a trained counselor, teacher, parent, or psychologist. There is absolutely no excuse for any boy to slap, hit, or physically abuse any girl, not even if he's drunk, upset, angry, or jealous. Even a simple smack on the face like we see in the movies can signal more trouble to come. "Guys who hit girls are a total turnoff to me," says Rita. "Some jocks I know do it. I have friends who've been hit and still go out with them, and I don't understand it. They don't beat them black and blue, but slap them around a little. I wouldn't take it; I don't even take insults!"

Carol found that one whack on the cheek was only the foreshadowing of worse problems. "Some of my boyfriends have hit me before," admits the waifish blonde, who seems so sweet and innocent it's hard to imagine her being hit by anyone. "One time my boyfriend Dennis, he lived in Boys' Town—a home for boys who are hard to handle—was staying at my house for Christmas and we got into a fight. He hit me so I ran into my room. I broke up with him and he took all the glasses from the kitchen shelf and started breaking them in my brother's room. Mom went up there and told him to leave right away and called Boys' Town. He came back a year later and called me a slut, because he was mad that I broke up with him and hurt his ego. He'd slapped me in the face and I'd let him know he couldn't do it again! My dad had to go outside and tell him never to come into our yard again.

"My new boyfriend Scott and I wrestle a lot when we're just playing. Once I hit him pretty hard—I didn't mean to—but it was in the face. And he said, 'I'd never hit you in the face. Never.' I felt so bad 'cause I didn't mean to do it. If he accidentally hurts me and it makes me cry, he hugs me and says, 'Oh, I'm sorry. I didn't mean to.' One time he almost broke my nose 'cause he came up with his head and hit me in the nose. But he didn't mean to."

He's so vain!

Every girl wants a guy who's secure and self-confident. But no one wants one whose self-adoration has run away with him. "I hate guys who act real snobby, like they own the place, or act like you're supposed to fall in love with them or go after their bodies," says one Strong Individualist. "I know lots of cute guys like that but their personalities ruin it!" Says another: "I don't like to hear about *him* all the time. If you talk to him and he's saying, 'I'm so good at this or that,' it gets boring. There's one guy, Max, and he's fourteen, my age. I don't know where he's from, maybe around here, maybe from New Jersey. He's like heavy metal—into concert T-shirts and jeans. He's good-looking, has short brown hair that's layered back. He can attract you but once you talk to him he doesn't. He's really pushy with his girlfriends—not so much sexually but emotionally. He always wants them to do something for him and is telling them, 'Don't touch this, don't touch that.' He's very demanding. He just thinks he's terrific. He basically loves himself and doesn't care what his girlfriend thinks.

One of my good friends went out with him, and he was always cheating on her. He played around with her head. He'd say, 'Me and my friend Rudy went to this party and got totally blitzed and I can't remember what happened.' People started talking about his antics and she eventually found out. It hurt her so much that they're not going out anymore."

But a lot of girls see right through the I-love-me image. "I don't like guys who think they're superior," says one. "They're always combing their hair, always primping. A lot of guys act conceited because they really want to be—but it's really just a cover-up for insecurity." Or says Helen quite bluntly: "Have you ever tried talking to a conceited guy? It's a lost cause! They're already convinced they're great so there's nothing new you can tell them. It's like talking to a brick wall; it's not fun at all."

(Of course, don't make the mistake of chalking off a shy guy to conceit or snobbishness. Really check it out. I've had more than one shy male friend say girls think he's snobby. Shy ones may appear cold and aloof on the surface, but they have very different reasons for acting that way.)

34

A Flirtatious Nature and Other Fatal Flaws

All girls agree flirts are fine—except when they're flirting with someone else! "I hate flirts," says Isabella, sixteen, a Strong Individualist from Clarksville, Tennessee. "The boyfriend I just broke up with flirted with everybody. I'd be standing there and he'd have his arm around someone else and it would really bug me! Other people would say, 'Oh, she's just being possessive.' But I felt anger; I was really mad. I'd go somewhere with him and he'd leave with another girl or flirt with her, when I'd rather have him flirting with me! It seemed like he wanted to get me mad." If it's any consolation to Isabella, the majority of girls dislike flirts for that very reason and 75 percent in the *TeenAge* Relationships Survey even admit flirts make them feel ignored or put down! Flirts are so universally unadored that "a flirtatious nature" gets a rock-bottom rating on the *TeenAge* list of male attributes, with only 20 percent saying it has any merit at all!

Like boys who try to impress us with their sense of control but end up overdoing it, many flirts just go overboard trying to impress us with their irresistibility. They think a little competition and jealousy keeps us interested. What they don't know is that it ends up making us confused and angry instead. "A guy who flirts with other girls gets me jealous," says Casey. "It's nice when a guy flirts with you but not with others. It gets annoying, because first you think they like you and then, when you see them acting the same way with other girls, you're not so sure. I'm still unsure about this guy I met last year. After a while he just started paying more attention to me. He'd already done the same thing with other girls—like he'd hold hands with them even when they weren't going out—and each one thought she was going out with him when she really wasn't. It got me really confused. To this day I don't know if he ever liked me or not. Other people said they thought he did, but no one could be sure."

In a relationship, flirting can be the seed of many fights. Virginia, who dates a handsome, green-eyed wrestler who's two years older, finds that his constant philandering gets to her so much that she occasionally has to put her foot down. "One summer our families rented houses next to each other at the shore so we saw a lot of each other and started fighting a lot," she says. "I left him at a party one night 'cause he was being jerky. I was driving 'cause he didn't have a car. But he was being really inconsiderate, saying, 'Drive me here, drive me there.' He'd assumed I wanted to drive him all over the place without asking. Then he started flirting with this other girl and it really got to me. I'm used to it. He never gets together with the girl afterwards, but that time I was like, 'Forget it.' It really wasn't fun. So I said, 'Let's go.' And he said no, he wasn't going to leave. So I gave him three minutes and left with the car. If he was being inconsiderate enough to let me wait in the car while he flirted with another girl, then I didn't feel like waiting!"

Not surprisingly, only an occasional girl finds flirts attractive at all. "I like flirts," says Norma. "They're not a turnoff at all. It simply shows the boy likes to have fun and is open." But what she really means is that he's fun because he's flirting with her!

Instant turnoffs

Also on the list of manly "can't stands" is a smattering of out-of-control behaviors that signal a boy is not interested in or really ready for a true relationship, because he's too immature, too self-involved, too uncouth to even pull it off. The following are, for almost all girls, instant turnoffs.

Immaturity: "I hate guys who are my friends and tell me all the things they do to get a girl in trouble," says April. "Then when they break up with her they ask me to go out with them. I think, 'You've got to be kidding! After all I know?' Like they take a girl to see a real pretty view somewhere and end up parking or set the clock in the car back an hour so she gets in late and gets in trouble. Or they tie your shoe laces together when you're not looking. We go to a very immature high school. If one guy cracks a joke, his friend tries to better it so everything turns into one big practical joke."

Loud or obnoxious behavior: "I don't like boys who show off all the time," says Linda, thirteen, a Modern Traditionalist from Ocala, Florida. "They brag about fights they get into, about how they won. It's just to impress me and it doesn't work. No guy is that great a hero!" Heidi agrees: "Most of the guys in our grade dance around saying, 'La-di-da, la-di-da.' They act between age two and twelve! I have an eight-year-old brother and they act just like him. If we go to the mall, this kid Duane will run around and throw stuff over the balcony. He'll go up to other girls and start making fun of them. He's just trying to get attention, but he's going about it the wrong way. It would be better to start up a conversation with me by saying, 'Oh, I like that sweater you're wearing. A friend of mine has one just like it.' A lot of immature guys I go to school with are really good-looking, but no girl will look at them because of the way they act."

Showoffs: "I hate it when guys have to show off to impress a girl," says Gia. "It's especially dumb when they try to play football in front of you to get your attention. Once this guy who liked me tried throwing me an unexpected pass when I was walking by. I dropped it of course! It was actually funny. He would have gotten so much further by just trying to talk to me."

Silliness: "I can't stand guys who act silly around me 'cause they like me," says Casey. "They don't know how to express it, so they tease me a lot and often carry it too far. Once I was fooling around with this guy Marvin at his house. We were in his mother's room making out on the bed and he kept joking around. I got angry and said, 'Stop it.' Then after a while he stopped. It feels good when a guy just sort of seduces you instead of joking around about it."

Hyperness: "The guy I like is really outgoing and really friendly and intelligent," says Janice. "The only thing I don't like is that he's too spastic—he's always running around and doing something. Everything he does is in high speed. He's hyper. He's got a real high energy level. That's okay for a while but after some time you want to tell him to slow down or sit still. I've told him that and he'll try to do it, but it doesn't work for long. Now I've just gotten used to it, so that if he gets upset or depressed he just kind of mopes around. Then I'd rather have him hyper!"

Possessiveness: "I hate it when a guy won't allow me to see other people," says Rita. "I had one boyfriend who went through my address book and saw a male name and had a fit. He told me he was the jealous type. I said okay, but it really began to bother me after that. Though we were the same age, that showed his immaturity."

35

Oh, no! It's Mr. Unreliable!

If success is "in" (94 percent in the *TeenAge* Relationships Survey say "dependability" is important), then it comes as no shock that boys who show signs of finishing last in the rat race are "out." It's no news that those who continuously disappoint us by not showing up for dates or canceling at the last moment make us cringe at the idea of another date with them, or at the notion of long-term commitment! Not only do we doubt their ability to "make it" in the adult world, but we end up questioning their underlying motives: are they just flakes and airheads or are they really self-centered or weak? No matter; inconsistent behavior quickly douses any flame we might carry and leaves us frustrated, hurt, and confused.

"I hate guys who make a lot of empty promises or don't follow through!" says Anita. "One guy I just finished dating would say on Monday, 'What are you going to do for the weekend?' And we'd make plans. Then one of his boyfriends would call and our plans would get rearranged. Then he would expect me, on a whim, to change all my plans. What was worse, if he didn't want to go out with me, then I was left to think up something else to do!

"Once when I was in the middle of cheering at a basketball game he came up to me and said he was going somewhere with his friends. But when his plans got canceled he suddenly decided he wanted to be with me. But I'd already made plans! My friends said it was okay to skip it with them if it was going to make him mad; I'm lucky to have such understanding friends. But guys who just expect you to drop all your plans for them make me mad!"

Joan agrees: "It's aggravating. Like he says, 'Do you want to go out Friday?' Then calls you up on Thursday and says, 'Well, sorry, but other plans came up so we can't go.' You just kind of smile and think, "Well, I still want to go out with him,' but it makes you not believe in him so much when he asks you out later. It doesn't put everything he does in doubt. Sometimes there are circumstances that you can understand—when something happens in the family and he absolutely can't go, but those times are really rare. The guys that really make me mad are those that cancel because they have better plans, because their friends call and they decide to get together that weekend."

Boys who never manage to be on time leave us dangling, interrupt our plans, and show a general lack of respect for how we run our lives. "I don't like to be stood up," says Carolyn. "That's never really happened, but Peter has the tendency not to be punctual and I've waited ten to thirty minutes for him to get somewhere. I'm very punctual and it really burns me when other people aren't, because it shows a lack of respect. Once it was freezing cold out and I told him to meet me at eleven. He didn't show up till twenty after, saying, 'Sorry, I'm late.' I know it's 'him'; it's just the way he is. I don't hold it against him but it's definitely annoying." She laughs. "I must admit though that when I dated one guy who was always five minutes early it was more annoying because sometimes I need the time to finish getting ready. With Peter, at least I know I have an extra twenty minutes!" Ginger says her boyfriend's constant excuses for being late began to make her feel foolish and eventually made their relationship crumble. "My boyfriend would say he was going to be at my house at a certain time and then he'd go off with friends and show up thirty minutes late," she says. "I would never have even cared if he'd called me, but once it happened that he was two hours late. He called and said there was something wrong with his car, but I heard the guys laughing in the background so I didn't believe him. I told him I was tired of it. He said, 'Tired of what?' I said, 'Tired of the way you treat me.' And he got so mad that we broke up. I felt bad later on when I found out his car really was messed up because he showed it to me."

Maddening miscellany

Then there's a barrage of assorted unclassified items that bear mentioning because of their paradoxical nature, i.e., that either too much or too little of it can drive a girl (sometimes even the same one) crazy!

The Constant Caller: "I hate when guys call a whole lot," says Joan. "Like every hour on the hour. They want to know where you are all the time. And if you go to someone's house they get mad when they call your house and you're not there. What do they want me to do? Call them and say, 'I'm going somewhere'? That's aggravating. If a guy I'm going out with has to call me ten times to get the plans straight—okay. But once a night is good enough. Not once at nine, once at ten, once at eleven. Or some call early in the afternoon, then late at night to check on you and see if you're still home. I think they're just bored and just want to prove they're interested. But when you're busy, it's hard to be nice and considerate and talk to them for a while on the phone each time."

Or the Inconstant Caller: "What I don't like about my boyfriend is that he doesn't call enough," says Kendal. "He kind of goes off and on. He kind of expects that we'll do something, like after a football game, instead of calling and asking. But I told him that I really didn't like that. It's not exactly macho—I just think that's the way he's used to doing it."

The Tongue-Tied Guys: "I hate guys who can't talk to me," says Claire. "I like guys who can gossip, not necessarily about other people, but who can talk about what they know about sex and birth control if I have some questions. It's not really girl-talk but close to that."

Or the Blabber Mouths: "I've gone out with guys who just talked my ear off and that can get boring," says Carolyn. "At the beginning of this year I went out for drinks with one guy from George Washington University, who went on and on about all his other dating experiences. I was so bored I never went out with him again. He called me twice until he finally got the picture. Perhaps he lost interest too, because I wasn't saying enough. I didn't get a chance to!"

The Unsavvy Asker: "It's really aggravating when a guy asks you out in front of other people. You want to turn him down because it's embarrassing," says Joan. "It's especially mortifying when it's in front of all his friends and they're going, 'Ooooo-h-h-h, ooooo-h-h-h! Get her.' Once a friend who was trying to set me up told me Ben was going to ask me out. It was no big deal—except that he did it in fifth period—in front of my whole class, in front of my teacher! Everybody in the class heard him and it got dead silent while they listened to my response. I said yes; I would have said yes even if he'd asked me somewhere else, but it was just aggravating—like a macho kind of thing. Like he was saying, 'Look at me; I'm great. I asked a girl out.' As it turned out, I didn't even go out with him because I got sick and had to stay in bed."

And yet from the same girl: "A boy shouldn't be afraid to ask a girl out. That's really ridiculous. There's always a way to find out ahead of time if she's going to say no. Then he can ask someone else. Ask her friend, 'Do you think she's going to say no?' I still think most guys are afraid. 'Cause you set them up or something and they say, 'I like her but I'm afraid to ask her out again.' I know there are not that many guys I would say no to—for one date. I would say no to a lot of guys about dating seriously forever and ever, but I can't think of many I would turn down the first time."

36

Falling for the Loser of the Pack

Suzanne is a chunky, pretty girl with glossy shoulder-length black hair, squinty, almond-shaped eyes, and a strong but flexible-fiberglass nature that attracts boys with a need to be mothered. Bright, quick, and full of adventure, Suzanne likes to party hard herself, but doesn't enjoy having to mop up socially after a boy who's constantly going overboard. "I hate guys who get really drunk!" exclaims the fourteen-year-old Pennsylvania pseudo-prep. "Every time my old boyfriend would go to a party, he'd get drunk and act crazy, you know, really get out of hand. I was embarrassed, very embarrassed. It got to the point where people would come up to me the next day and say, 'I don't believe he did it again!' And I hated having to baby-sit him, having to wake him up after the party and get him home every night. I don't drive yet so that meant walking him home myself or sending him with someone else. It was a big drag."

Like Suzanne, 76 percent of the girls in the *TeenAge* Relationships Survey find that a boy who smokes, drinks, or does drugs in excess is about as exciting as a wet sweater. Guys who pass out with their head in the fish tank are not funny or cute but "immature" and "uncool." Guys who can't remember where they've been or what they've done are not intriguing but show signs of "weakness" and "low self-esteem." Gone are the days when girls worshiped rebels like "The Leader of the Pack" or "A Rebel Without a Cause." We want boys who know what they're doing and can think for themselves. As Emily so succinctly puts it: "If a boy can't handle himself with smoking, drinking, or drugs, forget him! He probably does it from peer pressure. And if he needs to be cool or have friends that badly, then count me out!"

The drinking dilemma

One of the reasons why drinking gets so out of hand is that it has an air of acceptability about it. We see ads for beer on television, watch parents throw back Scotches, hear our older brothers crack a Schaefer while watching the football game. When we sneak into bars with fake IDs or stand around at parties with beers in our hands, we feel secure and adventuresome, like the adults we admire. Our fascination with alcohol is so consistent that the University of Michigan Institute for Social Research, which has surveyed 17,000 high-school seniors each year since 1975, reports that 93 percent of seniors have tried alcohol, 70 percent in the previous month, and 40 percent have had five or more drinks in a row—i.e., gotten drunk—in the previous two weeks! Drinking or partying is so indigenous to high-school life that Lloyd Johnston, Ph.D., director of the aforementioned study, says drinking has almost become normal, accepted behavior. What's more interesting, he reports that historically more boys have been drinkers than girls. Today, three times as many boys as girls are daily drinkers.

The most revealing clue to liquor's image appeal is that we don't even have to drink it to be considered cool; being around it is enough for some. "Yeah, drinking and keg parties are a big deal at our school," says Allison. "Getting it is the big deal. Whether you drink it or not is not the problem. No one cares if you get it and give it to someone else. But it's cool to have it 'cause the drinking age is twenty-one. The problem is that we just had a girl who decided to get drunk and nearly killed two people with her car. We have a big curve on Moosehead Lane and she plowed right into a mom and dad. She's getting sued beyond belief. So I think a lot of kids think getting drunk is not good."

Unlike Allison, who is a member of SADD (Students Against Drunk Driving), many girls and boys drink even when they don't want to, just to avoid looking like an outcast. "Many guys I know think that going out and getting drunk is the big thing," observes Gigi. "It makes them feel tough. They always talk about it. The girls, too, because it has a certain prestige. Lots of girls like to say they got drunk and a guy took advantage of them. They like to use it as a convenient excuse.

"There's a lot of peer pressure to drink. I'm just lucky that I'm outspoken and say what I think, do what I want. If my friends are talking about how drunk they got and think it's funny, I'll laugh with them but I won't do it. I guess some of them try to impress me with how much they drink and how much fun they have, but it doesn't sway me. I don't have any desire to. It's a moral reason. That's just the way I've been brought up, I guess, since my parents don't drink. But people accept it. I don't feel pressured at parties, but then I've never been to something really wild. If I ever feel out of place, I just carry around a soda or something."

Charlotte has a similar outlook. "Drinking is a big problem in our school. We have nothing else to do, so that's what we think up. I don't drink a lot because I'm really into basketball and I'm looking for a scholarship. I don't want to waste that. But there's so much pressure to conform! Sometimes people will say, 'Just hold this beer can and you'll be okay. No one will bother you that way.' Or I'll be at a party and feel I have to explain that I'm in basketball training right now so I can't drink. But if nothing's going on and I don't have an excuse, they'll push a little harder."

The pothead

Perhaps because girls are so conscious of the pressures to drink and be cool, they're intolerant of boys who seek manhood at the end of a roach clip or at the bottom of a Valium bottle. Types admired in the Sixties as avant-garde, hippies, or radicals, are called "burnouts" today. "The guy I just finished dating wasn't really my type," explains Bobbi. "He was just into more things than I could handle. Like drugs. Like pot. I really didn't know it at first, but when I found out I just didn't like the thought of it. It shocked me a bit. I mean I know a lot of people who do it but I just don't want to date them. It scares me. I also think he did more than pot, because he told me he took Valium a lot. He explained that he originally had a prescription for them, but that his mom had taken it away so he had to get them elsewhere. That didn't sound too good.

"He wasn't a druggie type of person but was easily manipulated by his friends. He lives with two big-time drug-doers and I think he just thought it was tough. But guys who do drugs just 'cause their friends do are stupid. They're weak in some way. My mom's twin brother has been in and out of rehabilitation centers because of drugs, because he was shooting up and tried to kill himself a couple of times. So I know what drugs can do to a person and to the people around him. It's not worth dating someone like that."

Marion watched a good friend sink slowly into the burnout sunset. "I had one close friend named Greg, who I grew up with. When we were two and three, we played together all the time and went to grade school together. But in junior high he got into drugs—coke, heroin, pot—you name it, he was into it. I could see him deteriorating. He was smart, very bright, but lost interest in his schoolwork. He had a lot of family problems too, but it was the drugs that changed his face. It really upset me because I cared about him. I don't even know what happened to him. Perhaps he dropped out of school. I don't know why any boy thinks drugs and liquor impress girls. I don't associate with that type of guy, because they can't accept that a girl likes them the way they are. I say if someone doesn't like you the way you are, don't lower yourself and change."

Curiously enough, according to the University of Michigan study, teen interest in all illicit drugs has diminished—the number of daily pot-smokers dropping drastically from an 11 percent peak in 1978 to 5.5 percent in 1983. And though the number of cocaine-users remains constant at 16 percent, it's more common in urban areas. "Drugs have never been widely accepted among teens," Michigan study director Johnston attests and speculates that the recent bad publicity given cocaine—Richard Pryor's free-basing incident that landed him in a hospital, and the speed-ball that killed John Belushi—has finally cracked its glamorous veneer. As

Helen says, drugs are a sure sign that a guy "is sizzling his brain and turning it to putty. A little is fun, but too much of anything is bad and some guys use it as a scapegoat. It's fine to sit there and notice the room spinning, but from nine to five every day it's not. They need to have a handle on it. Pot and cocaine are acceptable in my group but they're not considered 'cool.' Any drug is a waste of money." Or as one health-minded teen explains: "A lot of teenagers smoke pot and do coke but usually all drugs are considered stupid to take. They're not only bad for you but make you act very superficial."

The last tango with the Marlboro Man

Over half the girls I met say heavy cigarette smokers are a downer, often because kissing a boy who smokes is like "licking a dirty ashtray." Foul-smelling hair, clothes, and breath and nicotine-stained hands are romantically uninspiring as well. The University of Michigan study also finds that an increased concern about health, more militant non-smokers, and changing perceptions about smoking as "cool" have brought teen smoking, recently on the rise for girls, down a third since 1979. As for our perception of male smokers, instead of the Marlboro Man image, Johnston says girls say boys who smoke are less cool, tough, mature, sophisticated, independent, and secure than non-smokers. For that reason, 65 percent say they'd rather not date a smoker.

Smokers vs non-smokers

The *TeenAge* Relationships Survey shows that girls who smoke (29 percent overall; 49 percent among Supersonic Daters; and only 24 percent among Modern Traditionalists) are twice as tolerant of smoking and more lenient about other "fast-lane" behavior in boys they date as others, perhaps because they're more interested in looking "cool" (the reason many smokers start in the first place). They're also more likely to be attracted to cool, aloof guys who are a challenge, more prone to want an older boy, and more apt to judge a boy by his clothes than non-smokers. They're also twice as likely to be drinkers and drug experimenters.

The smokers in the survey are also more likely to be socially and sexually active. Sixty-eight percent are currently dating compared with only 56 percent of non-smokers) and many more have already asked a boy for a date, are not virgins, and feel premarital sex is fine. Interestingly enough, the smokers' group is more likely to complain they feel pressured into sexual contact by boys and sometimes admit they go further in sex than they'd like to. Rebels and rule-breakers maybe, but liberationists no. Smokers show an unexpected conservative streak as well and are less inclined than non-smokers to support a househusband! Drinkers (57 percent overall and highest among Supersonic Daters) present a similarly racy portrait, and are more likely than non-drinkers to smoke cigarettes and pot, and to have already asked a boy out. They are much more tolerant of religious differences, premarital sex, and boys with wild behavior.

Similarly, pot smokers (18 percent overall, 35 percent among Supersonic Daters) are more likely to drink, to smoke cigarettes, and to do cocaine or other drugs. They are also more likely to feel drugs are acceptable, and to give a boy with a wild partying nature a break. Sexually, they are much more liberal than non-pot-smokers and are less likely to be virgins, more likely to want to play the field before marriage, and often go further with sex than they want to.

Going for Mr. Straight

But would we date Mr. Straight? The answer from the *TeenAge* Relationships Survey is yes! Ninety percent of the girls said it wouldn't mean he was queer or square, and some even think "it's great if he hasn't submitted to all the peer pressure." But a few girls I interviewed disagree on the grounds that a straight guy would be rigid. "I wouldn't date Mr. Straight!" exclaims Marsha, "because he would be too pure if he'd never tried anything at least once! He'd be boring. He wouldn't want to be with my crowd that was drinking or doing drugs. Everyone has to try it at one point or another." Pamela, who doesn't over-indulge, agrees: "No, I wouldn't date Mr. Straight. He'd be too different. I've never met anyone like that. I wouldn't know how to act, especially if I wanted a drink. I like a guy who has some experience, but not a lot."

Cigarette Smokers vs. Non-Cigarette Smokers: Image Consciousness

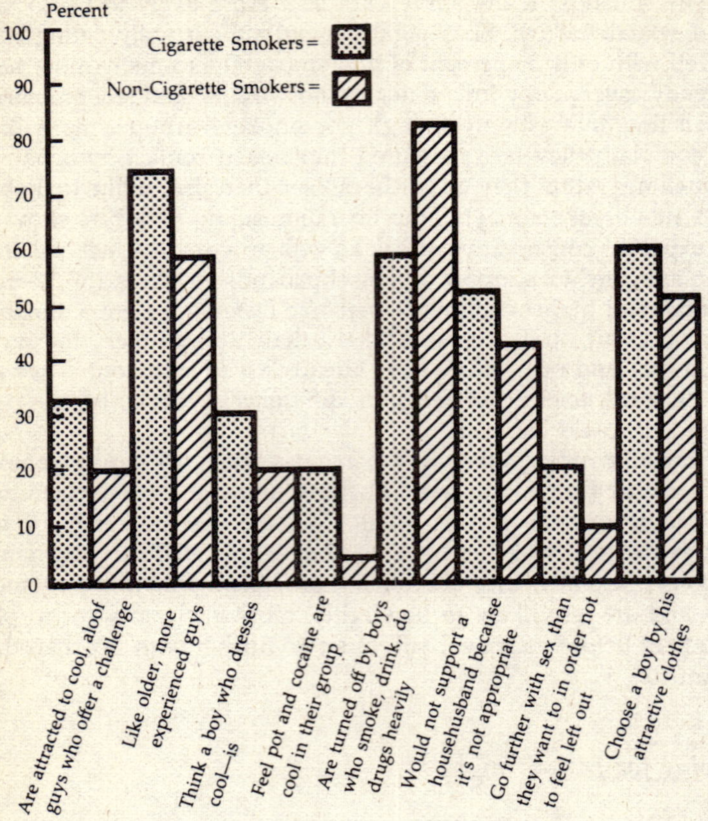

Cigarette smokers, 30% in total (49% among Super Sonic Daters) on The TeenAge *Relationships Survey, seem to be more concerned with image than non-smokers. Thirty-three percent of smokers are attracted to "cool, aloof" boys who offer a challenge while only 20% of non-smokers feel the same way; 31% think a boy who dresses "cool"—is, while only 20% of non-smokers agree. Not surprisingly, smokers are also attracted to older, more experienced boys by a difference of 74% to 58% and feel drugs like pot and cocaine are "cool" in their group by a difference of 20% to 4%. As part of the "cool" social image they cultivate themselves, only 59% of smokers say they are turned off by boys with wild behavior—those who smoke, drink and do drugs heavily—while 83% of others agree, and admit by a difference of 20% to 9% over non-smokers that they often go farther with sex than they really want to in order not to feel left out.*

Cigarette Smokers vs. Non-Cigarette Smokers: Who Are They?

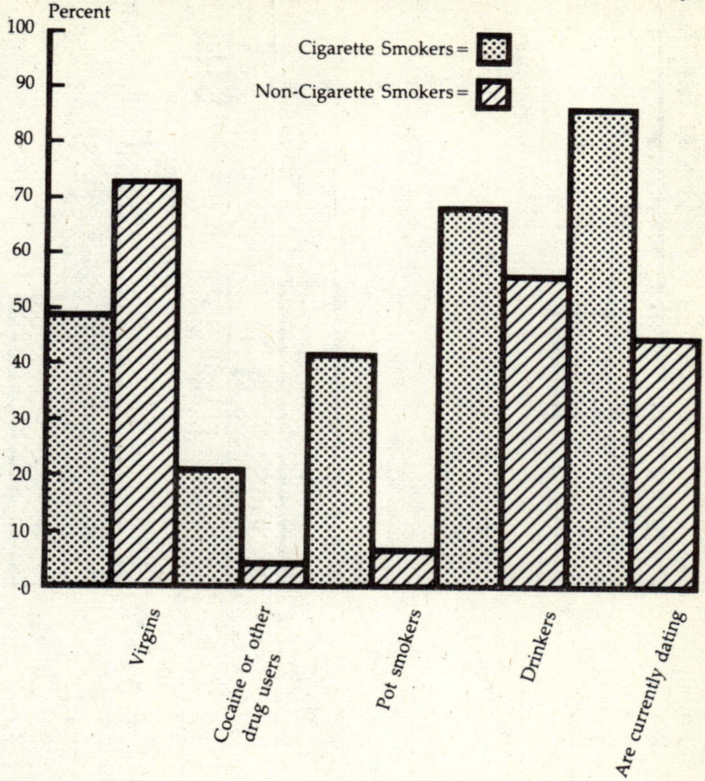

The TeenAge *Relationships Survey shows that cigarette smokers seem to be by nature more open to a racier lifestyle than non-cigarette smokers. For example, 68% of smokers date while only 56% of non-smokers do the same. And, probably because daters are more exposed to social pressure than non-daters, smokers are also more likely to have dabbled in recreational drugs: 42% of cigarette smokers smoke pot, compared with only 7% of non-cigarette smokers; and 21% of cigarette smokers have tried cocaine or other drugs, while only 4% of non-cigarette smokers have. Not surprisingly, cigarette smokers are also more likely to be drinkers—by a difference of 86% to 45%. And, they are more likely to have tried sex: only 49% of cigarette smokers are virgins compared with 73% of non-smokers.*

This, of course, does not imply that just because a girl smokes cigarettes she will try pot or cocaine or run out and lose her virginity. It merely shows that cigarette smokers, for whatever reason, seem to accept a more racy kind of social behavior than non-smokers.

Drinkers: Who Are They?

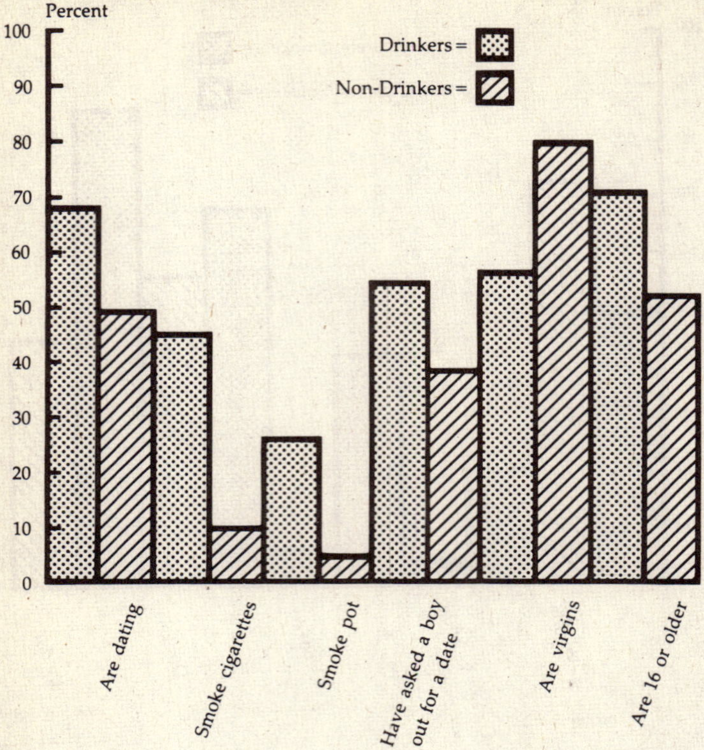

According to the TeenAge *Relationships Survey, drinkers, 57% of respondents, seem to have very different social habits and personalities than non-drinkers. For instance, 45% of drinkers smoke cigarettes but only 10% of non-drinkers smoke; 26% of drinkers smoke pot while only 5% of non-drinkers do the same. More drinkers seem to be dating as well, in this case by a margin of 68% to 49% and are more likely, by a lead of 54% to 38%, to have already asked a boy out. Perhaps because of more exposure to the dating scene in general, drinkers are also less likely to be virgins (56%) than non-drinkers (80%). And they tend to be older: 71% are age 16 or older compared to 53% of others. This does not mean, however, that girls who start drinking will suddenly become popular with boys, nor does it mean they will necessarily lose their virginity. It only suggests that drinkers have a more liberal attitude toward fast lane living, dating and experimentation than their non-drinking friends.*

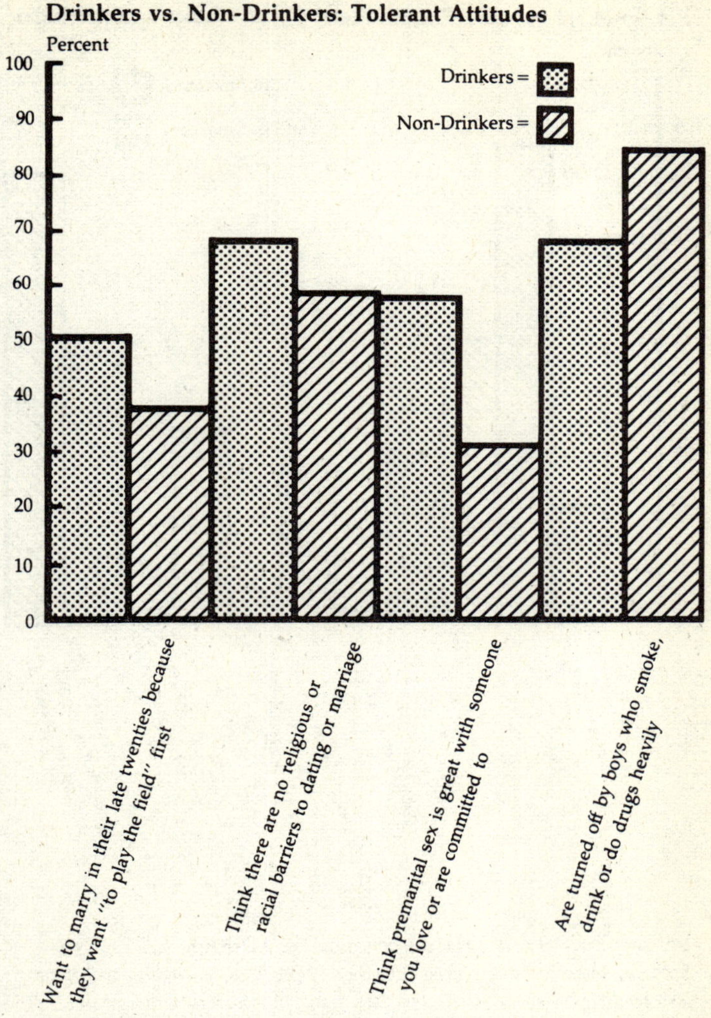

According to the TeenAge *Relationships Survey, drinkers are more tolerant than non-drinkers. For instance, only 69% of drinkers are turned off by a boy who smokes, drinks or does drugs heavily, while 85% of non-drinkers, who have more stringent rules to live by, are. And 69% of drinkers say there are no religious or racial barriers to dating or marriage, while only 59% of non-drinkers agree. Drinkers are also more liberal sexually, with 58% approving of premarital sex compared with only 32% of non-drinkers. And lastly, they are more apt, by a margin of 51% to 38% over non-drinkers, to want to "play the field" before tying the knot.*

Pot Smokers vs. Non-Pot Smokers: Social Habits and Attitudes

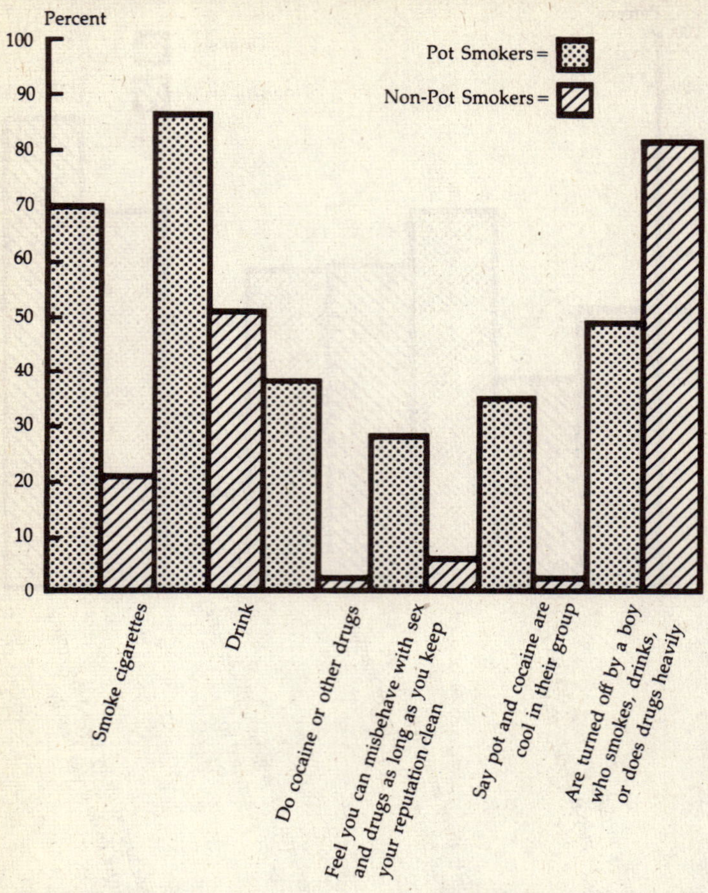

Pot smokers, 18% of those surveyed on the TeenAge *Relationships Survey, seem to have picked up other negative social habits and have less traditional social attitudes than non-pot smokers. For example, 70% of pot smokers also smoke cigarettes while only 21% of others do, and 86% of pot smokers drink while 51% of others do. Finally, 38% of pot smokers do cocaine or other drugs while only 3% of others do.*

Not surprisingly, pot smokers are more likely to feel that they can misbehave with sex and drugs as long as they keep their reputation clean by a margin of 28% to 6% over non pot smokers. And pot smokers are more tolerant of a boy with similar social behavior. Only 49% say they are turned off by a boy who smokes, drinks, or does drugs heavily, while 82% of others say the same.

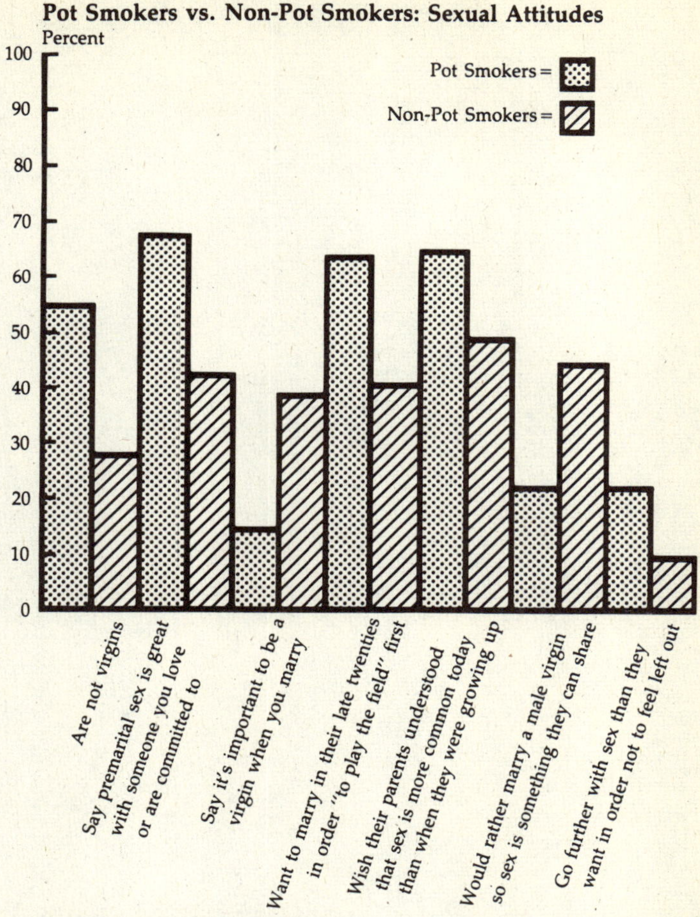

According to the TeenAge *Relationships Survey, pot smokers are more sexually active and liberal than non-pot smokers. For instance, 55% are not virgins while only 28% of non-pot smokers are not, and 68% say premarital sex is great with someone you love or are committed to, while only 43% of others feel the same way. Conversely, only 15% say it's important to be a virgin when you marry contrasted with 39% of others, and only 23% would like to marry a male virgin compared with 45% of others. Being a little more rebellious in nature, perhaps, pot smokers say by a margin of 64% to 41% over non-pot smokers that they would like to marry in their late twenties in order to "play the field first," and since pot smokers are more likely to be sexually active, 65% say they wish their parents understood that sex is more common today than when they were growing up compared with only 49% of others.*

Section Six

Dealing with Parents

37

Parents, Boys, and the Processes of Breaking Away

The teen years are a strange time, when we seem to be caught half-way between lifeless lumps of stone and beautiful sculptures bursting with energy. Sometimes it even feels as if we've been left alone in the studio while the artist takes a break, and we're caught with one leg, one arm, jutting out, trying to break away, trying to make a run for it. Yet at the same time we know we're really not free. Our parents are the sculptors and those with whom we have the best relationships are most willing at this stage to hand over the hammer and chisel and let us finish the masterpiece ourselves. It may be hard going, but the parent-teen relationships that evolve in this necessary change of command are very positive and rewarding.

Not surprisingly, mothers have the greatest impact on our dating habits and on the boys we eventually select. They act as a center of balance, a fulcrum against which we weigh old and new values, conventional and unconventional insights. But while we aim to please both parents by bringing home boys who meet their standards, we don't like to feel constrained by their demands; and though we like them to express interest, we don't want them to meddle; and though we want them to exercise a firm, confident hand in reining us in, we don't want them to pull the reins *too* tight. Maintaining this delicate balance during the breaking-away years is without doubt difficult, but it can make the difference between dating memories filled with joy and excitement, and those clouded by dread and misery.

"Mom's my best friend!"

Parents who score the highest marks from teens are those who convey above all else a sense of trust. They let us try out our new wings, yet are always there to catch us if we fall; boost our confidence, but don't praise us falsely. They never pass judgment about a boy we like—especially while we're dating him—and never try to impose their own generation's values on us. The happiest teen is the girl who knows that she can turn to her mom one day and say, "You know that guy I was dating? He was a creep!" and that her mother will say, "You're absolutely right!" instead of "I told you so."

Devon has just that sort of relationship. Though she hasn't officially dated much, she feels it's important that she and her parents see eye-to-eye about boys. "They don't impose on my dating, but their opinion has a lot to do with whom I see," she says. "I mean, if I bring a guy home and they like him, then I feel great. If they don't like him, I feel bad. I'll say, 'Hey, mom, did you like him?' She'll say, 'Oh, yeah, Dev.' Or, 'No, not really.' Though I like them to approve, they'd have to give me a pretty good reason to stop seeing someone. But anyway, they'd never tell me I couldn't date some guy, because they trust my judgment. I wouldn't go out with a real dip!" she laughs.

When they do comment, Devon continues, it's because "they see things that I don't, and when they give me a little insight I usually see it myself. Like once I was going with this guy Ricky and really liked him 'cause he was so good-looking—God, was he good-looking! I guess that's the reason I didn't see what a jerk he was! But when I brought him home my parents asked me if I realized how immature he was. I didn't. But once I started watching him I saw what a jerk he was. He was always picking on my little sister; nobody picks on my little sister! They see things like that faster than I do, because they know more."

Friendly, outspoken, confident, Devon, who attends a private Catholic girls' school in Florida, might be considered a little "straight" and "unsophisticated" by today's teen standards, but her relationship with her parents gives her another kind of confidence. "We talk about everything," she continues. "At the dinner table, if something comes up we'll talk about it for an hour. Or if I'm having problems we can sit down and discuss it after school. I recently went to visit colleges where all they did was go to five classes and get drunk for the rest of the day. I can't handle that, so I called dad and said, 'Dad, we're going to have to do some talking when you get home. You should hear the things they do here. If all schools are like this I'm going to have to get a job or go nuts!' He said, 'Okay, gotcha covered, kid.'

"My parents and I have an excellent relationship, we really do. I think I've been very lucky having parents like that. They're very—I can't say 'strict,' because I don't have a curfew—but then I don't stay out late enough for them to lose their trust in me."

And trust is the cornerstone of the best parent-daughter interactions. "My relationship with my parents is pretty easygoing," says Suzanne. "They just want to know the details of my dates—like where I'm going, what I'm doing, how I'll be getting home. Not the details of the relationship. They never get personal and ask prying questions. I don't think they worry about me either, because they know I have a head on my shoulders; they know I make decisions for myself, not because of friends."

And the best parents don't tell us their insights until he's long gone. "If my parents don't like who I'm dating they usually don't tell me until I'm not dating him anymore," says Isabella. "I like that 'cause I don't want to know his bad points ahead of time. After I broke up with Alfie my mom asked me if he was mean to me. Now that I'm dating one of his friends, she's always asking if Alfie is around. My dad tells me I shouldn't speak to him anymore. He never liked him because Alfie didn't treat me well, didn't care. Mom thought he didn't treat me like he wanted to date me a lot. And they were right. He was always nice and polite to my face, but really a jerk behind my back. He'd tell his friends things we did sexually. I never thought he'd be two-faced, but he was. I couldn't believe it! It was a bad sign that he was bragging;

it meant he only wanted sex so he could tell his friends about it."

Unfortunately, Isabella's relationship with them is not without some catches. "They trust me and let me do just about anything I want, but they won't let me go near alcohol. When I get back from a party my mom always asks if there was drinking and I always say no. It would be nice if she could understand that all kids drink, but she doesn't. She might have gone to drinking parties when she was in high school, but I'm not about to chance finding out because then she won't let me go. I don't go out and get wasted every night. That wouldn't be worth it. Then I'd have to sneak in and worry about getting caught. It's fun to drink sometimes, but I only do it when I'm sleeping at someone else's house."

Alexis also likes the way her parents manage to show concern without dictating to her. "They told me once that they didn't like my boyfriend because he didn't take me out enough. They like me to be spoiled. But they kept quiet until after the relationship was over and then said something. That was great, because then I could do whatever I liked and didn't have to worry, 'Maybe you shouldn't come over; my parents don't really like you.' My mom tries as hard as she can to like whoever I like, and I know that's not common. My best friend's mom doesn't like any of her boyfriends. She has to drive to my house to see them. She can't really go out on dates. I have to deliver his post cards and letters to her too, so her mom won't see them. I don't like mothers who run their girls' lives. They had their time, and I don't think they should have anything to do with ours."

Yet we do want their approval, especially if it's for the boy we're about to marry. "My mom didn't approve of my first boyfriend because she knew I could do better," says Marsha. "That guy was on drugs. Mom said she could tell by his actions that he did pot and speed, and made me be in at six every night. Once he did ask me to try speed! When I told her, she said she had known but wouldn't say. They love my present boyfriend and are very supportive. When my mom needs help in the house, she'll call him up and he'll come over. Mom even said we should get married. Now if I'm not in by midnight and haven't called, she knows I'm in good hands. She trusts me and it makes me feel good. I know other girls wish they could have a mother like her."

Even girls who aren't divulging their secrets to their parents like to know they could if they wanted to. "My parents don't interfere with my dating," says Jennifer. "At least not yet. They're really understanding, particularly my mom. I can't really talk to them about boys though. I really get uneasy when the subject comes up—not so much with my dad, but with my mom. My mother has had a lot of experience with guys though, so I think if I were to open up, she'd be able to relate to what I was going through."

Some even like knowing that they think exactly like their mothers. "My mom's pretty liberal-minded," says Helen. "We basically have the same feelings about guys. I haven't had that many experiences yet that I feel she would react differently to. The only difference is that she tells me I shouldn't be tied down to one guy and should try and experience other personality types. That's what she does, so she's probably right."

38

Parent/Teen Conflicts

If you talk to teens enough, you find a surprising amount of information comes belting forth about parents who are overly protective and refuse to let them fly, who refuse to believe in the importance of young love, or who try to push them into the kinds of relationships they wish they'd had as teens. Most culpable are mothers, who try to relive their own dating years through their daughters'. In some ways the parent-teen dance is as delicate as the gentle push-twist-pull of a champagne-cork extraction. Rush it or hesitate, and parents can end up with the whole bottle exploding right in their hands.

Rebels with a cause

What's most likely to cause an explosion? Lack of trust. For whatever reason, founded or unfounded, when parents don't give girls the green light to trust their own best instincts, they rebel. Such is the case of Colleen, a remarkably level-headed, clear-thinking individual who, though inclined to experiment, won't take unnecessary risks. Yet her parents, who tried to squelch her interfaith relationship (see Chapter 8), also try to keep her tied into their old value system, even though it's clear she's trying to develop one of her own. When she tried to share with them the new things she'd learned abroad in Denmark, she was stonewalled, almost alienated.

"I can't talk to my parents about any of the new things I learned during my year of life over there," she says sadly. "They've even said, 'We don't want to know what you did.' So I never came right out and said I had sex. But one night we were watching a movie together and during a sex scene between two people who weren't married I made a comment about how nice it would be to live together before marriage. They said, 'Where did you get that idea?' I felt like, 'Oh, no, I stuck my foot in it.'

"I'm not mad at them for not seeing my point of view because I know they love me so much that they're just trying to protect me. But I think they should just let me grow up, let me learn for myself. They had to learn for themselves, too. I just wish they'd step back a while because it seems like they want to make all my decisions—especially about where I should go to college—when that's really for me to do.

"They should also realize that even at their age there's a generation gap—especially with sex. We don't agree about marriage—or smoking either. Both of them smoke and I'm not allowed to—supposedly. While I was in Europe, forget it! I did what I wanted. I followed what my moral conscience said was right—not what they taught me. And I found that I liked it."

Colleen finds that most teens her age are like mercury—apply pressure on one end and you get an equal and opposite reaction on the other. "I guess I'm a rebeller," she confesses, "so the more they lean on me, the more I'll go the other way. I talked to my mom about it once—indirectly. We were at the kitchen table discussing the girl across the street, the sweetest girl in the neighborhood until she linked up with a strange crowd. Her mom was saying she couldn't understand what happened. I told her Bonnie had just gotten into a bad crowd. 'I told her not to do it,' her mother said. So I said, 'You know that we're going to do whatever we want, no matter what you say.' But she couldn't understand it. So I asked her if she wasn't ever a kid? 'Yes,' she said, 'but we got into an awful lot of trouble if we rebelled.' I told her that maybe our generation can just hide it better. Maybe we're just better liars. It's like riding a horse—if you pull the reins too tight, it's going to break free. If you leave them a little looser, it can go faster at its own speed. I think it's better that way. I don't think kids are naturally good, but by letting them go you can find out if they need restraint or not. I think an awful lot goes wrong if parents try to restrain you when you'd normally do something right.

"I'm not a bad kid. At least *I* don't think so. I can just imagine what would happen if a bad kid was told not to do something. She'd just keep doing it to get attention. I've given in a lot of times to their pressure. I do an awful lot of housework. Every time my boyfriend comes over he gets insane because I'm ironing, washing, or cooking dinner. He says, 'That's your mother's job' 'cause that's the way it is in his house. But my mom's been working since I can remember. And I have an eight-year-old brother. I was nine when he was born and used to pick him up from nursery school. My friends used to call me 'Little Mother.' I don't mind helping out, but other times I get mad and ask, 'Why did they do this to me when I was so young, and I could have gone out and had fun with my boyfriend?' And that makes me feel like rebelling, too."

Some girls rebel by dating a boy their parents reject—even if deep down inside they don't like him either. "My parents are very selective about who I date," says Dale, a beefy kind of girl with stringy blonde hair, jeans, a sweater, and beige espadrilles that she flicks nervously on and off her heel as we talk (she comes from one of the wealthiest families in the community). "The boys have to be the right age and of the right background. I get mad at them for screening my dates. I don't talk to them for days. I say, 'I can't wait to get out of this house!' They say, 'We'll ground you for a month.' But they only did that once. The guy I see now never finished high school and his name appeared recently in the newspaper for a robbery. His friend was accused of robbing a store and he was implicated. They told me not to see him but I do anyway. We meet secretly at the movies, the roller rink, go out to eat at prearranged places. He gets upset that he can't be seen with me in public. He would really like to pick me up but he can't. So we talk on the phone. His name's going to be cleared in December, I know. But if he really did rob the store with his friend, I won't go out with him. Even now I won't be with him alone. I meet him with other friends around in case he could be dangerous. I just like him 'cause he's fun."

Like Colleen, Dale rebels because she feels her parents don't trust her enough. "I wish my parents would give me more responsibility in who I date, where I go, and what time I get in, because I think I have good judgment," she says. "If they'd just let me try something new sometimes it would help. I'm not allowed to go to parties at all, but I do it anyway and don't come home drunk. I'm the first child, so they're the most cautious with me. Most kids, though, if you say no, will do it anyway. I don't look for something that they'll disapprove of, but if something comes up, there's a 75 percent chance I'll do it anyway."

Even worse are parents who make us feel we have to pick a boy to suit their personal tastes. Two sisters I met complained independently of a strangulating mother, who didn't want them to talk to me because the answers on the questionnaire were "too prying." They told her they were going to a church bazaar, saw me anyway, and gave some very revealing insights into the sort of mother who won't let go. "My mom would probably tease me if I'd told her about any of my crushes, so I haven't and won't," says Pamela. "I don't like to bring dates to the house for that reason. She doesn't tease my sisters because they're older, but to me she'll always say there's something she doesn't like about the boy I'm seeing. She says this one's too short, or that one's not reliable, or that one's just no good. I don't want to hear it if I like him! It makes me feel I constantly have to find someone good enough for her, when we really have different tastes in boys. I can't go out with superjocks like she wants me to, because I don't relate to them. I won't go against her wishes though, unless I really, really like the guy."

Her older sister, Barbara, who has talked happily up until now about her upcoming marriage, reveals that a bad family situation makes her feel pushed into it. "If my mother doesn't like a boy, I won't be able to go out with him," she begins. "She'll say, 'Be home at twelve,' and if I'm home at twelve-fifteen without calling she'll call me irresponsible. My friend died last year, but my mom thinks her boyfriend did it. If one of his friends calls me up, she'll tell me I can't see him. She associates people with their friends. When I break up with a guy, she'll talk about him forever and pick out every flaw he has. 'You shouldn't feel sorry,' she'll say. 'He's not like all the other guys out there.' Then she'll take me out to eat and make me not feel so bad.

"A guy also has to go in and shake hands with her and say, 'Hi. I'm Joe Shmo,' or she won't let me go out with him. I'm nineteen and dating this guy Richard for one year and she still makes him pick me up!

"I feel she trusts me but wish she'd understand that there are so many different guys out there that I'd like to try out. She should respect the way I feel. I only make fifty dollars a week, and so she pays for my car and insurance and I live at home. She said she'd pay for college and the car or just an apartment, but that's it. I have to be independent then or get a job or get married.

"When she yells it gets on my nerves. I say, 'Mom, you're forcing me to get married to get out of this house.' I never really wanted to get serious at this point in my life. I think I'm too young. I'm not really interested in one guy, just sick of the dating scene and her hassles."

Another common problem is parents pressuring teens to have more or fewer boyfriends than they already have. "I wish my mother would realize that if I wanted a steady boyfriend right now I would have one," says Christy. "But it's my senior year and I don't want to be held down. She thinks that every teenage girl should spend all of her time with a boy." Or: "My mother thinks I'm too young to have a serious relationship with one guy," says Ruth. "She wants me to be free, with no one cornering me. So I never feel I'm able to do what I want. She should understand that just because I date one guy it doesn't mean I'm going to marry him! I'm old enough to make the proper judgment and don't need her to hold my hand."

Conflicts in social values are a big point of friction: "My mother always thinks that every guy who calls is someone I like or who likes me," says Casey. "She seems to think that guys are just boyfriends and not friends. She gets all silly about it. Now that guys my age are getting deeper voices, she thinks they're men calling me. She always tries to impose her old values on me. When she goes away for weekends she says, 'Don't have your little boyfriends over!' And then I go ahead and do it anyway. At this age parents should realize that their girls are going to do it anyway. She says it too pejoratively.

"If I got pregnant," she continues, "I wouldn't go to her 'cause I can imagine the kind of looks she'd give me or what she'd say. She'd make me feel ashamed. She should understand that sex is more common these days. That sounds like a justification, I know, but really that's the way it is. If she'd just understand that I may not follow her value system, it would be easier."

In actuality, Casey would like to communicate with her mother about many aspects of dating but finds that all the roads have been blocked by estrangement. "I would like to talk to her about boys," she says wistfully. "We live in the same house but can't communicate. It's like living with a stranger. It would be easier for me to communicate with guys too, if she hadn't made such a big deal about the difference between the sexes. She made it sound like we're two different unapproachable kinds of beings. She says you can't be in a room with a boy without thinking about certain things."

Pamela agrees: "I wish my mother understood that boys and girls can be friends and that every time a boy takes me out it's not a date but just two friends getting together. Lots of boys can be friends if you treat them like girlfriends and just talk to them. She doesn't understand it. That's how I like it though. I'd rather be friends with guys than go out on dates. When I'm not on a formal date, I feel more comfortable."

But then amidst all the parents who take our relationships too seriously are those who don't take them seriously enough. "My dad thinks I'm too young to be going out with guys," says Noel, fifteen. "I'm never comfortable talking about boys with my parents. If I had a young mother I would. But she's forty-two. My aunt is twenty-eight and I love talking to her. My dad has forgotten what it's like. I don't know why they act the way they do. I never say, 'I'm going out with a boy.' I just say I'm going out with friends. Then they don't mind when I go out. When my sister began dating they made such a big deal about it and I hated it. They teased her about boys and I won't accept that at all."

Heidi has a similar gripe. "I want my parents to know that in this day and age people can fall in love at my age," says the fourteen-year-old. "They think that when I go out with a guy I'm just getting together. I love them dearly, but I could never tell them some of the things I've done; it would make me feel too awful. I have one friend though, who can tell her mom anything.

She caught us drinking once because someone threw up on her oriental rug. Before her mom even walked into the house and could smell it, Joanne said, 'Mom, we've been drinking . . .'

"I couldn't be open like that because I don't know how my parents would react. I think they'd be worried about me if they knew what I did. They feel I'm little innocent Heidi, because I'm the youngest. I look at them and think, 'If they only knew that I went to a party last month and really got drunk . . .' And then I feel guilty. Like I shouldn't be doing that."

But the biggest complaint of all is that parents don't understand the sex-and-drug culture of today. "I don't talk to my parents about boys," says Gigi. "I think I could, but I just don't. I talk to my friends. I guess I think my parents won't understand how I feel, that they'd be shocked at some of the things I do. I don't know if they just think you hold hands on a date or what. I wish they understood that sex is more common today. They're not old-fashioned, but they think it doesn't go on at my school. It's not as important as it is in big cities. But it happens just as much 'cause we don't have that much to do."

"I love/I hate strict parents"

One kink in the parent-daughter relationship is the ambivalent attitude toward strict parents. There were a startling number of teens who criticized their parents for being unreasonably strict about dating rules and regulations when they were younger, yet say they're glad now that they exercised such control. It's as if some of us are angry and happy at the same time to have someone caring enough to hold on tightly, even if it makes us scream, wince, yell in agony. These girls fall into a special category though, because they fear that if let loose they really would have had no sexual self-control—something they might well have regretted later.

"I couldn't officially date until I was sixteen," says Vanessa. "Then I had to be in at eleven o'clock. My parents were real strict and I hated it. But I'm glad they did it. I look at friends of mine and they're wild sexually, so I'm glad my parents didn't let that happen to me. I thought at the time I hated them. I cried all the time 'cause I couldn't go out. It didn't help that the first love of my life was pressuring me to go out—so we dated unofficially until I was a junior. I'd stay at my friend's house for the night and sneak out to see him. I don't think I was rebelling; I just wanted to see him. He was also dating someone else, another cheerleader, so it was a big rivalry. He was cute, not gorgeous, but very tall with sandy blond hair, glasses, and great clothes."

Ginger says her parents' strict rules kept her from becoming a sexual maniac. "My parents understand everything. I don't wish my dad had understood the sex thing when I was younger though. If he'd said, 'Go ahead and stay out till one in the morning, screw anybody you like,' I would have done it and wouldn't have worried about letting them down. But I would have been unhappy now, because I don't think it's right to go to bed with a lot of guys. I like the way I turned out." Jean agrees: "I'm glad my parents were strict when I was in junior high. I don't know what would have happened to me if I'd been allowed to carouse the way I wanted to. I might have gotten in trouble. I mean, I'd lived an isolated life until then. I didn't even know what a hard-on was until I was a freshman. I'm glad they were strict, even though I cried many nights away 'cause I had to be in early."

39

The Irony of Change

So what exactly would we like most to change about the dating system? First, slow the pace of relationships, make them more casual and friendly, not so serious, says girl after girl. "I'd like to see people go out with more than one person," says Janice. "Your teenage years are a kind of preparation, a way to get to know how different boys act in a relationship. It's like testing the waters. But where I live you're automatically going steady if you like each other. A lot of people get too serious just because of that." Kendal agrees. "It may be because I live in a small town, but it seems like if you date one guy no one else will ask you out at that time. I wish dating didn't have to be such a serious thing. There's nothing wrong with wanting to go out and have a nice time. Society and television have misled guys into thinking you have to jump right into romantic involvement."

Others would like to see the old stereotype of the "dumb broad" banished. "I hate it when girls lower themselves by making themselves look more stupid so guys look better," exclaims Pamela. "Like when a boy asks a question about a sport and they pretend they don't know the answer even if they do. I could never put myself in that position. I feel it should be total equality. I think most guys feel better too when girls act on their level, because then they can communicate with them; then the boy doesn't have to do all the talking. Girls don't learn to act dumb from parents, they pick it up in junior high from all the sex typing. It's subtle and people don't talk about it out loud, but girls get the message. They comply 'cause they're afraid of losing their boyfriends." Marion agrees: "My friend was the worst about acting dumb around guys. She did a Marilyn Monroe act every time a boy came up to her! I finally had to say, 'How can you do that; is it worth it?' "

But the most votes go to being more assertive. "I really like the fact that girls have recently started asking boys out," says Athena. "I think the boys like it, too. Then we're free to make a choice and don't have to sit there waiting and trying to beautify ourselves until that one guy asks us out. If we really want someone we can go for it. Once I decided to ask a guy out and just called him up. He sounded really surprised because he didn't expect it, but he told me later he was thinking of asking me to the same dance. So at least he wasn't saying, 'Oh, sick, sympathy, I guess I'll say yes just for the heck of it.' We had a good time and got along well. I paid for everything that night, and it felt weird because I'd never done it and wasn't sure how everything worked. It was a good change of roles for me though, 'cause now I know how guys feel dishing out money all the time. It's a big step to decide if they like a girl enough to spend all that money on her."

Devon agrees: "I don't see why guys have to ask girls out. I don't think the responsibility should be put on them. Women's lib has made a big change. If women work and have money, then why can't they ask boys out? It will have to change eventually. I'm positive. I don't know if it'll get to be like the television ads, where the girl just picks up the phone and calls a guy, but it might."

Still others want to tear apart the fabric of the entire social system."I'd change the pressure to go to bed," says Ginger. "There's one guy I've been dating here, and I wasn't with him for five minutes when he had his hands all over me. I wanted to tell him to get away. It was ridiculous. Pressuring sex is so stupid. It's not the only thing in the world. It was ridiculous to have all those repressed sexual feelings back in the Fifties, and openness is really good but now it's too much.

"I'd also like to get rid of the labels," she continues. "It's crazy, I know. I use labels too and I hate it. But I'd like guys to slow down and look at personalities. They seem just to date bodies. If a guy sees a girl who's relatively cute but not gorgeous, he won't go out with her, even if she's the neatest person in the world. That's crazy not to date somebody because they're not as terrific-looking as you are."

Noel agrees: "I'd change the looks factor. I'd make people understand it's not so important to be beautiful, social, to climb to the top of the social ladder. In New York it's especially exaggerated. I go to some other places and girls in ninth grade still have hair with a middle part and barrettes! They don't wear makeup yet, or else they think it's cool when they do. Everyone I know is so concerned with being social and looking much older than they are that I just can't stand it."

Revolution? Not quite. The majority of girls today seem quite content with the dating system as it is. A few are trying to push back the tide of male chauvinism, and more and more are looking for new ways to "be themselves" with boys, to close the teenage gender gap. Almost all females are looking for independence, room to date around, ways to make *their* likes and dislikes known.

And yet the kind of changes we say we want are riddled with contradictions. Some of us want parents to be more understanding of the new sexual mores; others want to erase the pressure to have sex. Some want a place to fit in, a label to hang their hat on; many want to cut away the confining molds of gossipy labels and stereotypes. Change in the teenage years is not unlike that in any other years—it's something a lot of us talk about but few of us actually do anything about.

APPENDIX I

The TeenAge *Relationships Survey*

Instructions: These are statements taken from girls just like you. Please read each one carefully and decide how much you agree or disagree with each one. You may agree with all of them, none of them, or feel indifferent about them. Be as honest as possible. Place a letter in front of each one. Remember this is an opinion poll—**There are no right or wrong answers.**

I. Choose the letter which best describes your feelings about the following statements:

A. Agree strongly C. Not sure E. Disagree strongly
B. Agree somewhat D. Disagree somewhat

_____ 1. I want a career (a job) because I want to be able to support myself in case of divorce.

_____ 2. A boy must have manners and be polite in order to make a good impression on my parents.

_____ 3. I wouldn't date a guy who smoked cigarettes because I would feel pressured to smoke, too.

_____ 4. I like my boyfriend to flirt with other girls; it shows he likes to have fun.

_____ 5. Humor is a cover-up for feeling uncomfortable with a girl.

_____ 6. I like a guy who is not a great "brain" but has a "good head" on his shoulders.

_____ 7. I'm attracted to cool, aloof guys because they're more of a challenge.

_____ 8. I like older boys because they're more mature, responsible, experienced.

_____ 9. It would be nice to go out with an intelligent guy because I want to marry someone who will be successful.

_____ 10. Money isn't that important for a date; if I really love someone who's poor, I won't say no.

_____ 11. I like to go out with athletes because I'm into sports myself.

_____ 12. Flirts get on my nerves; when they pay more attention to other girls it makes me feel like I'm being ignored or put down.

_____ 13. I'm not prejudiced, but I might feel uncomfortable dating or marrying someone of a different race.

_____ 14. I like a boy who sends me flowers, picks me up for a date, and opens doors, because I love to be pampered and flattered.

_____ 15. It's not embarrassing and unromantic to ask a boy out for the first date.

_____ 16. If a good-looking boy has a bad personality, I'll hang in there anyway for his looks.

_____ 17. A good sense of humor sets a relaxed atmosphere and makes problems easier to deal with.

_____ 18. If a boy asks me out, I'm his responsibility and he should pay.

_____ 19. I don't like to hang around guys with greasy hair, bad breath, or poor grooming, because they embarrass me.

_____ 20. I would like to date the captain of the football team.

_____ 21. A girl can ask for the first date; things are pretty liberated today.

_____ 22. I like a guy I date to have money because I like to have a good time and get great presents.

_____ 23. If a boy dresses cool—I think he is.

_____ 24. My friends pressure me to judge a boy by his looks.

_____ 25. I want the guy I marry to have a lot of money.

_____ 26. There are no religious barriers in dating or marriage because love counts more.

_____ 27. I'd date a guy who wasn't good-looking if his personality was great.

_____ 28. I'm not attracted to younger boys because girls mature faster.

_____ 29. A boy should make the first moves with kissing or making out because a girl who does will be called a "sleaze."

_____ 30. I want to be a housewife.

_____ 31. I wish my parents understood that sex is more common today than when they were growing up.

_____ 32. I don't like a guy who dresses terribly because it says he doesn't care about his self-image.

_____ 33. Group dates make me feel more comfortable; they get rid of the tension of being with boys.

_____ 34. I might ask a boy to the movies but never to "go steady."

_____ 35. I like splitting the cost of a date: it makes me feel independent.

_____ 36. I'd rather marry a man who's a virgin so sex will be something we share.

_____ 37. Macho behavior is neat because it shows a boy is in control and manly.

_____ 38. No girl is a virgin when she marries anymore.

_____ 39. Pot and cocaine are cool in my group.

_____ 40. A boy should make the first moves because I'd rather be the one to say "no."

_____ 41. I want a career that will make the most of my education.

_____ 42. There's no such thing as peer pressure when it comes to sex, drugs, and drinking.

_____ 43. I've often felt pressured into sexual contact by the boy I'm with because I don't know how to say "no."

_____ 44. Premarital sex is great with someone you love or are committed to.

_____ 45. It doesn't bother me if a boy smokes cigarettes.

_____ 46. A woman should put taking care of her kids and a home before a job or a career.

_____ 47. I still don't know enough about birth control to make an intelligent decision about sex.

_____ 48. It's important to be a virgin when you marry.

_____ 49. A conceited boy is not insecure.

_____ 50. Sexual behavior is acceptable at my age because sex is fun.

_____ 51. If a girl asks a boy out, she should pay.

_____ 52. A boy who drinks, smokes or does drugs heavily turns me off because it says he can't handle himself and needs to be cool to have more friends.

_____ 53. I wish I could talk to my parents about sex and birth control but that just isn't possible.

_____ 54. I wouldn't support a househusband because it's not appropriate; a man who marries should be prepared to work.

_____ 55. I would date a boy who never smoked, drank, or did drugs; it doesn't mean he's stupid or square.

_____ 56. I want to marry in my late twenties because I want to "play the field" first.

_____ 57. I would be willing to support a househusband if he could handle it.

_____ 58. I go further in sex than I feel comfortable with in order to feel experienced and not left out.

_____ 59. I want to marry in my late twenties because I want to work on my career first.

_____ 60. You can misbehave as much as you want with sex and drugs as long as you keep your reputation clean.

_____ 61. The thing I hate most about the dating system is that everybody dates just one person forever; there should be more dating "around."

II. Choose the answer that best describes yourself:

_____ 62. Are you currently dating? (1) ☐yes (2) ☐no

_____ 63. Are you dating just one boy? (1) ☐yes (2) ☐no

_____ 64. Do you smoke cigarettes? (1) ☐often (2) ☐sometimes (3) ☐never

_____ 65. Do you drink? (1) ☐often (2) ☐sometimes (3) ☐never

_____ 66. Do you smoke marijuana? (1) ☐often (2) ☐sometimes (3) ☐never

_____ 67. Do you do cocaine or other drugs? (1) ☐often (2) ☐sometimes (3) ☐never

_____ 68. Do you plan to ever get married? (1) ☐yes (2) ☐not sure (3) ☐never

_____ 69. At what age do you plan to marry? (1) ☐15–20 (2) ☐25–30 (3) ☐over 30 (4) ☐not sure

_____ 70. Do you want to have children? (1) □yes (2) □not sure (3) □no

_____ 71. Do you plan to work if you're married? (1) □yes (2) □not sure (3) □no

_____ 72. Who do you turn to for most of your advice on boys?
(1) □mother (4) □books (7) □religious leaders
(2) □father (5) □magazines (8) □other (explain) _____
(3) □friends (6) □teachers

_____ 73. Have you ever had a formal sex education course in school? (1) □yes (2) □no

_____ 74. Have you ever asked a boy out for a date? (1) □yes (2) □no

_____ 75. Would you like to? (1) □yes (2) □no

_____ 76. Are you a virgin? (1) □yes (2) □no

III. Choose the letter which best fits your feelings about the following qualities a boy must have:

A. Very important
B. Somewhat important
C. Not sure
D. Somewhat unimportant
E. Completely unimportant

_____ 77. Manners/politeness

_____ 78. Conversational ability

_____ 79. A flirtatious nature

_____ 80. A sense of humor

_____ 81. Warmth and sensitivity

_____ 82. Intelligence

_____ 83. Athletic ability

_____ 84. The same race

_____ 85. The same religion

_____ 86. The same age

_____ 87. A romantic nature: treating me like a lady (opening doors, bringing flowers)

_____ 88. Good grooming

_____ 89. Money

_____ 90. Attractive clothes

_____ 91. Good physical looks

_____ 92. Self-confidence

_____ 93. Dependability

_____ 94. Success-oriented

IV. Please answer the following questions about yourself:

_____ 95. How old are you?

(1) □12	(4) □15	(7) □18
(2) □13	(5) □16	(8) □19
(3) □14	(6) □17	(9) □over 19

_____ 96. What grade are you in?

(1) □8th or lower	(4) □11th
(2) □9th	(5) □12th
(3) □10th	(6) □other

_____ 97. What kind of school do you attend?

(1) □public	(3) □private Christian
(2) □private nonsectarian	(4) □private sectarian (other)

_____ 98. What state do you live in?_____________________________

_____ 99. How big is your town? (Please estimate if you don't know)

(1) □less than 1,000	(4) □31,000–50,000
(2) □1,000–10,000	(5) □51,000–100,000
(3) □11,000–30,000	(6) □more than 100,000

_____100. Are you willing to talk to the author of this book about these topics? This is entirely optional, and all responses will be kept strictly confidential.

APPENDIX II

The TeenAge *Relationships Survey Results*

Survey questions	ALL GIRLS Result	Percent	STRONG INDIVIDUALISTS Result	Percent	20TH-CENTURY FAST TRACKERS Result	Percent	MODERN TRADITIONALISTS Result	Percent	SWEET SOUTHERN BELLES Result	Percent	SUPERSONIC DATERS Result	Percent
1. I want a career (a job) because I want to be able to support myself in case of divorce.	(Of total 1006)		(Of total 493)		(Of total 163)		(Of total 76)		(Of total 103)		(Of total 171)	
No answer	3	.3	2	.4	1	.6	0	.0	0	.0	0	.0
A. Agree strongly	324	32.2	156	31.7	47	28.8	30	39.5	30	29.1	61	35.6
B. Agree somewhat	321	31.9	155	31.4	41	25.1	23	30.3	43	41.8	59	34.5
C. Not sure	78	7.8	45	9.1	13	8.0	1	1.3	6	5.8	13	7.6
D. Disagree somewhat	143	14.2	63	12.8	27	16.6	13	17.1	17	16.5	23	13.5
E. Disagree strongly	137	13.6	72	14.6	34	20.9	9	11.8	7	6.8	15	8.8
2. A boy must have manners and be polite in order to make a good impression on my parents.												
No answer	1	.1	1	.2	0	.0	0	.0	0	.0	0	.0
A. Agree strongly	464	46.1	216	43.8	61	37.4	51	67.2	62	60.2	74	43.3
B. Agree somewhat	401	39.8	204	41.4	71	43.6	19	25.0	35	34.0	72	42.1
C. Not sure	65	6.5	40	8.1	14	8.6	3	3.9	4	3.9	4	2.3
D. Disagree somewhat	61	6.1	23	4.7	15	9.2	3	3.9	2	1.9	18	10.5
E. Disagree strongly	14	1.4	9	1.8	2	1.2	0	.0	0	.0	3	1.8
3. I wouldn't date a guy who smoked cigarettes because I would feel pressured to smoke, too.												
No answer	1	.1	1	.2	0	.0	0	.0	0	.0	0	.0
A. Agree strongly	82	8.2	39	7.9	7	4.3	14	18.4	14	13.6	8	4.7
B. Agree somewhat	93	9.2	57	11.6	14	8.6	5	6.6	13	12.6	4	2.3

The TeenAge *Relationships Survey Results (continued)*

Survey questions	ALL GIRLS Result	Percent	STRONG INDIVIDUALISTS Result	Percent	20TH-CENTURY FAST TRACKERS Result	Percent	MODERN TRADITIONALISTS Result	Percent	SWEET SOUTHERN BELLES Result	Percent	SUPERSONIC DATERS Result	Percent
C. Not sure	106	10.5	59	12.0	15	9.2	9	11.8	10	9.7	13	7.6
D. Disagree somewhat	242	24.1	114	23.1	45	27.6	17	22.4	29	28.1	37	21.6
E. Disagree strongly	482	47.9	223	45.2	82	50.3	31	40.8	37	36.0	109	63.8
4. I like my boyfriend to flirt with other girls; it shows he likes to have fun.												
No answer	1	.0	1	.2	0	.0	0	.0	0	.0	0	.0
A. Agree strongly	16	1.6	6	1.2	2	1.2	2	2.6	3	2.9	3	1.8
B. Agree somewhat	34	3.4	16	3.2	10	6.1	2	2.6	4	3.9	2	1.1
C. Not sure	80	8.0	42	8.5	13	8.0	3	3.9	5	4.9	17	9.9
D. Disagree somewhat	222	22.1	112	22.7	44	27.0	16	21.1	16	15.5	34	19.9
E. Disagree strongly	653	64.9	316	64.2	94	57.7	53	69.8	75	72.8	115	67.3
5. Humor is a cover-up for feeling uncomfortable with a girl.												
No answer	0	.0	0	.0	0	.0	0	.0	0	.0	0	.0
A. Agree strongly	51	5.1	28	5.7	9	5.5	2	2.6	6	5.8	6	3.5
B. Agree somewhat	182	18.1	95	19.3	24	14.7	19	25.0	17	16.5	27	15.8
C. Not sure	269	26.7	152	30.9	17	10.4	21	27.6	32	31.1	47	27.5
D. Disagree somewhat	267	26.5	115	23.3	54	33.2	22	29.0	30	29.1	46	26.9
E. Disagree strongly	237	23.6	103	20.9	59	36.2	12	15.8	18	17.5	45	26.3
6. I like a guy who is not a great "brain" but has a "good head" on his shoulders.												
No answer	1	.1	1	.2	0	.0	0	.0	0	.0	0	.0
A. Agree strongly	446	44.3	212	43.1	65	39.9	41	54.0	57	55.3	71	41.5
B. Agree somewhat	381	37.9	189	38.3	63	38.7	26	34.2	35	34.0	68	39.8
C. Not sure	78	7.7	45	9.1	7	4.3	6	7.9	7	6.8	13	7.6
D. Disagree somewhat	79	7.9	35	7.1	23	14.1	1	1.3	3	2.9	17	9.9
E. Disagree strongly	21	2.1	11	2.2	5	3.0	2	2.6	1	1.0	2	1.2

Survey questions	ALL GIRLS Result	ALL GIRLS Percent	STRONG INDIVIDUALISTS Result	STRONG INDIVIDUALISTS Percent	20TH-CENTURY FAST TRACKERS Result	20TH-CENTURY FAST TRACKERS Percent	MODERN TRADITIONALISTS Result	MODERN TRADITIONALISTS Percent	SWEET SOUTHERN BELLES Result	SWEET SOUTHERN BELLES Percent	SUPERSONIC DATERS Result	SUPERSONIC DATERS Percent
7. I'm attracted to cool, aloof guys because they're more of a challenge.												
No answer	1	.1	1	.2	0	.0	0	.0	0	.0	0	.0
A. Agree strongly	57	5.7	24	4.9	3	1.8	4	5.3	12	11.7	14	8.2
B. Agree somewhat	181	18.0	96	19.5	18	11.0	12	15.8	19	18.4	36	21.1
C. Not sure	226	22.5	112	22.7	34	20.9	17	22.4	24	23.3	39	22.8
D. Disagree somewhat	294	29.2	137	27.8	57	35.0	26	34.2	23	22.3	51	29.8
E. Disagree strongly	247	24.5	123	24.9	51	31.3	17	22.3	25	24.3	31	18.1
8. I like older boys because they're more mature, responsible, experienced.												
No answer	3	.3	2	.4	1	.6	0	.0	0	.0	0	.0
A. Agree strongly	250	24.9	114	23.1	23	14.1	17	22.4	30	29.1	66	38.6
B. Agree somewhat	384	38.1	179	36.4	67	41.1	32	42.2	48	46.6	58	33.9
C. Not sure	148	14.7	82	16.6	20	12.3	9	11.8	15	14.6	22	12.9
D. Disagree somewhat	153	15.2	79	16.0	36	22.1	15	19.7	7	6.8	16	9.4
E. Disagree strongly	68	6.8	37	7.5	16	9.8	3	3.9	3	2.9	9	5.2
9. It would be nice to go out with an intelligent guy because I want to marry someone who will be successful.												
No answer	4	.4	3	.6	1	.6	0	.0	0	.0	0	.0
A. Agree strongly	296	29.4	142	28.8	36	22.1	33	43.5	45	43.7	40	23.4
B. Agree somewhat	409	40.7	212	43.0	56	34.4	28	36.8	43	41.8	70	40.9
C. Not sure	128	12.7	71	14.4	21	12.9	5	6.6	7	6.8	24	14.0
D. Disagree somewhat	116	11.5	41	8.3	33	20.2	8	10.5	6	5.8	28	16.4
E. Disagree strongly	53	5.3	24	4.9	16	9.8	2	2.6	2	1.9	9	5.3
10. Money isn't that important for a date; if I really love someone who's poor, I won't say no.												
No answer	3	.3	2	.4	1	.6	0	.0	0	.0	0	.0
A. Agree strongly	593	58.9	275	55.8	119	73.1	45	59.2	54	52.4	100	58.5

The TeenAge *Relationships Survey Results (continued)*

Survey questions	ALL GIRLS Result	Percent	STRONG INDIVIDUALISTS Result	Percent	20TH-CENTURY FAST TRACKERS Result	Percent	MODERN TRADITIONALISTS Result	Percent	SWEET SOUTHERN BELLES Result	Percent	SUPERSONIC DATERS Result	Percent
B. Agree somewhat	227	22.6	105	21.3	28	17.2	18	23.7	35	34.0	41	24.0
C. Not sure	112	11.1	68	13.8	10	6.1	5	6.5	8	7.8	21	12.3
D. Disagree somewhat	40	4.0	28	5.7	2	1.2	4	5.3	4	3.9	2	1.1
E. Disagree strongly	31	3.1	15	3.0	3	1.8	4	5.3	2	1.9	7	4.1
11. I like to go out with athletes because I'm into sports myself.												
No answer	3	.3	2	.4	1	.6	0	.0	0	.0	0	.0
A. Agree strongly	99	9.8	51	10.3	16	9.8	10	13.2	11	10.6	11	6.4
B. Agree somewhat	256	25.4	125	25.4	43	26.4	20	26.3	32	31.1	36	21.1
C. Not sure	145	14.4	74	15.0	19	11.6	4	5.2	18	17.5	30	17.5
D. Disagree somewhat	278	27.7	127	25.8	56	34.4	25	32.9	24	23.3	46	26.9
E. Disagree strongly	225	22.4	114	23.1	28	17.2	17	22.4	18	17.5	48	28.1
12. Flirts get on my nerves; when they pay more attention to other girls it makes me feel like I'm being ignored or put down.												
No answer	5	.5	1	.2	1	.6	0	.0	1	1.0	2	1.1
A. Agree strongly	447	44.4	223	45.3	57	35.0	37	48.7	57	55.3	73	42.7
B. Agree somewhat	308	30.6	154	31.2	57	35.0	21	27.6	24	23.3	52	30.4
C. Not sure	74	7.4	36	7.3	17	10.4	4	5.3	8	7.8	9	5.3
D. Disagree somewhat	105	10.4	45	9.1	21	12.9	5	6.6	8	7.8	26	15.2
E. Disagree strongly	67	6.7	34	6.9	10	6.1	9	11.8	5	4.8	9	5.3
13. I'm not prejudiced, but I might feel uncomfortable dating or marrying someone of a different race.												
No answer	3	.3	1	.2	2	1.2	0	.0	0	.0	0	.0
A. Agree strongly	333	33.1	159	32.3	32	19.6	24	31.6	64	62.1	54	31.6

Survey questions	ALL GIRLS Result	ALL GIRLS Percent	STRONG INDIVIDUALISTS Result	STRONG INDIVIDUALISTS Percent	20TH-CENTURY FAST TRACKERS Result	20TH-CENTURY FAST TRACKERS Percent	MODERN TRADITIONALISTS Result	MODERN TRADITIONALISTS Percent	SWEET SOUTHERN BELLES Result	SWEET SOUTHERN BELLES Percent	SUPERSONIC DATERS Result	SUPERSONIC DATERS Percent
B. Agree somewhat	229	22.8	104	21.1	41	25.2	19	25.0	23	22.3	42	24.6
C. Not sure	142	14.1	68	13.8	24	14.7	8	10.5	8	7.8	34	19.9
D. Disagree somewhat	95	9.4	49	9.9	16	9.8	8	10.5	3	2.9	19	11.1
E. Disagree strongly	204	20.3	112	22.7	48	29.5	17	22.4	5	4.9	22	12.8
14. I like a boy who sends me flowers, picks me up for a date, and opens doors, because I love to be pampered and flattered.												
No answer	2	.2	1	.2	1	.6	0	.0	0	.0	0	.0
A. Agree strongly	391	38.9	182	36.9	42	25.8	35	46.1	56	54.4	76	44.4
B. Agree somewhat	363	36.1	185	37.5	57	35.0	22	28.9	33	32.0	66	38.6
C. Not sure	91	9.0	53	10.8	17	10.4	7	9.2	5	4.9	9	5.3
D. Disagree somewhat	109	10.8	49	9.9	33	20.2	8	10.5	6	5.8	13	7.6
E. Disagree strongly	50	5.0	23	4.7	13	8.0	4	5.3	3	2.9	7	4.1
15. It's not embarrassing and unromantic to ask a boy out for the first date.												
No answer	1	.1	1	.2	0	.0	0	.0	0	.0	0	.0
A. Agree strongly	295	29.4	134	27.2	67	41.1	19	25.0	16	15.5	59	34.5
B. Agree somewhat	261	25.9	123	24.9	51	31.3	16	21.1	28	27.2	43	25.2
C. Not sure	175	17.4	95	19.3	20	12.3	12	15.8	23	22.4	25	14.6
D. Disagree somewhat	145	14.4	73	14.8	15	9.2	20	26.3	13	12.6	24	14.0
E. Disagree strongly	129	12.8	67	13.6	10	6.1	9	11.8	23	22.3	20	11.7
16. If a good-looking boy has a bad personality, I'll hang in there anyway for his looks.												
No answer	2	.2	1	.2	0	.0	0	.0	0	.0	1	.6
A. Agree strongly	24	2.7	17	3.4	1	.6	1	1.3	1	.9	4	2.3
B. Agree somewhat	47	4.7	26	5.3	1	.6	2	2.6	8	7.8	10	5.9
C. Not sure	90	8.9	52	10.5	10	6.1	3	4.0	7	6.8	18	10.5

The TeenAge *Relationships Survey Results (continued)*

Survey questions	ALL GIRLS Result	Percent	STRONG INDIVIDUALISTS Result	Percent	20TH-CENTURY FAST TRACKERS Result	Percent	MODERN TRADITIONALISTS Result	Percent	SWEET SOUTHERN BELLES Result	Percent	SUPERSONIC DATERS Result	Percent
D. Disagree somewhat	171	17.0	86	17.4	15	9.2	14	18.4	17	16.5	39	22.8
E. Disagree strongly	672	66.5	311	63.2	136	83.5	56	73.7	70	68.0	99	57.9
17. A good sense of humor sets a relaxed atmosphere and makes problems easier to deal with.												
No answer	2	.2	1	.2	0	.0	0	.0	0	.0	1	.6
A. Agree strongly	527	52.4	256	51.9	89	54.7	39	51.3	58	56.4	85	49.7
B. Agree somewhat	354	35.2	180	36.5	51	31.3	23	30.3	37	35.9	63	36.8
C. Not sure	73	7.3	30	6.1	11	6.7	10	13.2	6	5.8	16	9.4
D. Disagree somewhat	38	3.8	18	3.7	11	6.7	2	2.6	2	1.9	5	2.9
E. Disagree strongly	12	1.1	8	1.6	1	.6	2	2.6	0	.0	1	.6
18. If a boy asks me out, I'm his responsibility and he should pay.												
No answer	1	.1	1	.2	0	.0	0	.0	0	.0	0	.0
A. Agree strongly	165	16.4	89	18.1	0	.0	12	15.8	31	30.1	33	19.3
B. Agree somewhat	239	23.8	136	27.6	0	.0	25	32.9	26	25.2	52	30.4
C. Not sure	142	14.1	92	18.7	0	.0	12	15.8	14	13.6	24	14.0
D. Disagree somewhat	318	31.6	123	24.9	105	64.4	23	30.3	24	23.3	43	25.2
E. Disagree strongly	141	14.0	52	10.5	58	35.6	4	5.2	8	7.8	19	11.1
19. I don't like to hang around guys with greasy hair, bad breath, or poor grooming because they embarrass me.												
No answer	3	.3	3	.6	0	.0	0	.0	0	.0	0	.0
A. Agree strongly	461	45.9	220	44.7	54	33.1	40	52.6	58	56.3	89	52.1
B. Agree somewhat	261	25.9	126	25.6	52	31.9	16	21.1	28	27.2	39	22.8
C. Not sure	115	11.4	60	12.1	21	12.9	10	13.1	5	4.8	19	11.1

Survey questions	ALL GIRLS Result	Percent	STRONG INDIVIDUALISTS Result	Percent	20TH-CENTURY FAST TRACKERS Result	Percent	MODERN TRADITIONALISTS Result	Percent	SWEET SOUTHERN BELLES Result	Percent	SUPERSONIC DATERS Result	Percent
D. Disagree somewhat	99	9.8	50	10.1	27	16.6	5	6.6	4	3.9	13	7.6
E. Disagree strongly	67	6.7	34	6.9	9	5.5	5	6.6	8	7.8	11	6.4
20. I would like to date the captain of the football team.												
No answer	1	.1	1	.2	0	.0	0	.0	0	.0	0	.0
A. Agree strongly	136	13.5	70	14.2	11	6.7	8	10.5	25	24.3	22	12.9
B. Agree somewhat	147	14.6	73	14.8	26	16.0	10	13.2	18	17.5	20	11.7
C. Not sure	345	34.3	178	36.2	60	36.8	22	29.0	35	34.0	50	29.2
D. Disagree somewhat	116	11.5	49	9.9	25	15.3	9	11.8	8	7.7	25	14.6
E. Disagree strongly	261	26.0	122	24.7	41	25.2	27	35.5	17	16.5	54	31.6
21. A girl can ask for the first date; things are pretty liberated today.												
No answer	2	.2	1	.2	0	.0	0	.0	0	.0	1	.6
A. Agree strongly	450	44.7	216	43.8	89	54.6	22	28.9	36	35.0	87	50.9
B. Agree somewhat	309	30.7	141	28.6	60	36.8	31	40.8	33	32.0	44	25.7
C. Not sure	112	11.1	66	13.4	7	4.3	10	13.2	15	14.6	14	8.2
D. Disagree somewhat	69	6.9	34	6.9	6	3.7	8	10.5	9	8.7	12	7.0
E. Disagree strongly	64	6.4	35	7.1	1	.6	5	6.6	10	9.7	13	7.6
22. I like a guy I date to have money because I like to have a good time and get great presents.												
No answer	2	.2	2	.4	0	.0	0	.0	0	.0	0	.0
A. Agree strongly	50	5.0	20	4.1	4	2.5	5	6.6	7	6.8	14	8.2
B. Agree somewhat	194	19.3	90	18.3	18	11.0	15	19.7	37	36.0	34	19.9
C. Not sure	130	12.9	78	15.8	14	8.6	7	9.2	6	5.8	25	14.6
D. Disagree somewhat	343	34.1	157	31.8	62	38.0	28	36.9	33	32.0	63	36.8
E. Disagree strongly	287	28.5	146	29.6	65	39.9	21	27.6	20	19.4	35	20.5
23. If a boy dresses cool—I think he is.												
No answer	2	.2	2	.4	0	.0	0	.0	0	.0	0	.0
A. Agree strongly	51	5.1	26	5.3	1	.6	5	6.6	11	10.7	8	4.7

The TeenAge *Relationships Survey Results (continued)*

Survey questions	ALL GIRLS		STRONG INDIVIDUALISTS		20TH-CENTURY FAST TRACKERS		MODERN TRADITIONALISTS		SWEET SOUTHERN BELLES		SUPERSONIC DATERS	
	Result	*Percent*	*Result*	*Percent*	*Result*	*Percent*	*Result*	*Percent*	*Result*	*Percent*	*Result*	*Percent*
B. Agree somewhat	180	17.9	84	17.0	20	12.3	12	15.8	24	23.3	40	23.4
C. Not sure	175	17.4	88	17.9	24	14.7	13	17.1	19	18.4	31	18.1
D. Disagree somewhat	298	29.6	146	29.6	57	35.0	21	27.6	24	23.3	50	29.2
E. Disagree strongly	300	29.8	147	29.8	61	37.4	25	32.9	25	24.3	42	24.6
24. My friends pressure me to judge a boy by his looks.												
No answer	1	.1	1	.2	0	.0	0	.0	0	.0	0	.0
A. Agree strongly	189	18.8	94	19.1	33	20.3	13	17.1	23	22.3	26	15.2
B. Agree somewhat	280	27.8	141	28.6	37	22.7	20	26.3	31	30.1	51	29.8
C. Not sure	66	6.6	36	7.3	6	3.7	2	2.6	10	9.7	12	7.0
D. Disagree somewhat	182	18.1	86	17.4	32	19.6	11	14.5	20	19.4	33	19.3
E. Disagree strongly	288	28.6	135	27.4	55	33.7	30	39.5	19	18.5	49	28.7
25. I want the guy I marry to have a lot of money.												
No answer	1	.1	1	.2	0	.0	0	.0	0	.0	0	.0
A. Agree strongly	137	13.6	67	13.5	16	9.8	7	9.2	20	19.4	27	15.8
B. Agree somewhat	267	26.5	128	26.0	35	21.5	21	27.6	36	35.0	47	27.5
C. Not sure	230	22.9	126	25.6	32	19.6	16	21.1	21	20.4	35	20.5
D. Disagree somewhat	229	22.8	102	20.7	39	23.9	23	30.3	21	20.4	44	25.7
E. Disagree strongly	142	14.1	69	14.0	41	25.2	9	11.8	5	4.8	18	10.5
26. There are no religious barriers in dating or marriage because love counts more.												
No answer	2	.2	2	.4	0	.0	0	.0	0	.0	0	.0
A. Agree strongly	477	47.4	252	51.1	84	51.5	23	30.3	19	18.5	99	57.9
B. Agree somewhat	172	17.1	75	15.2	33	20.3	14	18.4	19	18.5	31	18.1
C. Not sure	109	10.8	66	13.4	9	5.5	9	11.8	9	8.7	16	9.3
D. Disagree somewhat	153	15.2	60	12.2	32	19.6	17	22.4	29	28.1	15	8.8
E. Disagree strongly	93	9.3	38	7.7	5	3.1	13	17.1	27	26.2	10	5.9

Survey questions	ALL GIRLS		STRONG INDIVIDUALISTS		20TH-CENTURY FAST TRACKERS		MODERN TRADITIONALISTS		SWEET SOUTHERN BELLES		SUPERSONIC DATERS	
	Result	*Percent*	*Result*	*Percent*	*Result*	*Percent*	*Result*	*Percent*	*Result*	*Percent*	*Result*	*Percent*
27. I'd date a guy who wasn't good-looking if his personality was great.												
No answer	1	.1	1	.2	0	.0	0	.0	0	.0	0	.0
A. Agree strongly	524	52.1	239	48.5	100	61.4	49	64.5	50	48.6	86	50.3
B. Agree somewhat	278	27.6	144	29.2	48	29.4	16	21.0	26	25.2	44	25.8
C. Not sure	153	15.2	78	15.8	14	8.6	7	9.2	22	21.4	32	18.7
D. Disagree somewhat	34	3.4	22	4.5	1	.6	3	4.0	3	2.9	5	2.9
E. Disagree strongly	16	1.6	9	1.8	0	.0	1	1.3	2	1.9	4	2.3
28. I'm not attracted to younger boys because girls mature faster.												
No answer	2	.2	1	.2	1	.6	0	.0	0	.0	0	.0
A. Agree strongly	208	20.7	96	19.5	25	15.4	14	18.4	27	26.2	46	26.9
B. Agree somewhat	209	20.8	91	18.5	39	23.9	17	22.4	29	28.1	33	19.3
C. Not sure	200	19.8	113	22.9	27	16.6	18	23.7	12	11.7	30	17.5
D. Disagree somewhat	229	22.8	117	23.7	39	23.9	18	23.7	11	10.7	44	25.8
E. Disagree strongly	158	15.7	75	15.2	32	19.6	9	11.8	24	23.3	18	10.5
29. A boy should make the first moves with kissing or making out because a girl who does will be called a "sleaze."												
No answer	2	.2	2	.4	0	.0	0	.0	0	.0	0	.0
A. Agree strongly	224	22.3	92	18.7	16	9.8	26	34.2	56	54.4	34	19.9
B. Agree somewhat	263	26.1	124	25.2	36	22.1	16	21.1	47	45.6	40	23.4
C. Not sure	202	20.1	120	24.3	36	22.1	14	18.4	0	.0	32	18.7
D. Disagree somewhat	186	18.5	94	19.1	42	25.8	12	15.8	0	.0	38	22.2
E. Disagree strongly	129	12.8	61	12.3	33	20.2	8	10.5	0	.0	27	15.8
30. I want to be a housewife.												
No answer	3	.3	2	.4	0	.0	0	.0	0	.0	1	.6
A. Agree strongly	65	6.5	33	6.7	4	2.4	10	13.2	8	7.7	10	5.8
B. Agree somewhat	117	11.6	52	10.5	13	8.0	17	22.4	17	16.5	18	10.5

The TeenAge *Relationships Survey Results* (continued)

Survey questions	All Girls Result	All Girls Percent	Strong Individualists Result	Strong Individualists Percent	20th-Century Fast Trackers Result	20th-Century Fast Trackers Percent	Modern Traditionalists Result	Modern Traditionalists Percent	Sweet Southern Belles Result	Sweet Southern Belles Percent	Supersonic Daters Result	Supersonic Daters Percent
C. Not sure	176	17.5	94	19.1	27	16.6	9	11.8	24	23.3	22	12.9
D. Disagree somewhat	135	13.4	60	12.2	13	8.0	15	19.7	12	11.7	35	20.5
E. Disagree strongly	510	50.7	252	51.1	106	65.0	25	32.9	42	40.8	85	49.7
31. I wish my parents understood that sex is more common today than when they were growing up.												
No answer	7	.7	2	.4	1	.6	1	1.3	2	1.9	1	.6
A. Agree strongly	265	26.3	113	22.9	38	23.3	18	23.7	22	21.4	74	43.3
B. Agree somewhat	255	25.4	130	26.4	45	27.6	9	11.8	30	29.1	41	24.0
C. Not sure	201	20.0	110	22.3	31	19.0	18	23.7	18	17.5	24	14.0
D. Disagree somewhat	135	13.4	60	12.2	27	16.6	14	18.4	13	12.6	21	12.3
E. Disagree strongly	143	14.2	78	15.8	21	12.9	16	21.1	18	17.5	10	5.8
32. I don't like a guy who dresses terribly because it says he doesn't care about his self-image.												
No answer	3	.3	2	.4	0	.0	0	.0	0	.0	1	.6
A. Agree strongly	317	31.5	143	29.0	28	17.2	37	48.7	46	44.7	63	36.8
B. Agree somewhat	392	39.0	202	41.0	71	43.6	24	31.6	37	35.9	58	33.9
C. Not sure	135	13.4	74	15.0	28	17.2	7	9.2	10	9.7	16	9.4
D. Disagree somewhat	108	10.7	53	10.8	21	12.8	6	7.9	6	5.8	22	12.9
E. Disagree strongly	51	5.1	19	3.8	15	9.2	2	2.6	4	3.9	11	6.4
33. Group dates make me feel more comfortable; they get rid of the tension of being with boys.												
No answer	2	.2	2	.4	0	.0	0	.0	0	.0	0	.0
A. Agree strongly	223	22.2	121	24.5	25	15.3	21	27.6	31	30.1	25	14.6
B. Agree somewhat	332	33.0	161	32.7	68	41.7	29	38.2	25	24.3	49	28.7

Survey questions	All Girls Result	All Girls Percent	Strong Individualists Result	Strong Individualists Percent	20th-Century Fast Trackers Result	20th-Century Fast Trackers Percent	Modern Traditionalists Result	Modern Traditionalists Percent	Sweet Southern Belles Result	Sweet Southern Belles Percent	Supersonic Daters Result	Supersonic Daters Percent
C. Not sure	163	16.2	88	17.9	27	16.6	5	6.5	14	13.6	29	17.0
D. Disagree somewhat	164	16.3	64	13.0	31	19.0	11	14.5	20	19.4	38	22.2
E. Disagree strongly	122	12.1	57	11.5	12	7.4	10	13.2	13	12.6	30	17.5
34. I might ask a boy to the movies but never to "go steady."												
No answer	2	.2	2	.4	0	.0	0	.0	0	.0	0	.0
A. Agree strongly	338	33.6	169	34.3	39	23.9	22	28.9	43	41.8	65	38.0
B. Agree somewhat	276	27.5	130	26.4	54	33.1	24	31.6	26	25.2	42	24.6
C. Not sure	199	19.8	113	22.9	32	19.6	11	14.5	16	15.5	27	15.8
D. Disagree somewhat	94	9.3	41	8.3	26	16.0	6	7.9	6	5.8	15	8.7
E. Disagree strongly	97	9.6	38	7.7	12	7.4	13	17.1	12	11.7	22	12.9
35. I like splitting the cost of a date; it makes me feel independent.												
No answer	2	.2	1	.2	0	.0	0	.0	0	.0	1	.6
A. Agree strongly	183	18.2	86	17.4	56	34.4	12	15.8	12	11.7	17	9.9
B. Agree somewhat	309	30.7	146	29.6	58	35.6	17	22.4	32	31.1	56	32.8
C. Not sure	239	23.8	129	26.2	22	13.5	16	21.1	26	25.2	46	26.9
D. Disagree somewhat	183	18.2	87	17.7	24	14.7	20	26.3	20	19.4	32	18.7
E. Disagree strongly	90	8.9	44	8.9	3	1.8	11	14.4	13	12.6	19	11.1
36. I'd rather marry a man who's a virgin so sex will be something we share.												
No answer	4	.4	3	.6	1	.6	0	.0	0	.0	0	.0
A. Agree strongly	234	23.3	117	23.7	37	22.7	36	47.4	40	38.8	4	2.3
B. Agree somewhat	178	17.7	86	17.4	35	21.5	19	25.0	17	16.5	21	12.3
C. Not sure	249	24.8	138	28.0	44	27.0	10	13.2	25	24.3	32	18.7
D. Disagree somewhat	173	17.1	77	15.7	28	17.2	8	10.5	13	12.6	47	27.5
E. Disagree strongly	168	16.7	72	14.6	18	11.0	3	3.9	8	7.8	67	39.2
37. Macho behavior is neat because it shows a boy is in control and manly.												
No answer	2	.2	1	.2	0	.0	0	.0	0	.0	1	.6

The TeenAge Relationships Survey Results (continued)

Survey questions	ALL GIRLS Result	Percent	STRONG INDIVIDUALISTS Result	Percent	20TH-CENTURY FAST TRACKERS Result	Percent	MODERN TRADITIONALISTS Result	Percent	SWEET SOUTHERN BELLES Result	Percent	SUPERSONIC DATERS Result	Percent
A. Agree strongly	29	2.9	10	2.0	0	.0	3	3.9	6	5.8	10	5.8
B. Agree somewhat	76	7.6	34	6.9	4	2.5	8	10.5	16	15.5	14	8.2
C. Not sure	108	10.7	65	13.2	7	4.3	10	13.2	14	13.6	12	7.0
D. Disagree somewhat	298	29.6	148	30.0	47	28.8	23	30.3	32	31.1	48	28.1
E. Disagree strongly	493	49.0	235	47.7	105	64.4	32	42.1	35	34.0	86	50.3
38. No girl is a virgin when she marries anymore.												
No answer	12	1.2	9	1.8	0	.0	0	.0	2	1.9	1	.6
A. Agree strongly	56	5.6	26	5.3	2	1.2	5	6.5	9	8.7	14	8.2
B. Agree somewhat	120	11.9	49	9.9	22	13.5	4	5.3	13	12.6	32	18.7
C. Not sure	126	12.5	73	14.8	15	9.2	4	5.3	14	13.6	20	11.7
D. Disagree somewhat	209	20.8	100	20.3	29	17.8	20	26.3	20	19.5	40	23.4
E. Disagree strongly	483	48.0	236	47.9	95	58.3	43	56.6	45	43.7	64	37.4
39. Pot and cocaine are cool in my group.												
No answer	2	.2	2	.4	0	.0	0	.0	0	.0	0	.0
A. Agree strongly	31	3.1	15	3.0	3	1.8	2	2.6	4	3.9	7	4.1
B. Agree somewhat	57	5.7	20	4.0	6	3.7	3	4.0	2	1.9	26	15.2
C. Not sure	37	3.7	24	4.9	3	1.8	1	1.3	2	1.9	7	4.1
D. Disagree somewhat	104	10.3	44	8.9	19	11.7	2	2.6	8	7.8	31	18.1
E. Disagree strongly	775	77.0	388	78.8	132	81.0	68	89.5	87	84.5	100	58.5
40. A boy should make the first moves because I'd rather be the one to say "no."												
No answer	3	.3	3	.6	0	.0	0	.0	0	.0	0	.0
A. Agree strongly	256	25.5	120	24.3	18	11.0	31	40.8	45	43.7	42	24.6
B. Agree somewhat	265	26.3	132	26.8	41	25.2	22	29.0	25	24.3	45	26.3
C. Not sure	240	23.9	136	27.6	35	21.5	9	11.8	21	20.4	39	22.8
D. Disagree somewhat	159	15.8	70	14.2	42	25.8	8	10.5	9	8.7	30	17.5
E. Disagree strongly	83	8.2	32	6.5	27	16.5	6	7.9	3	2.9	15	8.8

Survey questions	ALL GIRLS Result	Percent	STRONG INDIVIDUALISTS Result	Percent	20TH-CENTURY FAST TRACKERS Result	Percent	MODERN TRADITIONALISTS Result	Percent	SWEET SOUTHERN BELLES Result	Percent	SUPERSONIC DATERS Result	Percent
41. I want a career that will make the most of my education.												
No answer	3	.3	3	.6	0	.0	0	.0	0	.0	0	.0
A. Agree strongly	682	67.8	330	67.0	127	77.9	51	67.1	72	69.9	102	59.7
B. Agree somewhat	162	16.1	74	15.0	21	12.9	16	21.1	17	16.5	34	19.9
C. Not sure	107	10.6	58	11.8	7	4.3	7	9.2	8	7.8	27	15.8
D. Disagree somewhat	26	2.6	11	2.2	6	3.7	0	.0	5	4.9	4	2.3
E. Disagree strongly	26	2.6	17	3.4	2	1.2	2	2.6	1	.9	4	2.3
42. There's no such thing as peer pressure when it comes to sex, drugs, and drinking.												
No answer	3	.3	3	.6	0	.0	0	.0	0	.0	0	.0
A. Agree strongly	99	9.8	46	9.3	19	11.7	11	14.4	9	8.7	14	8.2
B. Agree somewhat	81	8.0	39	7.9	11	6.7	3	4.0	13	12.6	15	8.8
C. Not sure	75	7.5	42	8.5	6	3.7	8	10.5	7	6.8	12	7.0
D. Disagree somewhat	165	16.4	78	15.8	22	13.5	12	15.8	14	13.6	39	22.8
E. Disagree strongly	583	58.0	285	57.9	105	64.4	42	55.3	60	58.3	91	53.2
43. I've often felt pressured into sexual contact by the boy I'm with because I don't know how to say "no."												
No answer	8	.8	6	1.2	1	.6	1	1.3	0	.0	0	.0
A. Agree strongly	88	8.8	44	8.9	13	8.0	5	6.6	10	9.7	16	9.4
B. Agree somewhat	156	15.5	70	14.2	23	14.1	16	21.1	16	15.5	31	18.1
C. Not sure	103	10.2	63	12.8	17	10.4	5	6.6	10	9.7	8	4.6
D. Disagree somewhat	170	16.9	79	16.0	25	15.3	9	11.8	22	21.4	35	20.5
E. Disagree strongly	481	47.8	231	46.9	84	51.6	40	52.6	45	43.7	81	47.4
44. Premarital sex is great with someone you love or are committed to.												
No answer	7	.7	5	1.0	1	.6	0	.0	1	.9	0	.0
A. Agree strongly	246	24.5	97	19.7	38	23.4	12	15.8	14	13.6	85	49.7

The TeenAge *Relationships Survey Results (continued)*

Survey questions	ALL GIRLS		STRONG INDIVIDUALISTS		20TH-CENTURY FAST TRACKERS		MODERN TRADITIONALISTS		SWEET SOUTHERN BELLES		SUPERSONIC DATERS	
	Result	*Percent*	*Result*	*Percent*	*Result*	*Percent*	*Result*	*Percent*	*Result*	*Percent*	*Result*	*Percent*
B. Agree somewhat	226	22.4	103	20.9	42	25.7	9	11.8	19	18.5	53	31.0
C. Not sure	218	21.7	131	26.6	30	18.4	15	19.7	19	18.5	23	13.5
D. Disagree somewhat	98	9.7	54	10.9	20	12.3	6	7.9	13	12.6	5	2.9
E. Disagree strongly	211	21.0	103	20.9	32	19.6	34	44.0	37	35.9	5	2.9
45. It doesn't bother me if a boy smokes cigarettes.												
No answer	2	.2	2	.4	0	.0	0	.0	0	.0	0	.0
A. Agree strongly	211	21.0	86	17.4	26	16.0	13	17.1	17	16.5	69	40.4
B. Agree somewhat	204	20.3	105	21.3	29	17.8	11	14.5	23	22.3	36	21.1
C. Not sure	66	6.5	43	8.7	8	4.9	5	6.5	3	2.9	7	4.0
D. Disagree somewhat	220	21.9	112	22.7	41	25.1	18	23.7	22	21.4	27	15.8
E. Disagree strongly	303	30.1	145	29.5	59	36.2	29	38.2	38	36.9	32	18.7
46. A Woman should put taking care of her kids and a home before a job or a career.												
No answer	2	.2	2	.4	0	.0	0	.0	0	.0	0	.0
A. Agree strongly	192	19.0	70	14.2	18	11.0	40	52.6	34	33.0	30	17.5
B. Agree somewhat	207	20.6	90	18.3	22	13.5	36	47.4	25	24.3	34	19.9
C. Not sure	168	16.7	94	19.0	26	16.0	0	.0	17	16.5	31	18.1
D. Disagree somewhat	205	20.4	112	22.7	39	23.9	0	.0	19	18.4	35	20.5
E. Disagree strongly	232	23.1	125	25.4	58	35.6	0	.0	8	7.8	41	24.0
47. I still don't know enough about birth control to make an intelligent decision about sex.												
No answer	9	.9	6	1.2	1	.6	0	.0	0	.0	2	1.2
A. Agree strongly	151	15.0	90	18.3	19	11.6	11	14.5	21	20.4	10	5.8
B. Agree somewhat	186	18.5	105	21.3	26	16.0	18	23.7	17	16.5	20	11.7
C. Not sure	105	10.4	51	10.3	13	8.0	8	10.5	21	20.4	12	7.0

Survey questions	ALL GIRLS Result	ALL GIRLS Percent	STRONG INDIVIDUALISTS Result	STRONG INDIVIDUALISTS Percent	20TH-CENTURY FAST TRACKERS Result	20TH-CENTURY FAST TRACKERS Percent	MODERN TRADITIONALISTS Result	MODERN TRADITIONALISTS Percent	SWEET SOUTHERN BELLES Result	SWEET SOUTHERN BELLES Percent	SUPERSONIC DATERS Result	SUPERSONIC DATERS Percent
D. Disagree somewhat	173	17.2	84	17.0	28	17.2	14	18.4	14	13.6	33	19.3
E. Disagree strongly	382	38.0	157	31.9	76	46.6	25	32.9	30	29.1	94	55.0
48. It's important to be a virgin when you marry.												
No answer	2	.2	2	.4	0	.0	0	.0	0	.0	0	.0
A. Agree strongly	197	19.6	83	16.8	28	17.2	46	60.5	40	38.8	0	.0
B. Agree somewhat	151	15.0	82	16.6	19	11.7	30	39.5	20	19.4	0	.0
C. Not sure	212	21.0	160	32.5	30	18.4	0	.0	22	21.4	0	.0
D. Disagree somewhat	231	23.0	88	17.9	39	23.9	0	.0	13	12.6	91	53.2
E. Disagree strongly	213	21.2	78	15.8	47	28.8	0	.0	8	7.8	80	46.8
49. A conceited boy is not insecure.												
No answer	7	.7	4	.8	1	.6	1	1.3	0	.0	1	.6
A. Agree strongly	40	4.0	21	4.3	5	3.0	3	4.0	6	5.8	5	2.9
B. Agree somewhat	96	9.5	49	9.9	12	7.4	8	10.5	12	11.7	15	8.8
C. Not sure	324	32.2	185	37.6	44	27.0	28	36.8	23	22.3	44	25.7
D. Disagree somewhat	239	23.8	100	20.3	43	26.4	14	18.4	31	30.1	51	29.8
E. Disagree strongly	300	29.8	134	27.1	58	35.6	22	29.0	31	30.1	55	32.2
50. Sexual behavior is acceptable at my age because sex is fun.												
No answer	5	.5	3	.6	0	.0	0	.0	0	.0	2	1.1
A. Agree strongly	67	6.6	30	6.1	4	2.5	5	6.6	6	5.8	22	12.9
B. Agree somewhat	133	13.2	52	10.5	21	12.9	9	11.8	11	10.7	40	23.4
C. Not sure	199	19.8	109	22.1	25	15.3	11	14.5	23	22.3	31	18.1
D. Disagree somewhat	250	24.9	124	25.2	48	29.4	13	17.1	17	16.5	48	28.1
E. Disagree strongly	352	35.0	175	35.5	65	39.9	38	50.0	46	44.7	28	16.4
51. If a girl asks a boy out, she should pay.												
No answer	3	.3	3	.6	0	.0	0	.0	0	.0	0	.0
A. Agree strongly	250	24.9	131	26.6	30	18.4	16	21.1	26	25.2	47	27.5
B. Agree somewhat	305	30.3	130	26.4	68	41.8	30	39.5	29	28.2	48	28.1
C. Not sure	219	21.8	120	24.4	23	14.1	13	17.1	25	24.3	38	22.2

The TeenAge *Relationships Survey Results (continued)*

Survey questions	ALL GIRLS Result	Percent	STRONG INDIVIDUALISTS Result	Percent	20TH-CENTURY FAST TRACKERS Result	Percent	MODERN TRADITIONALISTS Result	Percent	SWEET SOUTHERN BELLES Result	Percent	SUPERSONIC DATERS Result	Percent
D. Disagree somewhat	142	14.1	65	13.1	24	14.7	17	22.3	13	12.6	23	13.5
E. Disagree strongly	87	8.6	44	8.9	18	11.0	0	.0	10	9.7	15	8.7
52. A boy who drinks, smokes, or does drugs heavily turns me off because it says he can't handle himself and needs to be cool to have friends.												
No answer	5	.5	5	1.0	0	.0	0	.0	0	.0	0	.0
A. Agree strongly	595	59.1	307	62.3	96	58.9	54	71.1	62	60.2	76	44.4
B. Agree somewhat	170	16.9	76	15.4	35	21.5	10	13.2	18	17.5	31	18.1
C. Not sure	68	6.8	37	7.5	8	4.9	4	5.2	4	3.8	15	8.8
D. Disagree somewhat	90	8.9	38	7.7	14	8.6	3	3.9	8	7.8	27	15.8
E. Disagree strongly	78	7.8	30	6.1	10	6.1	5	6.6	11	10.7	22	12.9
53. I wish I could talk to my parents about sex and birth control but that just isn't possible.												
No answer	5	.5	3	.6	0	.0	1	1.3	0	.0	1	.5
A. Agree strongly	258	25.7	127	25.8	31	19.0	22	29.0	27	26.2	51	29.8
B. Agree somewhat	206	20.5	104	21.1	27	16.6	12	15.8	23	22.3	40	23.4
C. Not sure	98	9.7	43	8.7	18	11.0	13	17.1	8	7.8	16	9.4
D. Disagree somewhat	175	17.4	81	16.4	31	19.0	14	18.4	20	19.4	29	17.0
E. Disagree strongly	264	26.2	135	27.4	56	34.4	14	18.4	25	24.3	34	19.9
54. I wouldn't support a househusband because it's not appropriate; a man who marries should be prepared to work.												
No answer	5	.5	2	.4	0	.0	0	.0	1	1.0	2	1.2
A. Agree strongly	265	26.3	124	25.2	0	.0	46	60.5	48	46.6	47	27.5

Survey questions	ALL GIRLS Result	Percent	STRONG INDIVIDUALISTS Result	Percent	20TH-CENTURY FAST TRACKERS Result	Percent	MODERN TRADITIONALISTS Result	Percent	SWEET SOUTHERN BELLES Result	Percent	SUPERSONIC DATERS Result	Percent
B. Agree somewhat	195	19.4	98	19.9	0	.0	30	39.5	25	24.3	42	24.6
C. Not sure	133	13.2	94	19.0	0	.0	0	.0	7	6.8	32	18.7
D. Disagree somewhat	195	19.4	85	17.2	68	41.7	0	.0	18	17.5	24	14.0
E. Disagree strongly	213	21.2	90	18.3	95	58.3	0	.0	4	3.8	24	14.0
55. I would date a boy who never smoked, drank, or did drugs; it doesn't mean he's stupid or square.												
No answer	2	.2	2	.4	0	.0	0	.0	0	.0	0	.0
A. Agree strongly	791	78.6	382	77.5	145	89.0	65	85.5	83	80.6	116	67.8
B. Agree somewhat	114	11.3	57	11.6	12	7.4	7	9.2	11	10.7	27	15.8
C. Not sure	45	4.5	22	4.5	2	1.2	1	1.3	7	6.7	13	7.6
D. Disagree somewhat	30	3.0	16	3.2	2	1.2	3	4.0	1	1.0	8	4.7
E. Disagree strongly	24	2.4	14	2.8	2	1.2	0	.0	1	1.0	7	4.1
56. I want to marry in my late twenties because I want to "play the field" first.												
No answer	2	.2	2	.4	0	.0	0	.0	0	.0	0	.0
A. Agree strongly	228	22.7	97	19.7	44	27.0	19	25.0	24	23.3	44	25.7
B. Agree somewhat	226	22.5	93	18.9	52	31.9	19	25.0	25	24.3	37	21.6
C. Not sure	235	23.4	150	30.4	24	14.7	10	13.1	22	21.4	29	17.0
D. Disagree somewhat	173	17.1	83	16.8	31	19.0	16	21.1	17	16.5	26	15.2
E. Disagree strongly	142	14.1	68	13.8	12	7.4	12	15.8	15	14.5	35	20.5
57. I would be willing to support a househusband if he could handle it.												
No answer	5	.5	3	.6	0	.0	0	.0	0	.0	2	1.1
A. Agree strongly	259	25.7	112	22.7	88	54.0	10	13.2	12	11.6	37	21.6
B. Agree somewhat	211	21.0	107	21.7	47	28.8	8	10.5	20	19.4	29	17.0
C. Not sure	227	22.6	132	26.8	14	8.6	22	28.9	21	20.4	38	22.2
D. Disagree somewhat	121	12.0	50	10.1	8	4.9	13	17.1	14	13.6	36	21.1
E. Disagree strongly	183	18.2	89	18.1	6	3.7	23	30.3	36	35.0	29	17.0

The TeenAge *Relationships Survey Results (continued)*

Survey questions	ALL GIRLS Result	ALL GIRLS Percent	STRONG INDIVIDUALISTS Result	STRONG INDIVIDUALISTS Percent	20TH-CENTURY FAST TRACKERS Result	20TH-CENTURY FAST TRACKERS Percent	MODERN TRADITIONALISTS Result	MODERN TRADITIONALISTS Percent	SWEET SOUTHERN BELLES Result	SWEET SOUTHERN BELLES Percent	SUPERSONIC DATERS Result	SUPERSONIC DATERS Percent
58. I go further in sex than I feel comfortable with in order to feel experienced and not left out.												
No answer	6	.6	5	1.0	1	.6	0	.0	0	.0	0	.0
A. Agree strongly	40	4.0	26	5.3	5	3.1	2	2.6	2	1.9	5	2.9
B. Agree somewhat	85	8.5	39	7.9	5	3.1	9	11.8	12	11.7	20	11.7
C. Not sure	108	10.7	59	12.0	15	9.2	8	10.5	6	5.8	20	11.7
D. Disagree somewhat	168	16.7	89	18.1	27	16.5	11	14.5	15	14.6	26	15.2
E. Disagree strongly	599	59.5	275	55.7	110	67.5	46	60.6	68	66.0	100	58.5
59. I want to marry in my late twenties because I want to work on my career first.												
No answer	5	.5	3	.6	0	.0	1	1.3	1	1.0	0	.0
A. Agree strongly	423	42.0	179	36.4	111	68.1	31	40.8	40	38.8	62	36.3
B. Agree somewhat	233	23.2	107	21.7	52	31.9	17	22.4	22	21.4	35	20.5
C. Not sure	182	18.1	119	24.1	0	.0	11	14.5	23	22.3	29	17.0
D. Disagree somewhat	83	8.2	38	7.7	0	.0	10	13.1	13	12.6	22	12.8
E. Disagree strongly	80	8.0	47	9.5	0	.0	6	7.9	4	3.9	23	13.4
60. You can misbehave as much as you want with sex and drugs as long as you keep your reputation clean.												
No answer	5	.5	4	.8	0	.0	0	.0	0	.0	1	.6
A. Agree strongly	51	5.0	21	4.2	4	2.5	9	11.8	5	4.8	12	7.0
B. Agree somewhat	52	5.2	26	5.3	3	1.8	3	4.0	6	5.8	14	8.2
C. Not sure	73	7.3	36	7.3	9	5.5	3	4.0	7	6.8	18	10.5
D. Disagree somewhat	157	15.6	71	14.4	29	17.8	9	11.8	12	11.7	36	21.1
E. Disagree strongly	668	66.4	335	68.0	118	72.4	52	68.4	73	70.9	90	52.6

Survey questions	ALL GIRLS Result	Percent	STRONG INDIVIDUALISTS Result	Percent	20TH-CENTURY FAST TRACKERS Result	Percent	MODERN TRADITIONALISTS Result	Percent	SWEET SOUTHERN BELLES Result	Percent	SUPERSONIC DATERS Result	Percent
61. The thing I hate most about the dating system is that everyone dates just one person forever; there should be more dating "around."												
No answer	45	4.4	18	3.6	6	3.7	1	1.3	5	4.8	15	8.8
A. Agree strongly	250	24.9	124	25.2	35	21.5	26	34.2	30	29.1	35	20.5
B. Agree somewhat	242	24.1	122	24.7	42	25.8	16	21.0	25	24.3	37	21.6
C. Not sure	183	18.2	102	20.7	33	20.2	11	14.5	14	13.6	23	13.5
D. Disagree somewhat	164	16.3	71	14.4	30	18.4	11	14.5	15	14.6	37	21.6
E. Disagree strongly	122	12.1	56	11.4	17	10.4	11	14.5	14	13.6	24	14.0
62. Are you currently dating?												
No answer	5	.5	5	1.0	0	.0	0	.0	0	.0	0	.0
A. Yes	602	59.8	228	46.3	95	58.3	44	57.9	64	62.1	171	100.0
B. No	399	39.7	260	52.7	68	41.7	32	42.1	39	37.9	0	.0
63. Are you dating just one boy?												
No answer	72	7.1	39	7.9	17	10.4	9	11.8	7	6.8	0	.0
A. Yes	390	38.8	158	32.1	58	35.6	28	36.8	38	36.9	108	63.2
B. No	544	54.1	296	60.0	88	54.0	39	51.4	58	56.3	63	36.8
64. Do you smoke cigarettes?												
No answer	3	.3	2	.4	0	.0	0	.0	0	.0	1	.6
A. Often	82	8.1	28	5.6	10	6.1	7	9.2	8	7.8	29	17.0
B. Sometimes	214	21.3	94	19.1	31	19.0	11	14.5	23	22.3	55	32.2
C. Never	707	70.3	369	74.9	122	74.9	58	76.3	72	69.9	86	50.2
65. Do you drink?												
No answer	1	.1	1	.2	0	.0	0	.0	0	.0	0	.0
A. Often	71	7.1	22	4.4	5	3.1	6	7.9	5	4.9	33	19.3
B. Sometimes	505	50.2	194	39.4	90	55.2	36	47.4	47	45.6	138	80.7
C. Never	429	42.6	276	56.0	68	41.7	34	44.7	51	49.5	0	.0

The TeenAge *Relationships Survey Results (continued)*

Survey questions	All Girls Result	All Girls Percent	Strong Individualists Result	Strong Individualists Percent	20th-Century Fast Trackers Result	20th-Century Fast Trackers Percent	Modern Traditionalists Result	Modern Traditionalists Percent	Sweet Southern Belles Result	Sweet Southern Belles Percent	Supersonic Daters Result	Supersonic Daters Percent
66. Do you smoke marijuana?												
No answer	4	.4	2	.4	0	.0	0	.0	0	.0	2	1.2
A. Often	38	3.8	21	4.3	1	.6	2	2.6	2	1.9	12	7.0
B. Sometimes	138	13.7	49	9.9	23	14.1	9	11.8	10	9.7	47	27.5
C. Never	826	82.1	421	85.4	139	85.3	65	85.6	91	88.4	110	64.3
67. Do you do cocaine or other drugs?												
No answer	2	.2	1	.2	0	.0	0	.0	0	.0	1	.6
A. Often	28	2.8	14	2.8	3	1.8	4	5.2	2	1.9	5	2.9
B. Sometimes	63	6.2	28	5.7	4	2.5	3	4.0	4	3.9	24	14.0
C. Never	913	90.8	450	91.3	156	95.7	69	90.8	97	94.2	141	82.5
68. Do you plan to ever get married?												
No answer	6	.6	5	1.0	0	.0	1	1.3	0	.0	0	.0
A. Yes	775	77.0	362	73.4	121	74.3	60	78.9	92	89.3	140	81.9
B. Not sure	200	19.9	110	22.3	40	24.5	12	15.8	11	10.7	27	15.8
C. Never	25	2.5	16	3.3	2	1.2	3	4.0	0	.0	4	2.3
69. At what age do you plan to marry?												
No answer	11	1.1	4	.8	3	1.8	1	1.3	2	1.9	1	.6
A. 15–20	149	14.8	83	16.8	5	3.1	10	13.2	20	19.4	31	18.1
B. 25–30	621	61.7	278	56.4	131	80.4	45	59.2	63	61.2	104	60.8
C. Over 30	29	2.9	15	3.0	7	4.3	1	1.3	0	.0	6	3.5
D. Not sure	196	19.5	113	23.0	17	10.4	19	25.0	18	17.5	29	17.0
70. Do you want to have children?												
No answer	7	.7	5	1.0	1	.6	0	.0	1	1.0	0	.0
A. Yes	735	73.1	353	71.6	112	68.7	67	88.2	81	78.6	122	71.4
B. Not sure	197	19.6	94	19.1	41	25.2	8	10.5	15	14.6	39	22.8
C. No	67	6.6	41	8.3	9	5.5	1	1.3	6	5.8	10	5.8

Survey questions	ALL GIRLS		STRONG INDIVIDUALISTS		20TH-CENTURY FAST TRACKERS		MODERN TRADITIONALISTS		SWEET SOUTHERN BELLES		SUPERSONIC DATERS	
	Result	*Percent*	*Result*	*Percent*	*Result*	*Percent*	*Result*	*Percent*	*Result*	*Percent*	*Result*	*Percent*
71. Do you plan to work if you're married?												
No answer	8	.8	6	1.2	1	.6	1	1.3	0	.0	0	.0
A. Yes	791	78.6	379	76.9	148	90.8	53	69.7	73	70.9	138	80.7
B. Not sure	184	18.3	96	19.5	12	7.4	16	21.1	29	28.2	31	18.1
C. No	23	2.3	12	2.4	2	1.2	6	7.9	1	.9	2	1.2
72. Who do you turn to for most of your advice on boys?*												
No answer	28	2.8	18	3.7	2	1.2	4	5.3	2	1.9	2	1.2
1. Mother	294	29.2	151	30.6	51	31.3	28	36.8	29	28.2	35	20.5
2. Father	33	3.3	18	3.7	6	3.7	5	6.6	1	1.0	3	1.8
3. Friends	715	71.1	347	70.4	118	72.4	51	67.1	73	70.9	126	73.7
4. Books	93	9.2	49	9.9	14	8.6	5	6.2	9	8.7	16	9.4
5. Magazines	160	15.9	80	16.2	21	12.9	9	11.8	21	20.4	29	17.0
6. Teachers	31	3.1	18	3.7	6	3.7	2	2.6	3	2.9	2	1.2
7. Religious leaders	14	1.4	8	1.6	0	.0	2	2.6	3	2.9	1	.6
8. Other (explain) ______	148	14.7	77	15.6	28	17.2	8	10.5	6	5.8	29	17.0
73. Have you ever had a formal sex education course in school?												
No answer	3	.3	2	.4	0	.0	0	.0	0	.0	1	.6
A. Yes	617	61.3	302	61.3	112	68.7	49	64.5	59	57.3	95	55.6
B. No	386	38.4	189	38.3	51	31.3	27	35.5	44	42.7	75	43.8
74. Have you ever asked a boy out for a date?												
No answer	5	.5	2	.4	1	.6	1	1.3	0	.0	1	.6
A. Yes	476	47.3	216	43.8	89	54.6	21	27.6	43	41.7	107	62.6
B. No	525	52.2	275	55.8	73	44.8	54	71.1	60	58.3	63	36.8
75. Would you like to?												
No answer	85	8.5	38	7.7	17	10.4	3	4.0	8	7.7	19	11.1

* Numbers do not add up to 100% because in many cases, more than one answer was given.

The TeenAge *Relationships Survey Results (continued)*

Survey questions	ALL GIRLS Result	Percent	STRONG INDIVIDUALISTS Result	Percent	20TH-CENTURY FAST TRACKERS Result	Percent	MODERN TRADITIONALISTS Result	Percent	SWEET SOUTHERN BELLES Result	Percent	SUPERSONIC DATERS Result	Percent
A. Yes	645	64.1	317	64.3	126	77.3	40	52.6	59	57.3	103	60.2
B. No	276	27.4	138	28.0	20	12.3	33	43.4	36	35.0	49	28.7
76. Are you a virgin?												
No answer	17	1.7	10	2.0	3	1.8	1	1.3	1	1.0	2	1.1
A. Yes	664	66.0	360	73.1	120	73.7	58	76.3	77	74.8	49	28.7
B. No	325	32.3	123	24.9	40	24.5	17	22.4	25	24.2	120	70.2
77. Manners/politeness												
No answer	1	.1	1	.2	0	.0	0	.0	0	.0	0	.0
A. Very important	617	61.3	313	63.5	86	52.8	60	79.0	72	69.9	86	50.3
B. Somewhat important	362	36.0	165	33.5	72	44.2	14	18.4	31	30.1	80	46.8
C. Not sure	13	1.3	5	1.0	3	1.8	2	2.6	0	.0	3	1.7
D. Somewhat unimportant	11	1.1	8	1.6	2	1.2	0	.0	0	.0	1	.6
E. Completely unimportant	2	.2	1	.2	0	.0	0	.0	0	.0	1	.6
78. Conversational ability												
No answer	3	.3	2	.4	1	.6	0	.0	0	.0	0	.0
A. Very important	467	46.4	208	42.2	83	51.0	40	52.7	54	52.4	82	48.0
B. Somewhat important	467	46.4	240	48.7	73	44.8	33	43.4	45	43.7	76	44.4
C. Not sure	33	3.3	22	4.5	2	1.2	1	1.3	2	1.9	6	3.5
D. Somewhat unimportant	31	3.1	18	3.6	3	1.8	2	2.6	1	1.0	7	4.1
E. Completely unimportant	5	.5	3	.6	1	.6	0	.0	1	1.0	0	.0
79. A flirtatious nature												
No answer	2	.2	2	.4	0	.0	0	.0	0	.0	0	.0
A. Very important	46	4.6	17	3.5	6	3.7	3	4.0	8	7.8	12	7.0
B. Somewhat important	155	15.4	66	13.4	20	12.3	18	23.7	17	16.5	34	19.9
C. Not sure	173	17.2	105	21.3	24	14.7	9	11.8	10	9.7	25	14.6
D. Somewhat unimportant	318	31.6	155	31.4	58	35.6	18	23.7	36	34.9	51	29.8
E. Completely unimportant	312	31.0	148	30.0	55	33.7	28	36.8	32	31.1	49	28.7
80. A sense of humor												
No answer	1	.1	0	.0	1	.6	0	.0	0	.0	0	.0
A. Very important	446	44.3	205	41.6	71	43.6	32	42.1	55	53.4	83	48.5

Survey questions	ALL GIRLS Result	Percent	STRONG INDIVIDUALISTS Result	Percent	20TH-CENTURY FAST TRACKERS Result	Percent	MODERN TRADITIONALISTS Result	Percent	SWEET SOUTHERN BELLES Result	Percent	SUPERSONIC DATERS Result	Percent
B. Somewhat important	494	49.1	248	50.3	86	52.8	39	51.4	44	42.7	77	45.0
C. Not sure	22	2.2	13	2.6	2	1.2	2	2.6	3	2.9	2	1.2
D. Somewhat unimportant	36	3.6	23	4.7	2	1.2	2	2.6	1	1.0	8	4.7
E. Completely unimportant	7	.7	4	.8	1	.6	1	1.3	0	.0	1	.6
81. Warmth and sensitivity												
No answer	1	.1	0	.0	1	.6	0	.0	0	.0	0	.0
A. Very important	863	85.8	415	84.2	143	87.8	69	90.8	92	89.3	144	84.2
B. Somewhat important	123	12.2	66	13.4	16	9.8	7	9.2	10	9.7	24	14.0
C. Not sure	7	.7	5	1.0	0	.0	0	.0	0	.0	2	1.2
D. Somewhat unimportant	10	1.0	7	1.4	3	1.8	0	.0	0	.0	0	.0
E. Completely unimportant	2	.2	0	.0	0	.0	0	.0	1	1.0	1	.6
82. Intelligence												
No answer	2	.2	0	.0	0	.0	0	.0	1	1.0	1	.6
A. Very important	335	33.3	156	31.6	61	37.4	25	32.9	43	41.8	50	29.2
B. Somewhat important	551	54.8	273	55.4	90	55.2	46	60.6	47	45.6	95	55.6
C. Not sure	51	5.1	33	6.7	5	3.1	1	1.3	6	5.8	6	3.5
D. Somewhat unimportant	51	5.1	23	4.7	5	3.1	2	2.6	6	5.8	15	8.8
E. Completely unimportant	16	1.5	8	1.6	2	1.2	2	2.6	0	.0	4	2.3
83. Athletic ability												
No answer	2	.2	2	.4	0	.0	0	.0	0	.0	0	.0
A. Very important	39	3.9	18	3.7	4	2.4	2	2.6	10	9.7	5	2.9
B. Somewhat important	289	28.7	144	29.2	44	27.0	18	23.7	38	36.9	45	26.4
C. Not sure	138	13.7	78	15.8	15	9.2	9	11.8	12	11.7	24	14.0
D. Somewhat unimportant	338	33.6	149	30.2	63	38.7	34	44.8	32	31.1	60	35.1
E. Completely unimportant	200	19.9	102	20.7	37	22.7	13	17.1	11	10.6	37	21.6
84. The same race												
No answer	3	.3	2	.4	0	.0	1	1.3	0	.0	0	.0
A. Very important	298	29.6	130	26.4	23	14.1	27	35.5	70	68.0	48	28.1
B. Somewhat important	221	22.0	102	20.7	26	16.0	17	22.4	33	32.0	43	25.1
C. Not sure	166	16.5	88	17.9	36	22.0	10	13.2	0	.0	32	18.7
D. Somewhat unimportant	158	15.7	85	17.2	34	20.9	11	14.4	0	.0	28	16.4
E. Completely unimportant	160	15.9	86	17.4	44	27.0	10	13.2	0	.0	20	11.7

The TeenAge *Relationships Survey Results (continued)*

Survey questions	ALL GIRLS Result	Percent	STRONG INDIVIDUALISTS Result	Percent	20TH-CENTURY FAST TRACKERS Result	Percent	MODERN TRADITIONALISTS Result	Percent	SV EET SOUTHERN BELLES Result	Percent	SUPERSONIC DATERS Result	Percent
85. The same religion												
No answer	1	.0	1	.2	0	.0	0	.0	0	.0	0	.0
A. Agree strongly	79	7.9	27	5.4	2	1.2	9	11.8	35	34.0	6	3.5
B. Agree somewhat	162	16.1	56	11.4	13	8.0	11	14.5	68	66.0	14	8.2
C. Not sure	112	11.1	70	14.2	12	7.4	18	23.7	0	.0	12	7.0
D. Disagree somewhat	249	24.8	130	26.4	45	27.6	25	32.9	0	.0	49	28.7
E. Disagree strongly	403	40.1	209	42.4	91	55.8	13	17.1	0	.0	90	52.6
86. The same age												
No answer	3	.3	1	.2	0	.0	1	1.3	1	1.0	0	.0
A. Agree strongly	15	1.5	7	1.4	0	.0	2	2.6	3	2.9	3	1.8
B. Agree somewhat	183	18.2	96	19.5	28	17.2	13	17.1	28	27.2	18	10.5
C. Not sure	62	6.2	37	7.5	5	3.1	6	7.9	7	6.8	7	4.1
D. Disagree somewhat	304	30.2	144	29.2	48	29.4	29	38.2	37	35.9	46	26.9
E. Disagree strongly	439	43.6	208	42.2	82	50.3	25	32.9	27	26.2	97	56.7
87. A romantic nature: treating me like a lady (opening doors, bringing flowers)												
No answer	1	.0	1	.2	0	.0	0	.0	0	.0	0	.0
A. Agree strongly	275	27.3	132	26.8	33	20.3	26	34.2	44	42.7	40	23.4
B. Agree somewhat	499	49.6	254	51.5	77	47.2	36	47.4	42	40.8	90	52.6
C. Not sure	83	8.3	41	8.3	18	11.0	5	6.6	10	9.7	9	5.3
D. Disagree somewhat	118	11.8	52	10.6	26	16.0	8	10.5	7	6.8	25	14.6
E. Disagree strongly	30	3.0	13	2.6	9	5.5	1	1.3	0	.0	7	4.1
88. Good grooming												
No answer	1	.1	1	.2	0	.0	0	.0	0	.0	0	.0
A. Very important	536	53.3	248	50.3	74	45.4	44	57.9	76	73.8	94	55.0
B. Somewhat important	410	40.8	212	43.0	79	48.5	30	39.5	26	25.2	63	36.8
C. Not sure	28	2.8	16	3.3	4	2.5	0	.0	1	1.0	7	4.1
D. Somewhat unimportant	24	2.4	13	2.6	5	3.0	2	2.6	0	.0	4	2.3
E. Completely unimportant	7	.6	3	.6	1	.6	0	.0	0	.0	3	1.8

Survey questions	ALL GIRLS Result	ALL GIRLS Percent	STRONG INDIVIDUALISTS Result	STRONG INDIVIDUALISTS Percent	20TH-CENTURY FAST TRACKERS Result	20TH-CENTURY FAST TRACKERS Percent	MODERN TRADITIONALISTS Result	MODERN TRADITIONALISTS Percent	SWEET SOUTHERN BELLES Result	SWEET SOUTHERN BELLES Percent	SUPERSONIC DATERS Result	SUPERSONIC DATERS Percent
89. Money												
No answer	1	.1	1	.2	0	.0	0	.0	0	.0	0	.0
A. Very important	58	5.8	27	5.5	5	3.1	5	6.6	7	6.8	14	8.1
B. Somewhat important	406	40.4	187	37.9	48	29.4	33	43.4	63	61.2	75	43.9
C. Not sure	134	13.3	79	16.0	18	11.0	10	13.1	9	8.7	18	10.5
D. Somewhat unimportant	292	29.0	141	28.6	64	39.3	23	30.3	16	15.5	48	28.1
E. Completely unimportant	115	11.4	58	11.8	28	17.2	5	6.6	8	7.8	16	9.4
90. Attractive clothes												
No answer	1	.1	1	.2	0	.0	0	.0	0	.0	0	.0
A. Very important	71	7.1	32	6.4	4	2.4	5	6.6	18	17.5	12	7.0
B. Somewhat important	477	47.4	238	48.3	55	33.7	37	48.7	60	58.3	87	50.9
C. Not sure	100	9.9	57	11.6	19	11.7	4	5.3	3	2.9	17	9.9
D. Somewhat unimportant	276	27.4	124	25.2	65	39.9	22	28.9	21	20.4	44	25.8
E. Completely unimportant	81	8.1	41	8.3	20	12.3	8	10.5	1	.9	11	6.4
91. Good physical looks												
No answer	1	.1	0	.0	0	.0	0	.0	1	1.0	0	.0
A. Very important	119	11.8	56	11.3	11	6.7	7	9.2	19	18.5	26	15.2
B. Somewhat important	560	55.7	275	55.8	81	49.7	39	51.4	68	66.0	97	56.8
C. Not sure	101	10.0	53	10.8	20	12.3	9	11.8	7	6.8	12	7.0
D. Somewhat unimportant	185	18.4	89	18.1	43	26.4	15	19.7	6	5.8	32	18.7
E. Completely unimportant	40	4.0	20	4.0	8	4.9	6	7.9	2	1.9	4	2.3
92. Self-confidence												
No answer	1	.1	1	.2	0	.0	0	.0	0	.0	0	.0
A. Very important	493	49.0	241	48.9	88	54.0	40	52.7	50	48.5	74	43.3
B. Somewhat important	441	43.8	219	44.4	66	40.5	33	43.4	46	44.7	77	45.0
C. Not sure	45	4.5	19	3.9	6	3.7	1	1.3	5	4.8	14	8.2
D. Somewhat unimportant	23	2.3	11	2.2	3	1.8	2	2.6	1	1.0	6	3.5
E. Completely unimportant	3	.3	2	.4	0	.0	0	.0	1	1.0	0	.0
93. Dependability												
No answer	1	.1	1	.2	0	.0	0	.0	0	.0	0	.0
A. Very important	671	66.7	309	62.7	108	66.3	57	75.1	82	79.6	115	67.3
B. Somewhat important	273	27.1	150	30.4	47	28.8	15	19.7	17	16.5	44	25.7
C. Not sure	37	3.7	19	3.9	6	3.7	1	1.3	3	2.9	8	4.7

The TeenAge *Relationships Survey Results (continued)*

Survey questions	ALL GIRLS Result	Percent	STRONG INDIVIDUALISTS Result	Percent	20TH-CENTURY FAST TRACKERS Result	Percent	MODERN TRADITIONALISTS Result	Percent	SWEET SOUTHERN BELLES Result	Percent	SUPERSONIC DATERS Result	Percent
D. Somewhat unimportant	14	1.4	8	1.6	1	.6	2	2.6	0	.0	3	1.8
E. Completely unimportant	10	1.0	6	1.2	1	.6	1	1.3	1	1.0	1	.5
94. Success-oriented												
No answer	4	.4	4	.8	0	.0	0	.0	0	.0	0	.0
A. Very important	324	32.2	143	29.0	51	31.3	29	38.2	44	42.7	57	33.3
B. Somewhat important	433	43.0	222	45.1	65	39.9	29	38.2	47	45.7	70	40.9
C. Not sure	147	14.6	77	15.6	25	15.3	8	10.5	9	8.7	28	16.4
D. Somewhat unimportant	82	8.2	38	7.7	19	11.7	9	11.8	3	2.9	13	7.6
E. Completely unimportant	16	1.6	9	1.8	3	1.8	1	1.3	0	.0	3	1.8
95. How old are you?												
No answer	1	.1	0	.0	0	.0	0	.0	0	.0	1	.6
A. 12	22	2.2	15	3.0	2	1.2	0	.0	3	2.9	2	1.2
B. 13	46	4.6	29	5.9	5	3.1	3	3.9	3	2.9	6	3.5
C. 14	117	11.6	70	14.2	20	12.3	8	10.5	7	6.8	12	7.0
D. 15	183	18.2	93	18.9	25	15.3	12	15.8	27	26.3	26	15.2
E. 16	234	23.3	98	19.9	44	27.0	23	30.3	20	19.4	49	28.7
F. 17	198	19.7	96	19.5	30	18.4	11	14.5	23	22.3	38	22.2
G. 18	128	12.7	65	13.2	22	13.5	9	11.8	11	10.7	21	12.3
H. 19	54	5.4	20	4.0	13	8.0	5	6.6	7	6.8	9	5.3
I. Over 19	23	2.2	7	1.4	2	1.2	5	6.6	2	1.9	7	4.0
96. What grade are you in?												
No answer	7	.6	2	.4	1	.6	3	3.9	1	1.0	0	.0
A. 8th or lower	56	5.6	36	7.3	9	5.5	3	3.9	5	4.8	3	1.8
B. 9th	120	11.9	75	15.2	17	10.4	8	10.5	7	6.8	13	7.6
C. 10th	170	16.9	79	16.0	25	15.4	14	18.4	24	23.3	28	16.4
D. 11th	232	23.1	109	22.1	41	25.2	16	21.1	16	15.5	50	29.2
E. 12th	201	20.0	91	18.5	31	19.0	20	26.4	28	27.2	31	18.1
F. Other	220	21.9	101	20.5	39	23.9	12	15.8	22	21.4	46	26.9

Survey questions	ALL GIRLS Result	ALL GIRLS Percent	STRONG INDIVIDUALISTS Result	STRONG INDIVIDUALISTS Percent	20TH-CENTURY FAST TRACKERS Result	20TH-CENTURY FAST TRACKERS Percent	MODERN TRADITIONALISTS Result	MODERN TRADITIONALISTS Percent	SWEET SOUTHERN BELLES Result	SWEET SOUTHERN BELLES Percent	SUPERSONIC DATERS Result	SUPERSONIC DATERS Percent
97. What kind of school did you attend?												
No answer	41	4.1	13	2.6	8	4.9	5	6.6	6	5.8	9	5.5
A. Public	804	79.9	402	81.6	125	76.7	63	82.9	78	75.8	136	79.3
B. Private nonsectarian	42	4.2	22	4.5	8	4.9	1	1.3	4	3.9	7	4.1
C. Private Christian	92	9.1	46	9.3	14	8.6	6	7.9	13	12.6	13	7.6
D. Private sectarian (other)	27	2.7	10	2.0	8	4.9	1	1.3	2	1.9	6	3.5
98. What state do you live in?												
No answer	16	1.6	3	.6	0	.0	1	1.3	0	.0	1	.6
North East:	265	26.3	135	27.4	50	30.7	12	15.8	18	17.5	50	29.2
Mid West:	315	31.3	141	28.6	54	33.1	27	35.6	35	34.0	60	35.1
South:	165	16.4	86	17.4	15	9.2	9	11.8	27	26.2	27	15.8
South West:	59	5.9	24	4.9	16	9.8	6	7.9	7	6.9	7	4.1
West:	186	18.5	104	21.1	28	17.2	21	27.6	16	15.5	26	15.2
99. How big is your town? (Please estimate if you don't know)												
No answer	35	3.5	15	3.0	5	3.1	2	2.6	0	.0	13	7.6
A. Less than 1,000	88	8.7	45	9.1	13	8.0	12	15.8	7	6.8	11	6.4
B. 1,000–10,000	296	29.5	135	27.4	50	30.7	18	23.7	41	39.8	52	30.4
C. 11,000–30,000	212	21.1	98	19.9	33	20.2	20	26.3	21	20.4	40	23.4
D. 31,000–50,000	135	13.4	82	16.7	18	11.0	5	6.6	8	7.8	22	12.9
E. 51,000–100,000	93	9.2	43	8.7	15	9.2	8	10.5	13	12.6	14	8.2
F. More than 100,000	147	14.6	75	15.2	29	17.8	11	14.5	13	12.6	19	11.1